HEAVENLY LIGHTS

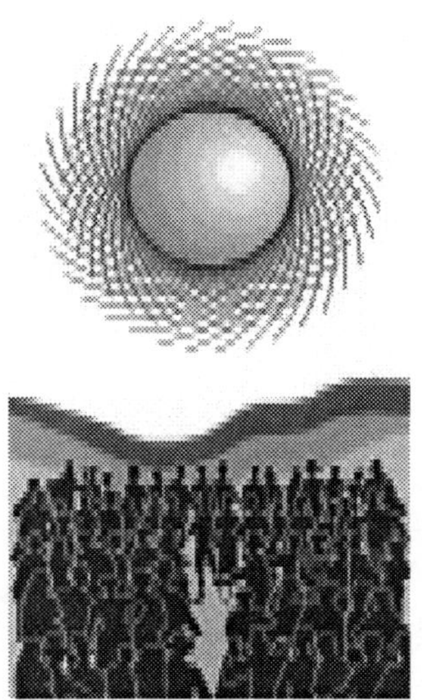

Other books in this series

Celestial Secrets: The Hidden History of the Fátima Incident

Fátima Revisited: The Apparition Phenomenon in Myth, Religion, and Science

HEAVENLY LIGHTS

The Apparitions of Fátima and the UFO Phenomenon

DR. JOAQUIM FERNANDES
& FINA D'ARMADA

Translated from Portuguese and Edited by
ANDREW D. BASIAGO & EVA M. THOMPSON

Foreword by
DR. JACQUES F. VALLÉE

Anomalist Books
San Antonio • New York

Heavenly Lights: The Apparitions of Fátima and the UFO Phenomenon

This book was originally published by EcceNova, Victoria, BC, Canada in 2005.

This Anomalist Books edition was published in 2007:
ISBN: 1933665211

Cover art by Roy Young
Cover design by Seale Studios

For information about Anomalist Books, go to anomalistbooks.com or write to:

Anomalist Books
5150 Broadway #108
San Antonio, TX 78209

Anomalist Books
PO Box 577
Jefferson Valley, NY 10535

AUTHORS & CONTRIBUTORS

JOAQUIM FERNANDES, Ph.D. and FINA D'ARMADA, M.A. are Portuguese historians who have researched and written about the Fátima case for more than 25 years. Their works *As Aparições de Fátima e o Fenómeno OVNI* and *Fátima: Nos Bastidores do Segredo* are definitive histories of the Fátima Incident of 1917.

ANDREW D. BASIAGO, J.D. is an American lawyer, journalist, and environmental scholar educated at UCLA and Cambridge. He has investigated historical aspects of the UFO cover-up. He is now writing a book about secret time-space exploration activities undertaken in the United States by the Defense Advanced Research Projects Agency.

EVANGELINE M. THOMPSON is an accomplished poet, singer/songwriter, translator, and interpreter fluent in the Romance languages. She has translated essays, poems, lyrics, musicals, operas, television scripts, and feature films, including works by Bertolucci, Diegues, Herzog, Kurosawa, Malle, Wajda, and Zhang.

JACQUES F. VALLÉE, Ph.D. is a distinguished researcher who has authored over 20 books on such subjects as UFO sightings and claims of human contact with alien beings. He inspired the French scientist played by François Truffaut in Steven Spielberg's classic film about the alien-human contact phenomenon, *Close Encounters of the Third Kind.*

STEVE NEILL is one of the world's most prominent UFO artists. He drew the illustration of an alien found on the cover of Whitley Strieber's celebrated account of alien contact, *Communion.* He was also the artistic genius behind the NBC program *Confirmation*, which was a landmark production about ETs by a major media company.

CAROL F. SHELLEY, B.A. is a creative and accomplished graphic artist with a broad range of skills and interests. Her artistic metiers include airbrush and water colours. Many of her illustrations in this work were computer-designed based on Claro Fângio's drawings for the original Portuguese edition of this book.

DEDICATION

CLARO FÂNGIO (1944-1998) was a versatile Portuguese artist. He was a painter, a sculptor, a painting restorer, and an exquisite designer. He illustrated eleven books and over 800 articles in more than 25 newspapers. He exhibited extensively throughout Portugal and was a well known artist in other European countries. In 2000, a street was named after him, in the Portuguese city of Rio Tinto. This English translation of a book first illustrated by Claro Fângio is dedicated to him *in memoriam*.

CONTENTS

FOREWORD

This book is the product of an analysis of perceived "apparitions," whether religious or profane in nature, and their interpretation in a rational, scientific context. Such an effort is long overdue. By bridging the gap between the vast domain of spiritual miracles (illustrated here by the Fátima events of 1917) and the equally immense amount of data recorded by investigators of unidentified flying objects, Joaquim Fernandes and Fina d'Armada have opened up an important new avenue of research. In the process, they tell the fascinating story of a global phenomenon that reaches far beyond the boundaries of Portugal and stretches through centuries of passion and puzzlement.

The facts they have uncovered bring new light to the age-old problem of unexplained aerial phenomena. This neglected area of research is fundamental to our understanding of the physical universe, of human consciousness, and of the role played by spiritual movements in shaping human history.

Consider the statement made by the three children of Fátima who, while watching their sheep on May 13, 1917, said they first saw lightning, and then, "As we arrived at the middle of the ranch, another flash of lightning struck again, and we saw a lady on top of an oak tree. We were very frightened at seeing the resplendency that enveloped her."

Now compare this statement with the report provided by the Arias family of Nicanor-Olivera, Argentina, who, on August 31, 1978, were awakened by an intense luminosity outside their house. An egg-shaped object, they said, hovered over a nearby eucalyptus tree. From one edge, the object emitted a circular light. At the end of this beam, they saw "two bulky beings" that carried, at chest height, a red light that "seemed to run as if falling from a small waterfall." The entities moved in a rigid fashion, like "floating travelers, seated on something."

The burden falls on the scientific community to explain why these seemingly absurd observations arise so often from frightened and sincere witnesses, and how they can have such a powerful influence on our belief systems. But what should the professional scientist or the curious amateur do when faced with events that seem to contradict everything we know about "normal" reality?

The easiest path is a well-worn one, and that is to flatly deny the facts. Perhaps the witnesses are deluded individuals, or liars. Indeed, this accusation was made against the shepherds of Fátima, until the final sighting, when over 60,000 witnesses observed the luminous display, and the physical effects were such that no one could deny them any longer. The scientific consensus, and the majority view in educated circles, however, still hold that the events in question "must have been" ordinary, and mistakenly observed. This is certainly the most parsimonious assumption.

A second way of interpreting incidents like Fátima is held in respect throughout much of the world. It does not deny the facts but instead carefully reframes them within the structure of dogma and belief. This cosmology assumes that the witnesses were privileged to take part in a miracle, a signal sent uniquely to them from a divine level of such spiritual intensity that it would be folly to try to understand it, blasphemy to challenge the wisdom of its pronouncements. This is the religious path. In this view, God, or His messengers, are so far above the human level that we would display silly arrogance if we did more than record the events and cower in obedience before them.

For those who, like the authors of this work, refuse to follow either one of these convenient paths, the challenges become enormous. They involve detachment and critical analysis of difficult material; correlation of testimony from many independent parties; and confrontation between two sets of physical descriptions, namely, those of religious events, like Fátima, and those of more mundane but equally puzzling unidentified aerial phenomena, like the reports of the Arias family of Argentina. As the authors show, it is in this manner that genuine research can go forward. The result is a new awareness of the complexity of consciousness.

Modern laboratory research has shown that our perceptions are highly vulnerable to changes in our physical environment. They can be altered by drugs, hypnosis, and electromagnetic fields. They are shaped by language, culture, and education. They are subject to social pressure.

As we enter an age when the functions of the brain can be studied in real time with sophisticated instruments, academic research is beginning to seriously consider a range of consciousness phenomena that earlier scientists discounted. In this context, percipients of unusual events are becoming participants in a novel and exciting field rich in potential scientific breakthroughs. The authors of this book analyze such events, and they go on to establish relevant linkages between various classes of unexplained facts. Their work makes an important contribution to our understanding of the human condition and of the universe in which we live.

Jacques F. Vallée, Ph.D.

INTRODUCTION

Unexpectedly and surprisingly, critical acclaim resulted from the publication of our work, *Extraterrestrial Intervention at Fátima: The Apparitions and the UFO Phenomenon*, in 1982. Public interest followed, and two subsequent editions quickly sold out. We now have the opportunity to re-edit the essential parts of our work, improved in small but important ways by the contributions made by other investigators since our work first appeared.

On that occasion, technical demands necessitated a reduction in the size of the manuscript after it had already gone to print. This meant a painstaking reading of obscure or unknown original documents, which had been kept within the archives at the Sanctuary of Fátima. Moreover, it required, over a six-year period, a detailed, systematic, chronological reconstruction of the testimony of the day, most of it firsthand.

In this version, we have opted to maintain the phenomenological assessments that sustain the nucleus of our hypothesis: similarities and parallelisms exist between the syndromes and processes that support either interpretation of the event. Whereas, when seen from a religious perspective, they were "Marian Apparitions" or visions, when informed by the secular worldview of our technological society and urban sub-culture they involved manifestations characteristic of "unidentified flying objects," defined globally as the UFO phenomenon.

That a proliferation of works, of the most diverse types, was inspired by the events at Cova da Iria in 1917 is well known. The overwhelming majority of these have been apologetic and confessional in nature and have lacked objectivity, whether in terms of historical rigor or interdisciplinary factual analysis. The fact that objectivity was not their aim is understood. The same thing, however, has also occurred at the opposite end of the spectrum, where a positivist ideological reading, prompted by anti-clerical sentiment, sweeps from its path whatever intelligible trace of the events do not conform to the contemporary scheme of skeptical reference.

Between the two extremes of irrational pity and rational intolerance, viewed in the long tradition of "the manque," there lies a vast no-man's-land, where the practice of a "third way" is beginning to find legitimacy in academic circles. For the authors, the Fátima phenomena – not to be considered in isolation, but to be examined alongside the impressive body of "anomalous" and "atypical" experiences to be found in the record of other cultural and time-space contexts

– constitute a promising field of investigation and analysis in the human and social sciences. As we attempt to demonstrate, the Fátima incident is also germane to the physical disciplines.

Do not invoke the "moral legitimacy" that has tended to sustain the exclusively religious context within which the phenomenology of the established historical "Marian" apparitions has tended to be examined. Rather, the most recent examples in this epiphanic tradition, so fundamentally inscribed in the social and cultural archetypes of the world of Catholic expression (such as the apparitions at Medjugorje), deserve active study by scientists, including medical specialists. If we are to develop optimal information about the processes involved, it is essential to remember that popular forms of religious devotion do not amount to "revealed truth" in a dogmatic sense, but rather, favor an investigation of their cultural and anthropological contents. Only in this manner, can we gird ourselves with a reliable and verifiable view of the world.

The objective of our work is not to debate with the attitudes of the faithful, which we respect. But, indeed, it is to recover on behalf of the critical and scientific debate a theme that we understand contains within itself other potentials beyond the mere tenet of "Believe and Abstain" that most devout individuals will consider the end of the dialogue. The fact is that a reasonable and honest attitude can tolerate a reconsideration of the postulates and analogies implied by the inescapable facts that remain unchanged in time and space.

The tendency of orthodoxy to resist the examination of "religious and supernatural experiences and manifestations" by science was identified almost a century ago by the philosopher Emile Durkheim, in an essay entitled *Les formes élémentaires de la vie religieuse* (1912). Only the growth of global information and working hypotheses (accumulated at various levels, namely, in the arena of the investigation of the "frontier" of the transpersonal, for example, in parapsychology) have justified a progressive commitment to the "neutral" treatment of these sources by independent and university scientific centers on the vanguard of research. These promise the eventual enrichment of a plurality of wisdoms.

In this manner, the "Marian Apparitions" of Fátima, censored in their sacred translation, yield an informative richness that inspires, indeed, compels, a detailed and attentive comparison with the mass of evidence already gathered about the contemporary, uncommon spacecraft known by the initials "UFO," whose morphology, complex behavior, and effects merit a detailed, competent, and thorough scientific exploration. This was not accomplished in its essential terms in 1917. As far as we are concerned, however, the evidentiary similarities that exist between these two realms speak for themselves without elaboration.

Lastly, we should recall that as recently as 1979, Pope John Paul II admitted, for the first time publicly, before the Papal Academy of Sciences, the errors and injustices committed by the Roman Catholic Church against Galileo. His late Holiness commented, "As with any truth, the scientific truth need not... answer to anyone but itself." In this spirit, let us try to take one step beyond, in the just precariousness of the worldly quest for knowledge, in pursuit of what is hiding behind the perpetual mysteries of human existence.

Joaquim Fernandes, Ph.D.
Fina d'Armada

PART ONE

PORTRAIT OF THE LADY WHO DESCENDED FROM THE SKY

Phenomena Associated with the Being of Fátima

1. THE DAY OF MAY 13TH

"If the kids saw a woman dressed in white,
who else could she be but Our Lady?"
– António dos Santos

"O, mother! I saw Our Lady at Cova da Iria," affirmed Jacinta, upon her return home, on May 13, 1917.[1]

Soon, a lonely and rocky part of the parish of Fátima, where not a single family resided, would become the wellspring of hope for believers, the center of attention for newspapers, and the source of agitation for politicians. Portuguese history found, on that Sunday afternoon, another course, perhaps even a new destiny.

"If the kids saw a woman dressed in white, who else could she be but Our Lady?" asked António dos Santos, as if to himself.[2] António was Lúcia's father and the brother of Jacinta and Francisco's mother. The heavenly visitor, however, did not disclose her identity to the little shepherds. Naturally, for a girl named "Jacinta," born into an ancient Celtic civilization, the Blue Lady would be Belísama – also known as Minerva, goddess of light and fire, forging and craft – who in that tradition was "The Being of the Flame." For Jacintas who once lived in Syria, Greece, Rome, and Bolivia, she would have been one of the other feminine deities who have descended from the sky, such as Astarte, Aphrodite, Venus, and Orejona.

In truth, in 1917, "*it could be no other.*" Lúcia, however, the principal seer and the one who dialogued with the "Lady," was not convinced of that. She remained quiet. Maria Rosa, her mother, who believed little in the supernatural, learned of the visitation, and decided to question her daughter about the alleged apparition of the previous day:

> "Lúcia, I heard it said that you saw Our Lady at Cova da Iria," her mother asked.
>
> "Who told you so?" Lúcia answered.
>
> "It was Jacinta's mother, whose daughter told her. Is it true?"
>
> Lúcia corrected: "I never said that it was *Our Lady* — rather, a small, pretty lady. I even asked Jacinta and Francisco to say nothing. They could not hold their tongues!"
>
> "A small lady?"

"Yes, mother."

"Then speak up and tell me what the lady told you."

"She told me that we should continue to go there for six consecutive months, on the 13th of each month, and that at the end of that time, she would tell us who she was and what she wanted of us."[3]

The Apparition had not identified herself, after all. She had promised to do so six months later. Jacinta, however, already "knew" that she was the Virgin Mary, and everyone followed suit. Quickly, the news spread beyond the obscure village, carrying with it the name of the Virgin. It was spoken everywhere that, at the Mount of Air, the Mother of Jesus was frequently seen. The newspapers and the politicians soon entered the fray. But the children continued without knowing the identity of the small lady.

Carlos de Azevedo Mendes, a young lawyer of 29 years of age, who would later be named deputy to the Portuguese national assembly, resolved to visit the locale of the much-acclaimed prodigies. It was in September that he, an imposing figure on horseback, arrived at Cova da Iria. Mendes lived alongside the seers and their families and accompanied the young shepherds to the famous stand of oak trees. In a letter addressed to his fiancée, he described the ritual preparation for the visions, and added:

"The children always say that the lady appears to them. They don't know who she is. Only after the sixth visit, on October 13th, will she tell them who she is and what it is that she wants."[4]

Once again it is established that while all of Portugal "knew" whom the small lady was who descended at Cova da Iria, the principal players wrestled with their doubts.

September 13th arrived, and Lúcia dialogued with the heavenly apparition. Two weeks later on the 27th, the Canon Formigão entered Fatimist history, adopting the pseudonym "the Viscount of Montelo." He would become the first chronicler of Fátima and the promoter of it as a Marian shrine.[5] On this day, he asked the seer Lúcia:

"Did you ever ask her who she is?"

"I asked, but she declared that only on October 13th would she say."[6]

Unintentionally, such affirmations fed the hunger of a populace avid for the supernatural, and commercial men thirsting for business began raising images of the Apparition, with designations such as "Lady of Peace" and "Lady of the Rosary" printed at the foot of already consecrated Catholic deities, on altars across the country.

October 13th arrived and with it the promised identification of the Being.

But the novelty was gone, for everyone "knew" whom the Lady was – she was the Virgin Mary, Mother of Jesus. Among the 50,000 Portuguese who journeyed to Fátima, eager for an encounter with the miraculous, walking vendors circulated, shouting out to prospective buyers about "an image of the Virgin as being the figure of the visions," a reporter for *O Seculo* [*The Century*] wrote in his newspaper's October 15th edition. A person from Leiria – we are told by Inácio António Marques[7] – "came to distribute illustrations with the pictures of the three children and Our Lady."

Yet non-believers, too, were gripped by the common religious fever. Alfredo Carvalho, in an article published in the Lisbon newspaper *A Lucta* [*The Struggle*] on the 18th, noted the fervor among atheists:

> I was informed that an illustrious doctor from my hometown, a member of the local Jacobin elite, was screaming as if possessed, with his hands crossed, and his eyes rolling back into his head, then fixed in space as if staring at something, as he shouted:
>
> "There goes the Virgin! There she is!"
>
> And a businessman, who is from Mação and an atheist, but considers himself to be no fool, hawked blessings and good luck charms to Catholic laborers, and it seems to me that in Fátima he has had great luck.

The children's doubts were, nonetheless, clearly expressed by their parish priest, who, after each visitation, kept a written record of the words told to him by the seers. In the *Parish Inquiry*, a passage from his interview with Lúcia was recorded on the 16th: "Build a chapel here to Our Lady of the Rosary." Lúcia had her doubts if that was what the Lady had said, or if it was, "Build a chapel here. I am the lady of the Rosary."[8]

The uncertainty remains until the end. In Portuguese, *rosario*, the rosary, also means *capela*, the chapel. Was this a play-on-words, simple confusion, or a red herring? The process was unstoppable, and no one would have been willing to turn back, even if Lúcia had discovered that the Apparition was the spirit of her grandmother. "Who else could it be but Our Lady?" repeated the inhabitants of the small-minded town, isolated from the higher society of 1917. For mostly illiterate townspeople, now returned to a religious devotion, who else could she have been? Likewise, for the educated, Our Lady surged forward as the only feminine inhabitant of a world different from ours. The long-forgotten goddesses of ancient civilizations, deemed pagan and false, did not fit into the universal culture of 1917; no other Lady could exist and appear in space dressed in white.

Nonetheless, having crossed the threshold of the 21st century, after first breaking the barrier of our atmosphere, and embarking on the pathways which lead to the stars, shouldn't we be asking if the "small, pretty lady" was *something else, another being*?

THE LITTLE SHEPHERDS

Let us return then to 1917, in search of the principal figures of this celebrated encounter with an Unidentified Being. Portugal would soon be swept into the maelstrom of the war raging in Europe. In the province of Estremadura, in a town like so many others, people continued to fight only for survival. Fátima, while a village of great expanse, was comprised, at that time, of no more than 32 residences.

At Aljustrel, a tiny hamlet of Fátima, lived two ordinary families. Maria Rosa and António dos Santos, known by the nickname "Pumpkin," were raising six children. Lúcia, age ten, was their seventh and final child. In a house nearby lived Manuel Pedro Marto and his wife, Olímpia de Jesus, together with their nine children. As she was a widow with two children when she married Manuel, Francisco was her seventh child and Jacinta was his seventh. In 1917, Francisco and Jacinta were nine and seven years old, respectively, and were Lúcia's cousins, for Olímpia was the sister of António dos Santos. Curiously, the three little shepherds of Fátima were all seventh born children.

Considering, for a moment, some of the characteristics of the young witnesses, we find that Francisco and Jacinta were illiterate and subject to beliefs, often blind in nature, which they got from their father. The priest of Fátima, during the course of his inquiries, would note that Manuel Marto was either "an over-believer, [or] otherwise, insane." Jacinta showed she was clever. She saw and heard the Lady. Francisco was an apathetic figure at the time of the visions, and this caused journalists to ignore him on the day of "The Miracle of the Sun." The newspapers of the time – *O Seculo*, *Liberdade* [*Liberty*], and *O Mensageiro* [*The Messenger*] – referred only to "the young girls." They reported: "He [Francisco] was of few words and, in general, imitated what his sister and cousin did. Rarely did he take any initiative."[9] He merely supplied some relevant declarations to the Viscount of Montelo, who somehow must have managed to persuade him of what had happened, for he failed to provide any interesting information to any of the other inquirers of 1917.

As for Jacinta, the editor of *O Mensageiro* wrote:

> [S]he responded in my ear what she remembered of the Apparitions, having

> as her unshakable response, the majority of the time, only silence or "I don't remember"... When I ask her some question about the words the Lady uttered, Jacinta responds, "I don't remember... Lúcia is the one who must know."[10]

Excluding, for the time being, the interrogations performed by the Viscount of Montelo in 1923, Lúcia is, therefore, the point of departure for the reconstruction of the events. How can we develop a proper profile of this seer? What kind of child was she, and how did she channel her behavior as an adult?

It is not easy to paint Lúcia's psychological portrait today, given that, all these many years, different authors have deified or denigrated her according to the taste of their own conceptions. There are those who have labeled her "the child of an alcoholic" and those who attribute to her virtues of saintliness, beyond the appropriate conveniences. She appears to us to have been an intelligent, fearless, and happy individual when she was a child, with nothing in her to define her as being "saintly" or "holy." "As is the case with all girls from the mountain country," Father João de Marchi wrote, "Lúcia liked to dress up when there were holidays, with gold chains and large earrings that fell to her shoulders and a cute hat adorned with golden beads and feathers of various colors."[11]

At the time of the Apparitions, Lúcia's level of culture was minimal. There being no school in the area for girls, few women knew how to read. The seer's teacher was her own mother. According to Costa Brochado, "Maria Rosa knew how to read a little print and was a devout Catholic, educating in that faith her children, to whom she taught the doctrine and read adequate passages of the lives of saints and of Scripture."[12]

Lúcia's mother also habitually read to her children from another book – *Missão Abreviada* [*The Abbreviated Mission*] – which speaks of Hell in mediaeval terms, describes the horrible tortures inflicted on sinners, and contains passages bordering closely on other Marian apparitions. The Viscount of Montelo believed that this book could have influenced the young Lúcia, and on October 11th put this question to the seer's mother. Maria Rosa confirmed that she had regularly shared these readings with her children, and that they included the vision of La Salette. She denied, however, that this last case involving an apparition of the Virgin Mary had particularly captured the interest of her daughter, and insisted, "I never heard her mention it." When the Canon Formigão posed the same question to the main seer, Lúcia reiterated her mother's opinion, adding: "I wasn't thinking of that story, nor did I retell it to anyone."[13]

The certainty is that, unconsciously or not, Lúcia appears to have been knowledgeable of other classical visions regarded as the Mother of Christ. It was natural for deep memories regarding them to resurface when, for the first time, she came face-to-face with the strange Lady, dressed in white, above the oaks. On the one hand, she would have to consider such facts to be normal once the most educated people that she knew – the priests – considered them so. On the other hand, she had never been told that creatures from outside the Catholic pantheon could descend from the sky.

The young seer could not surpass herself, ignorant, as she was, of everything that existed beyond the bounds of her small village. Her environment was eminently religious, and that influence was reflected in the message that it would transmit to the outside world.

The same sensibility can be found in the exhortation of Pope Benedict XV referred to in the Homily delivered during the Mass on May 13th by the priest of Fátima, in which he showed himself to be quite concerned about the worldwide conflict. The pontiff had endeavored unsuccessfully to mediate an end to World War I. In his papal message, *Urbi et Orbi*, for 1917, he invited Catholics to pray directly to the Virgin Mary in order to bring about "the end of the war." Everything leads us to believe that the parish priest must have divulged to his congregation of simple and rustic people the objective of the Church's new invocations and litanies. This is not altogether a despicable fact – one that will become one of the principal components of the Fátima message, channeled through Lúcia.

The truth is that the young girl maintained her ignorance about the identity of the strange celestial visitor. Among other things, Antero de Figueiredo, Father João de Marchi also testified that she affirmed, after the first visitation, "I don't know if she is Our Lady… she was a small, very pretty lady."[14] But, in June, the first pilgrims gathering beside the oaks were already speaking openly of "the Vision of our Lady." The entire atmosphere of this would resound in the questions that Lúcia asked the Being and in the interpretation of her subsequent answers.

As time went by, the youngster became ever more subjugated by the religious culture in which she found herself, until, at age 14, "it was arranged, in secret, that she be boarded at a school far from Fátima, which (was) unknown to everyone," we are told by Antero de Figueiredo.[15] On the eve of her departure, Lúcia listened reverently to the strict orders of the bishop, which, as repeated by the seer, included three admonishments: do not tell anyone where you are going; do not tell anyone whom you are; do not speak again of the Apparitions.

It was not an easy retreat, nor one done without injury, for a young person to leave behind the people and the places familiar to her. Antero de Figueiredo concludes, as the finishing touch to several dramatic pages, that following her sequestration, Lúcia's "obedient self (would) tomorrow be a dead thing that others (would) guide."[16]

In her retreat, Lúcia learned to read and write. She wrote letters and memoirs, and took charge of the mission to tell us "another story" – one in which "the woman" of her illustrious past was, after all, the Virgin Mary. Whatever she wrote had to first pass through the bishop's hands before it was read. Whosoever wished to contact her had to first obtain the permission of the religious authorities. When the authors attempted to do so in 1976, the prioress of her community sent us this amiable response:

> With religious compliments from the votaries of Saint Pascal, we hereby inform you that we have no jurisdiction to authorize visits to Sister Lúcia, with the exception of members of her family and friends. The Holy See corroborated the desire of the Sister, upon entering the Convent, to live in solitude and silence, and, thereby, only permits the Holy Congregation for the Doctrine of the Faith to grant authorization for other visits. Coimbra, April 16, 1976.

It is to be understood in our day. In 1929, however, a professor of theology from Bamberg University in Germany was unable to speak to her despite the recommendations he brought with him, which included a letter from the Superior Cardinal of Toledo. "It was told to me that it was absolutely impossible to speak with Lúcia," he wrote.[17]

One day, in May 1946, the seer returned to her land, and found her little village nearly transformed into a city. The Viscount of Montelo, who exclusively questioned Lúcia in 1917, wanted to speak to her again. In the magazine *Stella* [*Star*], supplied with a new pseudonym, "Mira Ceti," he recounted the adventures of the residence of the Dorotea Sisters, where Lúcia was cloistered, and his difficulties arranging a new interview.[18] The Canon Formigão himself, redactor of the principal documents of the Fátima incident, required permission from the bishop to question the Sister, who was no longer the brave young girl that he once knew. Would Lúcia keep to her original version of the events?

As a general rule, Lúcia's writings and declarations as an adult are in conflict with her testimony of 1917. An example, overstated perhaps, is that of her always altered version of "the end of the war." On October 19th, she told the Viscount of Montelo that the Lady had affirmed on October 13th: "The war will end even this day." In point of fact, this never came to pass. This detail is embarrassing if compared to another statement, recorded in the magazine *Brotéria*, in May 1951, by the pen of Father Luís Gonzaga da Fonseca. Therein, the now Sister Lúcia affirms, in a letter written on June 26, 1947 to the Reverend Dr. José Pedro da Silva, a future bishop of Viseu, that "I did not hear her say 'a war ends today,' but did hear, 'if they shall do penance, a war will end.'" Still, on September 25, 1948, Canon Barthas related that the seer denied having heard the phrase "a war ends today."

We conclude from this that the later memories of the principal seer cannot serve unconditionally as an infallible source for investigators of the events of 1917. For this reason, we turn, during the course of this work, mostly to the original statements of that time, which can preferentially constitute a body of more refined perceptions, given the young age and inherent incapacity of the witnesses to remember. We do so with the tacit proviso that perhaps even these may not convey the whole truth of the Fátima incident. Each person's truth carries with it the cultural charge of the individual, the influence of his or her environment, and the logic of the circumstances.

THE ENCOUNTER WITH THE LADY

One more Sunday would dawn on the mountain, that Sunday of May 13, 1917. As Lúcia walked to Mass like all of her neighbors, her thoughts were far from imagining that that day would alter the destiny of the people who surrounded her, and, among other things, as a matter of fact, her own destiny. It was, when it began, a Sunday like so many others. After Mass would come Lúcia's return home, and her departure with her cousins toward the ashen gray rocks, laden with their always-scarce provisions.

Lúcia decided that morning that the grazing of the herds would take place at Cova da Iria, one of her parents' properties, situated some two kilometers from Aljustrel, the tiny hamlet where the three children made their home.[19] Our young shepherds set their sheep to pasture among the groupings of oak trees and rocks, scattered on poorly cultivated agricultural land, according to the opinion of Dr. Pereira Gens, who was present at the events of 1917.[20] After taking their lunch, the young shepherds quickly prayed *O Terco* [*The Rosary*] and began to play their games.

Suddenly, an explosion of heavenly lights flooded the arid landscape. In 1922, Lúcia told us of the beginning of the phenomenon in this way:

> I was watching the sheep, at Cova da Iria, in the company of my cousins Francisco and Jacinta, playing, making a wall around a thicket, and we saw lightning.
>
> I said to Francisco: "Let's get out of here, because there is lightning, and a thunderstorm could come."

> We returned to the sheep so we could leave. As we arrived at the middle of the ranch, another flash of lightning struck again, and we saw a Lady on top of an oak tree. We were very frightened at seeing the resplendency that enveloped her.
>
> Then she said to us: "Do not be afraid, because I will do you no harm."[21]

The question as to the deity's origin sprang immediately to Lúcia's mind. In the *Parish Inquiry*, written 15 days after the first encounter, the seer would have heard the Lady say: "Her place is in the heavens." In *The Official Interrogations of 1923*, however, the young woman's mother would testify as follows: "She said that she saw a small, pretty lady; that her dress was completely white; and that to the question, 'Where are you from?' she had pointed to the sky, saying she was from there."[22]

To the seer's question regarding what she had come to do, the Lady responded: "I have come here to tell you to come here every month until six months have passed, and at the end of the six months I will tell you what I want." As for the end of the war, she gave only a vague response: "I cannot tell you yet, as long as I have not told you what I want."

The priest Manuel Ferreira Marques reconstituted the remainder of their dialogue. Jacinta merely testified: "When [the Lady] spoke to Lúcia, [Jacinta] heard a merciful voice, but does not remember hearing anything besides that [the seers] were going to the sky." Apart from that, this same priest was certain, Francisco heard nothing.

In 1941, after many years had passed, Lúcia offered a new version of this initial encounter with the Being.[23] The description this time would be much more vivid:

> We saw a Lady over an oak tree, dressed all in white, more brilliant than the Sun, sparkling with a light more clear and intense than a crystal glass full of water shot through by the most ardent rays of the Sun. We stopped, surprised by the Apparition. We were so close that we were within the light that enclosed her, or which she scattered, perhaps a meter and a half away, more or less.

In this version, Lúcia confirmed that the Being told her that she was "from the sky," that she would return a seventh time, and that each of them would go to heaven, even though Francisco still needed to "pray many *tercos* [rosaries]." New questions about the destiny of two dead girlfriends likewise were added. The final part of this version, in which reference was made to "the Grace of God," was also absolutely new, relative to the data of 1917.

According to Lúcia in this 1941 version, the Being asked them "if they wanted to offer themselves to God to bear all the sufferings in reparation of sins." The Lady then "opened her hands for the first time, transmitting to us an intense light, as if a reflection had issued from them, which penetrated our chests and into our innermost soul...."

In the presence of a painting depicting this scene, the authors pondered the reasons why doubts existed in 1917 as to the actual identity of the Apparition. Intentionally, or not, Lúcia pretends to insinuate that the Being was the Virgin Mary. Her characterization of God as a divinity thirsty for human suffering already harmonized with Lúcia's conventional religious outlook and with the new personality that she had acquired by that point.

We have no reason to value too highly Lúcia's capacity to remember as an adult, and, in this way, we contradict some Fatimist authors. She demonstrated, for example, that she was not able to remember the date of her father's death, a detail that anyone would not easily forget. In the inquiry directed by the aforementioned bishop of Viseu, José Pedro da Silva, the seer showed herself to have forgotten facts that anyone would remember.[24]

Having established that Lúcia's memories are but an approximation of the actual event, a factor which is important to our characterization of the first encounter, let us return again to 1917, so we may better arrive at a full-length portrait of the small, pretty Lady "more brilliant than the Sun."

2. WHAT WAS THE BEING LIKE?

"Her skirt was white and gold, little threads were strung along its length and throughout, and it was short...the coat was white..."
– Parish Inquiry

The statue which can be found in front of the Basilica of Fátima, which has a heart outside its chest, as well as the image venerated in the local area, follow the essential outline of the Catholic Virgin and her multiple personalities seen on altars around the globe. The classic cape over her head, a dress down to her feet, and rosary beads between her raised hands – these have been constants down through the ages. Nonetheless, when we consulted the primordial documents, the inexorable descriptions made at Fátima's original hour, we began perceiving the differences between the real and the imaginary. Let us paint, then, the "small, pretty Lady" who made Lúcia so ecstatic.

PHYSICAL ASPECTS

"Some kind of very pretty doll" was one of Lúcia's descriptions that *O Seculo* reproduced on its pages for June 23rd. In the *Parish Inquiry*, it can be read that she "had black eyes and a pretty face such as no other woman she had ever seen." The seer's cousins agreed with her.

The parish priest, Manuel Ferreira Marques, then drew some comparisons with various ladies of appreciable beauty, one of whom, a young lass of 15 years, was brought before Jacinta on August 21st. "[Our Lady] was none of these… [she] is much more lovely," was Jacinta's response, after the beauty pageant was completed. Not even the young woman, dressed in white, could match the image of beauty that persisted in the mind of the young seer. Francisco, urged by the Viscount of Montelo on September 27th, would repeat Jacinta's encomium about the heavenly beauty of the "small Lady," and deny any comparison to her earthly neighbors.

What age might the "little Lady" have been?

The investigators of 1917 did not precisely discern that detail. On October 11th, Lúcia informed the Viscount of Montelo that the Lady "seems to be about 15 years old." To the editor of *O Mensageiro*, the seer compared her to a young girl who lived in her village named Virginia, a neighbor of 12 years of age.[1] By that route, it is not surprising that the Canon Barthas described the Being as "the marvelous [young] girl,"[2] thus comparing her to Mary, mother of Jesus, an historical figure that died already idolized.

By way of Father Lacerda, of the aforementioned newspaper, we learn that Virginia, the 12-year-old, "was about 1.10 meters in height," an estimate which coincides with the one that can be read in the *Parish Inquiry*: "Lúcia said that the Lady that she and her cousins saw was a little over one meter in height…." Canon Barthas agreed that this strange lady was "not similar in appearance to any of the images of Our Lady or of other saints that they might have seen until then."[3]

The seers insisted repeatedly that they were not only awestruck by the Lady's appearance; they were "blinded" by it. Lúcia, by way of the Viscount of Montelo, said that the heavenly light that enfolded the Lady was "more beautiful than the light of the Sun and very bright." Two days after the "last encounter," the seer complained to the priest that "this time she also blinded" and that "from time to time I had to rub my eyes." According to Francisco, "the Lady's face was more clear than the Sun." And Jacinta complained on October 11th that she could not look directly at the Being "because she is hard on my eyes."

Gilberto Fernandes dos Santos, a businessman from the town of Torres Novas, spoke to the young seers in Aljustrel two years after the events, and their description to him is available to us today: "Our Lady was a very pretty lady. She wore a white dress that covered her from neck to feet, but it was a white that radiated light. She wore over her dress a white mantle, but of a white that gave off light." He added that when Lúcia saw the image suddenly, she declared "she was most lovely, because she was white, but of a white that gave off light."[4]

THE WARDROBE

Herein, we confront one of the major inconsistencies in the children's tale relative to the totality of descriptions typically given the Virgin Mary. What the Lady was seen to be wearing comprises, in our opinion, a major flaw in the classic theory of the Apparition. Let us take a look at what the diligent parish priest left written in his important narrative:

> Lúcia said that the Lady whom she and her cousins saw... was dressed in white when she appeared. Her skirt was white and gold, had threads along its length and across its width, and was short – that is, her skirt did not descend to her feet. The coat was not gold, but a white cape that fell from her head to the hem of the skirt, gold on top and on the bottom, cross-woven with threads. At the hem, the gold was more tightly woven. The coat had two or three cords at the wrists. It had no sash, ribbon, or belt. It seemed to Lúcia that she was wearing white stockings, not gold ones, but she was not certain of this, because she looked at little else but the Lady's face.

In point of fact, this description does not correspond to any Lady found within the Catholic culture. It may be that the parish priest described her with a view to historical accuracy, and thereby allowed his doubts that the Lady was the Virgin Mary of scripture to appear in his account. His subsequent departure from the parish may indicate that he disagreed with the direction the church's investigation was taking, and that he washed his hands of the matter, like Pontius Pilate.[5]

But it was not solely Lúcia who referred to the intriguing vestments of the Lady. Jacinta repeated this description to the parish priest, and Francisco communicated the same account to the Viscount of Montelo on September 27th. In her memoirs, Lúcia would come to supposedly correct Francisco's observation, putting forward that the gold appearance of the embroidery on the lady's dress were caused by "the undulation of light which formed the fullness of the dress."[6]

Even still, the seer's adult memory shows itself to be unstable, in that she reaffirmed to the editor of *O Mensageiro* that the Lady wore a skirt *without fullness*. And before that, the seer herself mimicked the pose of the Lady. She was the same height as Virginia. The dress was all white. The skirt fell to her ankles and she had on white stockings.

The detail of the stockings, as a matter of fact, varied in the interrogations. Some times the Lady appeared barefoot, other times, she wore stockings, even though, in the classical image they would have shod her in sandals. In her 1922 account, Lúcia admitted that they could have been stockings or her bare feet, "because I could not make out her toes."[7]

Concerning her head, we find various terms in the evidentiary record – veil, mantle, brilliance, *cestinho*. In the body of testimony, the same picture based on limited notions emerges, preconceptions supplied by Lúcia's enabling environment. But the idea of a type of headdress that would remind inhabitants of today's Space Age of a "space helmet" borders on something more plausible. It was Lúcia herself who expressed to Father Humberto Pasquale: "About her head, she had what seemed a *cestinho* of gold, tremendously rich and dazzling."[8] Whatever it may have been, it left the head of the Being in view, while her hair remained covered by the robe.

By means of this "portrait," we can deduce that as far as the outward appearance of the Being of Fátima is concerned, the notion that the Lady embodied classical representations of the Virgin Mary is only a remote possibility at best.

THE ADORNMENTS

While Jacinta and Francisco affirmed that they did not see the ears of the Being, Lúcia would affirm to the Viscount of Montelo, on September 27th, that she saw on her "some small hoop *earrings*." Lúcia would give another interpretation later of something that had appeared to her to be hoops: "[T]he cord of gold that, in the manner of an ardent ray of sunlight, seemed to embroider her robe, as it fell from her head to her shoulders onto the brilliance of the Lady, made some very varied undulations in the light itself, so that it sometimes called to mind small hoop earrings." Hoop earrings or something similar did not hang then from any ears, but were situated at the confluence of her neck and shoulders.[9]

The rosary, the element incongruent with the classical images of Fátima, is susceptible to several interpretations as to its significance. Jacinta communicated to the priest of Fátima that the Lady "held some very white beads, which she carried from her hands and were secured firmly between her index fingers and the thumbs of both hands, which she had raised to her waist." Alternately, Gilberto Fernandes dos Santos found substantial support for the assertion that "the beads hanging from her hands (they said carried *in* her hands), were also white and emitted light."[10] The choice between "*hang*" and "*brought*" can lead us to draw interesting inferences from a symbolic point-of-view.

As other adornments continue to flow, for example, from the first manuscript of the seer, dated 1922, they compel us to ponder what the Lady was actually wearing. Again we are presented with the question of language, and its manipulation vis-a-vis the cultural context. P.O. Faria has noted that the first chronicler of Fátima – the Viscount of Montelo – "left accounts that he had tidied-up as editor and in a language not that of the seers."[11] Thus, transcribing a response from Lúcia on September 27th, he affirmed: "They see on it [the dress], in front, two golden cords which fall from the neck and which are rejoined by a *ball*, also golden, at the height of mid-body." Returning to the manuscript of 1922, we read the following: "[A]t the neck, a cord with a *ball* reached her waist." From then on, a question of a ball and not a spherical adornment would persist, by force of convention, because this conformed to the accepted image of the Virgin.

When asked, Francisco stated "Our Lady held a heart in her hand, which

Fig. 1 – "She opened her hands and transmitted to us… the reflection of that infinite light… Jacinta and Francisco seemed to be within that part of the light that was rising to the sky, while I was in the light that was spreading along the ground. In front of her right hand, Our Lady held a heart surrounded by spines that seemed to be riveted onto it. We understood that it was the Immaculate Heart of Mary outraged by the sins of humanity that call for repentance." – Lúcia, in her *Memorias*, Part IV.

(The figures are not from Fátima, but from an incident reported in Argentina in 1968. It was this kind of "ball" that later inspired the devotion to the Immaculate Heart of Mary and informed one of the parts of the Secret. The figures are taken from the book *Encounters with Humanoids* by the Spanish author Antonio Ribera.)[12]

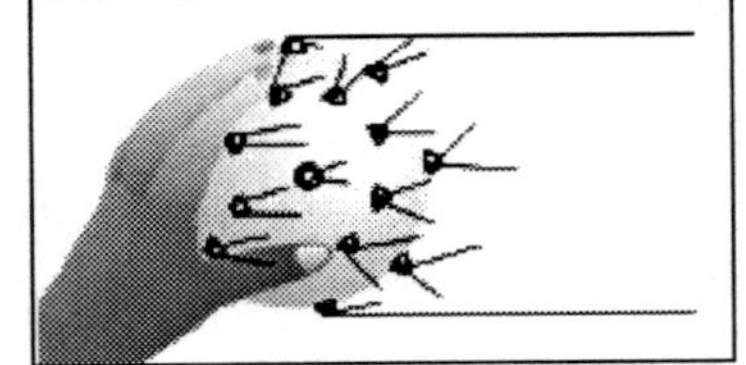

spread throughout the world that great light which is God."[13] Translated, by dint of logic, we can see that he spoke euphemistically of the manipulation of the ball by the Lady, which allows us to suppose that it remained near her waist. Notice the conceptual complexity of Francisco's speech, and review what we have said about the temporal and symbolic adaptability of the way language was used to describe the events at Fátima.

If this "ball" of 1922 is transformed into a "heart" in 1941, 74 pages later, this "heart" is converted into "the Immaculate Heart of Mary."[14]

THE MOVEMENTS

The seers agree that the Being "never smiled nor looked sad, but was always serious." Furthermore, she never directed her gaze toward the multitude of onlookers, nor did she perform the sign of the cross, pray, or unravel the beads of the Rosary. Francisco, who could not hear the Lady, noticed another detail: *the immobility of her mouth.*

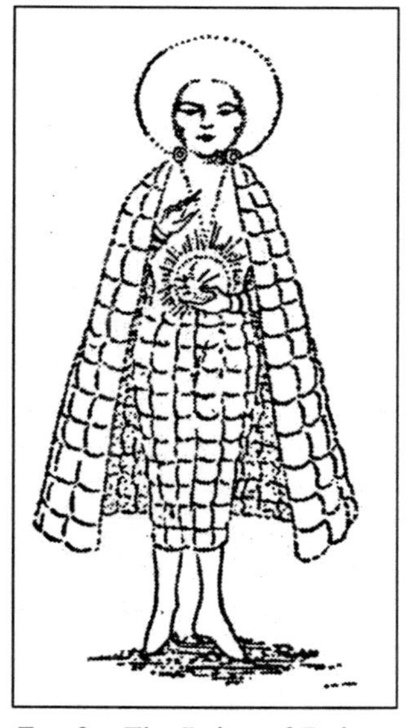

Fig. 2 – The Being of Fátima, as drawn by Claro Fângio, according to the initial description provided by Lúcia to the *Parochial Inquiry.*

And as for her hands? At least she moved them when she manipulated the ball. When she spoke, Lúcia told the priest of the parish "*she separated her hands a little more or less the distance of her shoulders.*" To the Dutch priest, Huberto Iongen, Lúcia allows us to perceive that on the fourth and fifth visits, the Lady did not move her hands,[15] while during the sixth "she turned the palms of her hands upward, and the rays which flowed from them seemed reflected by the Sun."[16]

On October 19th, Jacinta informed the Viscount of Montelo "the Lady pointed with her finger to a band where the Sun is."Hours after the final apparition, Francisco gave us another clue: "*She did not walk. She went certain where she was going. She did not move her feet.*" He described how she glided in the direction of a point in the sky, but curiously, that she departed *with her back to them*, which suggests that she moved to make a half-turn. The Being left, retreating with her back to the witnesses, by disappearing a little at a time, as if fading. First "her head, then the body, the last thing I saw were the feet," Lúcia explained.

Summarizing, therefore, the principal outlines of the "portrait" of the Being "that descended from the sky," we find that:

- *She was an apparently feminine and very beautiful figure*
- *She was wrapped in a light "that blinded"*
- *She measured approximately 1.10 meters tall*
- *She appeared to be between 12 and 15 years old*
- *She wore a skirt, a coat, a robe, and maybe a cape, which were white*
- *Her skirt and robe had checkered strands of gold*
- *Her coat had two or three cords at the wrists*
- *She wore something on her head that covered her ears and hair*
- *She had black eyes*
- *She had with her a strand of beads resembling a rosary, some type of hoop earrings at her neck, and a luminous ball at her waist*
- *She came from above and disappeared, little by little, in the inverse direction*
- *She made no facial movements, nor articulated her inferior limbs when moving*
- *She spoke without moving her lips*
- *She moved only her hands, once in a while*
- *She turned her back on the seers when departing*

3. WHO WAS THE BEING?

"Most Holy Father:
On September 19, 1846, a Lady appeared to me;
They say she is the Blessed Virgin;
You judge, by what follows,
if it might have been She."
– Seer at La Salette

The apparent morphological diversity of the beings that act in the context of apparitions of a religious nature and the tenor of the message they leave their human percipients – assuming different intrinsic and extrinsic factors – appear to point to a multiplicity of typologies. The only visible thing that links these types of manifestations is that they adopt the persona of a celebrated female, different from our known world.

Common sense tells us that a human being that died 2000 years ago, in old age, cannot circulate among us today with the features of a 15-year-old girl. Sometimes a being identified as the Virgin Mary is a common person, knocking on doors, as happened in San Damiano. Other times, she allows herself to be touched, and her body is clearly made of flesh, even emitting heat (L'Ile-Bouchard, December 1947). In Sicily, in 1950, 12-year-old Maria Pina saw such a Lady. "She placed her hand on my shoulder. Her hand was living flesh, I touched it. Her dress was very white." In turn, Brazilian doctor Fausto de Faria (1967-68) said, "a lady (dressed 'as the Virgin') appeared distinctly to be flesh and bone."[1]

The stature of these "Virgins" varied between the height of the young girls of the town (San Damiano) and that of a "bottle of wine" (France, Hydrequent, 1953); some are large (Dr. Fausto de Faria), or larger than normal (La Salette); others are the small size of the seers, 1.10 – 1.20 meters (as found in the majority of cases, Lourdes, Fátima).

If the believers do not doubt that these are somehow the multiple representations of the Mother of Christ, the most direct interpreters of these cases have publicly manifested their doubts. It was so in La Salette, Lourdes, and Fátima. What would cause illiterate children, whose only culture is that of their indigenous religion, to doubt the identity of a being that has appeared before them?

THE SEERS' DOUBTS

La Salette

Five years after La Salette, when Melanie, 15 years old, the principal seer, wrote to the Pope, giving an account of the classic "secrets," she began by saying: "Most Holy Father: on September 19, 1846, a Lady appeared to me; they say she is the Blessed Virgin; *You judge, by what follows, if it might have been She*."[2] In other words, the seer transferred the lady's identification to the Pope, alleviating herself of that responsibility.

Lourdes

"Bernadette never gave the Lady the name of Holy Virgin at the height of the Apparitions," wrote Father Cros, who questioned her and wrote the history of this well-known case in France.[3] After various encounters with the being, the young woman insisted: "It is the others who say that she is the Virgin

Mary."[4] Before the image of the Lady of Lourdes sculpted by J. Fabisch, Bernadette is said to have exclaimed in awe: "It is beautiful… *but that is not She*."[5] That Bernadette made this statement is supported by Professor Xavier Coutinho, docent of the Faculty of the School of Letters of Porto and its Greater Seminary, a member of the Academy of Sciences.

Fátima

Maria dos Anjos, sister of Lúcia, reaffirmed, in May 1979, to a journalist writing for the *Jornal de Notícias* [*News Journal*] the initial opinion of the seer when asked what had happened.[6] After 62 years, Maria remembered that her sister had told her how "a very pretty Lady" had appeared to her, "although she never referred to Her as being Our Lady."

In her *Memórias* [*Memoirs*], the seer managed to confess that, after the Apparitions of May and June 1917, she considered absenting herself from the "encounters," out of fear that they could be the work of the Devil.[7] She reconsidered, however, as if "impelled by a strange force," which is, as we shall see, a component that is omnipresent in human confrontations with other intelligent life forms. But, why these doubts?

As with Lourdes, the image of the Chapel of the Apparitions offered in 1920 by Gilberto dos Santos does not correspond to the initial description of the Being. Yet, it is She who is worshipped at Cova da Iria. Professor Coutinho recorded that dos Santos interviewed the seers and commissioned an image for the House of Fânzeres, in Braga.[8] The artisan to whom fell the execution of the task, J. Thedim, had no major difficulties in the realization of this work. "[H]e was inspired by an image of Our Lady of Lapa, of Casa Estrela, who corresponded with evident faithfulness to the description given by the seers of Fátima," Father dos Santos concluded."In this image, which is part of *Catálogo da Casa Estrela* [*The Catalogue of the House of*

Fig. 3 – On the left, a pamphlet of the Virgin of Fátima from 1927, placed side-by-side with the image upon which it was based, Our Lady of Lapa, as depicted in a pamphlet from 1914 (Courtesy of Dr. Xavier Coutinho).

Estrela], published in 1914, *with small modification of the details*… was found the solution, which had great success at the Sanctuary at Cova da Iria."

All of this leads us to conclude that the experiences of the young shepherds were overtaken by popular belief – by the distorted, underlying idea of the reality. The supernatural is an artificial, confused notion, a realm wherein live creatures that need, perhaps, to be "humanized" and made more palatable. The images construct themselves, the cult of worship surges. Sanctuaries are built, channeling to themselves the flow of multitudes intimidated by the present and ignorant of the future. As to the seers, secluded from the world, they find themselves trapped in the layers of the imaginary that they themselves helped to cultivate, while, unhappily, they are kept from the gaze of objective investigators. Afterwards, institutionalized belief becomes rarefied, until it is considered a crime *les majeste* to seek the truth in its original form rather than substitute instead a truth "supernatural" and credible.

THE ENDURING FACTS OF THE MESSAGE OF FÁTIMA

We know how very difficult it is to interpret what is not understood. Before the "Marian" messages, we have the pure sensation of a certain inability to reconcile it with the teachings of the Roman Catholic Church. Father André Richard addressed this preoccupation, when he wrote of what "a great effort was made in our time to integrate the Marian doctrine into the theological."[9]

For that reason, the message translated by Lúcia cannot, in its entirety, be understood literally. An entire semantic process was set in motion during the course of time. On the other hand, a fair approximation of the content of the Fátima message will have to bear in mind the relative faithfulness of the original testimony of 1922. We have seen how the dialogue was blocked on May 13th. The paranormal became the supernatural, and the supernatural became the religious.

In the following months, the vagaries continued, focusing the conversation between the Being and Lúcia around the following central themes: setting the date of the next encounter (the 13th of each month); recitation of the Rosary; construction of a wooden platform of the kind used to carry religious icons in parades; suggestions that Lúcia learn to read and write; requests of the priests; offers of gifts to the Lady; construction of a chapel; and promise of a miracle concerning the end of the war.

Strictly speaking, there was not an explicit expression during the six months that would permit a clear identification of the heavenly visitor. It is odd that we should be struggling with a phrase of the dialogue from October 13th. On that date, the Lady would tell Lúcia: "Make a chapel here to Our Lady of the

Rosary." The seer thought that it might have been: "Make a chapel here. I am the Lady of the Rosary." We think that these doubts may be logical, in that, as previously noted, "capela" and "rosario" share the same meaning in the Portuguese language, as they do in others. The Being may have included them in the same phrase, thereby provoking Lúcia's doubts.

Thus, availing ourselves a third time of Professor Coutinho, we can verify that "etymologically, *chapelle* (or chapel) is nothing more than a grouping of flowers around the head, exactly as Our Lady had on as seen by the seers of La Salette; not missing at her chest was a cross pendant of the *rosary* of flowers. *Rosary* and *chapel* are synonyms."[10]

In this detail, we can extract from the message of Fátima four designations that point to one meaning: – *capela* [chapel]; *rosário* [rosary]; *terço* [rosary]; *arco de flores de roda* [flower wreath].

Perhaps it is of some importance to say that a wreath of flowers and a rosary, when open and not suffering the effects of gravity, form the same symbol.

In our culture, this symbol (right) represents:

- the goddess Venus (a mother-goddess)
- the planet Venus
- the Morning Star (which designates the same planet and the Virgin Mary)
- all that is considered feminine
- the female chromosome

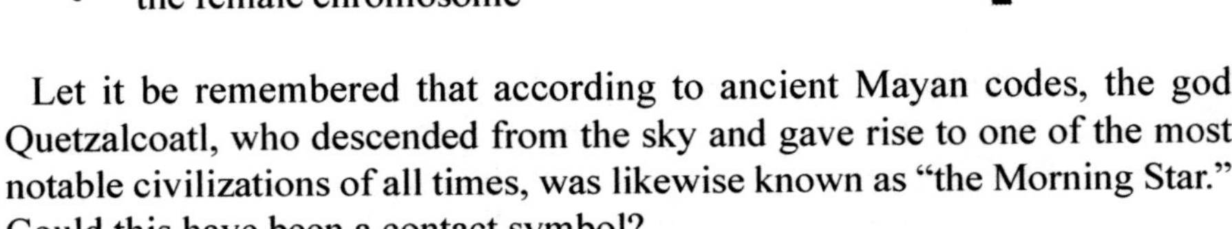

Let it be remembered that according to ancient Mayan codes, the god Quetzalcoatl, who descended from the sky and gave rise to one of the most notable civilizations of all times, was likewise known as "the Morning Star." Could this have been a contact symbol?

THE UNIDENTIFIED BEING

It was not merely at Fátima that the Being kept her identity secret. The other apparitions of the same typology also remained nameless. In his work *Les Apparitions de la Vierge* [*The Apparitions of the Virgin*], Tizané studied 57 cases involving sudden apparitions, and explored, among other things, the question of the refusal of identification by the being.[11] Assuming, for the sake of argument, that the Lady of Fátima failed to identify herself and that the remaining cases of identification submitted were true, we take note of the fact that in the seven apparitions recognized by the Church, the Lady identified herself in only three cases (43%). In the other 50 cases of unrecognized apparitions, she identified herself in only 27 (54%).

Table 1: Identifications

Apparitions Recognized			**Apparitions not Recognized**		
Identified	*Unidentified*	*Total*	*Identified*	*Unidentified*	*Total*
3	**4**	**7**	**23**	**27**	**50**

In Beauraing, children see a white mass transporting itself in space and exclaim: "Look! The Most Holy Virgin is passing over the bridge!" In this fatal manner, all the strange ladies that appear among us are identified as the Virgin Mary. It has become a fact acquired by force of habit. In some cases, the heavenly visitors appear, cure someone (almost always a woman), and then disappear without leaving their calling card.

WHAT ORIGINS?

In light of the fact that it is impossible, immediately, to establish the space-time limits of this type of being, we will attempt to draw the boundaries of the apparition phenomenon itself, which, in agreement with Salvador Freixedo, has been characterized in all eras, religions, or environments, as being:

- a real phenomenon, that is not precisely what we are seeing and hearing
- a phenomenon of the physical order (radiations, vibrations, etc.), but governed by physical laws with which we are, as of yet, unfamiliar
- a phenomenon that completely alters the normal functioning of our senses and our brains, inducing (intentionally or not) cognitive error.[12]

While some authors, such as Bertrand Méheust, totally reject the extraterrestrial hypothesis of the first degree, on the grounds that it posits entities manning material crafts,[13] others, notably the French investigator Aimé Michel, have gravitated towards the advanced para-physical dominions, or the physics of interactions between mind and matter. The UFO phenomenon, and, by association, the apparition phenomenon, could, perhaps, be a fantastic *poltergeist* – in which an object dislocates itself spontaneously in space, as if under the psychic direction of someone at a distance....[14]

Freixedo hypothesizes several possible solutions to the origin (or origins) of UFOs. They might be:

- projections of the collective unconscious of humanity
- manifestations of entities or intelligent energies from other dimensions
- manifestations of other physical inhabitants of our world
- nuclei of almost intelligent residual psychic energy, acting automatically
- visits by extraterrestrial beings[15]

Other investigators, within a more rational and economic prism, systematize their ultimate origins in three large groups:

- somewhere in this universe (our solar system, our galaxy, or others);
- in a universe:

1st – parallel to ours in space-time
2nd – parallel to our space but not contemporaneous
3rd – or parallel to our time but not in space

- intelligent processes beyond our own space-time *continuum*.[17]

Dr. Jacques Vallée and the late Dr. J. Allen Hynek have advanced similar parameters. In a work jointly authored,[17] they propose four hypotheses:

1A – extraterrestrials
1B – extra-human terrestrials
2A – beings from a secret human base
2B – genetic programming

They put forward still, as their working hypothesis, the interaction of universes with quantum laws different from ours, our space-time *continuum* being simply one cross-section of a universe with a multiplicity of dimensions.

But what other phenomena, pray tell, were observed at Fátima that support our suspicion that it was not an apparition of the Virgin Mary?

Notes

1. THE DAY OF MAY 13TH

[1] MARCHI, João de, *Era uma Senhora Mais Brilhante que o Sol* [*It was a Lady Brighter than the Sun*], 8th ed., Fátima, Missões Consalata, 1966, p. 83.

[2] BROCHADO, Costa, *As Aparições de Fátima* [*The Apparitions of Fátima*], Lisbon, Portugalia Editora, 1952, p. 52.

[3] FIGUEIREDO, Antero de, *Fátima (Gracas, Segredos, Mistérios)* [*Fátima (Graces, Secrets, and Mysteries)*], 14th ed., Lisbon, Bertrand, 1945, pp. 34-35.

[4] BROCHADO, Costa, op. cit., p. 59.

[5] Manuel Nunes Formigão (1883-1958) was born at the Monastery of Christ in the town of Tomar, a domain of the well-known medieval religious order the Templars. He was educated at the Gregorian University in Rome, where he earned a doctorate in Theology and Canon Law. He once stayed at the Lourdes Sanctuary for a month. In 1917, he was a professor at the Santarém High School and Seminary. He later became a member of the Committee for the Canon Process of Fátima, for which he wrote the document that led the Catholic Church, in 1930, to recognize the Marian nature of the Apparitions.

[6] The interrogations of the Canon Formigão (also known as the Viscount of Montelo) were included in his book *As Grandes Maravilhas de Fátima* [*The Great Wonders of Fátima*], Lisbon, 1927, and also in REIS, Sebastião Martins dos, *A Vidente de Fátima Dialoga e Responde pelas Aparicoes* [*The Seer of Fátima Dialogues and Answers for the Apparitions*], Braga, ed. Franciscana, 1970, pp. 89-114.

[7] The newspaper *A Voz de Fátima* [*The Voice of Fátima*], no. 3, December 13, 1922.

[8] Although we have consulted the original, the excerpts from the Parish Inquiry published in this work are taken from d'ARMADA, Fina, *Fátima – O Que se Passou em 1917* [*Fátima – What Happened in 1917*], Amadora, Bertrand, 1980.

[9] PASQUALE, Humberto, *Eu Vi Nascer Fátima* [*I Saw the Birth of Fátima*], Porto, Salesians, 1967, p. 91.

[10] The newspaper *O Mensageiro* [*The Messenger*], November 29, 1971.

[11] MARCHI, João de, op. cit., p. 49.

[12] BROCHADO, Costa, op. cit., p. 14.

[13] MONTELO, Viscount of, op. cit, resp. pp. 87 and 91.

[14] MARCHI, João de, op. cit., p. 86.

[15] FIGUEIREDO, Antero de, op. cit., resp. pp. 78-79 and 358.

[16] Ibid.

[17] FISCHER, Louis, *Fátima, a Lourdes Portuguesa* [*Fátima, the Portuguese Lourdes*], 1929, p. 19.

[18] The magazine *Stella* [*Star*], no. 114, June 1946, pp. 18-19.

[19] BARTHAS, Canon, *Fátima*, Lisbon, Aster, 1967, p. 37.

[20] GENS, José Pereira, *Fátima – Como Eu a Vi e como a Sinto (Memórias de um Médico)* [*Fátima – As I Saw It and as I Feel It (Memoirs of a Physician)*], 1967, preface.

[21] REIS, Sebastião Martins dos, *Uma Vida ao Servico de Fátima – Deus e o Diabo na Quinta do Inferno* [*Life of Service to Fátima – God and the Devil in Hell's Farm*],

Évora, 1973, pp. 304-321.

[22] All of the excerpts are quoted from *The Official Interrogations of 1923*, as cited in d'ARMADA, Fina, *supra.*

[23] *Memórias e Cartas da Irmã Lúcia* [*Memoirs and Letters of Sister Lúcia*], Porto, 1973, p. 331.

[24] The inquiry of 1947. REIS, Sebastiao Martins dos, *A Vidente de Fátima Dialoga e Responde pelas Aparicoes*, op. cit., pp. 55-64.

2. WHAT WAS THE BEING LIKE?

[1] The inquiry conducted by Father José Ferreira de Lacerda, probably in October, was published in his newspaper in its editions of November 8th, 15th, 22nd, and 29th for 1917. The reference relating to the Being's age and height, by comparison to the patterns of Lúcia's friend Virginia, was published in the November 15th edition.

[2] BARTHAS, Canon C., *Fátima*, Lisbon, Aster, 1969, p. 39.

[3] Ibid., p. 40.

[4] *Os Grandes Fenómenos da Cova da Iria e a História da Primeira Imagem de Nossa Senhora de Fátima* [*The Great Phenomena at Cova da Iria and the History of the First Images of Our Lady of Fátima*], 1956, pp. 47 and 60.

[5] *Memórias e Cartas da Irmã Lúcia*, op. cit., resp. pp. 179 and 367.

[6] Ibid.

[7] The first report of the seer remained unknown until 1973 or 1974, in the hands of her confessor, at the Vilar Asylum, Monsignor Dr. Manuel Pereira Lopes (23.07.1880/18.06.1069.) It was given to the public by REIS, Sebastiao Martins dos, *Uma Vida ao Serviço de Fátima*, op. cit., pp. 320-321.

[8] PASQUALE, Humberto, op. cit., p. 57.

[9] *Memórias e Cartas da Irmã Lúcia*, op. cit. p. 367.

[10] *Os Grandes Fenómenos da Cova da Iria...*, op. cit., p. 47.

[11] FARIA, P.O., *Perguntas sobre Fátima* e *"Fátima Desmascarada"* [*Questions about Fátima* and *"Fátima Unmasked"*], Porto, 1975, p. 174.

[12] Barcelona, ed. Planeta, 1982, pp. 166-169.

[13] *Memórias e Cartas da Irmã Lúcia*, op. cit., p. 263.

[14] Ibid., p. 337.

[15] The magazine *Médiatrice et Reine* [*Mediatrix and Queen*], nos. May-October 1946, cit. *Stella*, February 1947, no. 122, p. 18.

[16] REIS, Sebastiao Martins dos, *A Vidente de Fátima Dialoga e Responde pelas Aparições,* Braga, ed. Franciscana, 1970, p. 81.

3. WHO WAS THE BEING?

[1] TIZANÉ, E., *Les Apparitions de la Vierge: un enquêteur laïc s'interroge* [*The Apparitions of the Virgin: a lay investigator asks himself*], Tchou, 1977, pp. 198-199.

[2] ULLATHORNE, *A Santa Montanha de La Salette* [*The Holy Mountain of La Salette*], 1858, p. 107, cit. por ILHARCO, João, *Fátima Desmascarada* [*Fátima*

Unmasked], Coimbra, 1971, p. 168.
[3] TIZANE, E., op. cit., p. 54.
[4] LASSERE, Henri, *Notre Dame de Lourdes* [*Our Lady of Lourdes*], cit. por ILHARCO, João, op. cit., p. 180.
[5] COUTINHO, Xavier, *Nossa Senhora na Arte* [*Our Lady in Art*], Porto, Associação Católica do Porto, 1959, p. 139.
[6] The newspaper *Jornal de Notícias* [*News Journal*], Porto, May 13, 1979.
[7] *Memórias e Cartas da Irmã Lúcia*, op. cit., p. 137.
[8] COUTINHO, Xavier, op. cit., p. 141.
[9] RICHARD, André, *Sinais para o Nosso Tempo, Fátima – Vaticano II* [*Signs for Our Times, Fátima – Vatican II*], Lisbon, Circulo de Estudos Sociais, Vector, 1972, p. 19.
[10] COUTINHO, Xavier, *La Salette, Mensagem Marial do Seculo XIX* [*La Salette, a Marian Message from the 19th Century*], Porto, 1970, p. 40.
[11] TIZANE, E., op. cit., pp. 86-90.
[12] FREIXEDO, Salvador, *La Religion entre la Parapsicologia y los Ovnis* [*Religion within Parapsychology and Ufology*], Mexico, Orion, 1977, p. 220.
[13] MÉHEUST, Bertrand, *Science fiction et soucoupes volantes* [*Science fiction and flying saucers*], Mercure de France, 1978.
[14] MICHEL, Aimé, *Mysterieux objects celestes* [*Mysterious celestial objects*], Seghers, 1977, p. 341.
[15] FREIXEDO, Salvador, op. cit., p. 161 *et seq.*
[16] *UFO Investigation*, BUFORA, England, Newchapel, 1979.
[17] HYNEK, J. Allen and VALLÉE, Jacques, *Aux limites de la realite* [*To the limits of reality*], Paris, Albin Michel, 1978, p. 250.

PART TWO

THE UNUSUAL THAT COULD NOT BE MADE UP

Phenomena Associated with Cova da Iria

1. LIGHTNING

"All three ran to the oak tree with us behind them....
Then, we began to hear something akin to a fine voice.
But what it said could not be understood;
It was like the buzzing of bees."
– Maria Carreira

The editor of *O Mensageiro*, Father José Ferreira de Lacerda, questioned Lúcia in 1917, as we know. He asked her: "What were you doing when you saw Our Lady for the first time?"

> We were watching the sheep. It was sunny. *There was a flash of lightning*, and I said: 'O, Francisco, we had better go, because a thunderstorm is coming.' "There was another flash of lightning. I looked toward the oak tree, and I saw a lady on top of it.[1]

Lightning, on a sunny day and without thunder, was the first unusual phenomenon observed at Cova da Iria. During that first apparition, because the seers were alone, they were the only ones who witnessed it.

In subsequent months, it was the lightning that announced the arrival of the Being.In September, "around noon, we were there, waiting for the Lady to come. *Then, there was a flash of lightning*, and the Lady appeared."[2]

According to Lúcia, *the lightning always occurred prior to the Apparitions*. She observed it from May through October and on August 19th, in the Valinhos. Later, the seer found other terms with which to describe the lightning. "The flashes of lightning were not actually lightning," she wrote in her *Memórias*, "but a reflection of a light that was drawing near. Seeing that light is the reason we said, sometimes, that we would see Our Lady; but more accurately, we could only distinguish Our Lady in that light when it was already atop the oak tree."[3]

In relation to the June apparition, for example, Lúcia continued: "After praying the Rosary with Jacinta and Francisco and the others present, we again saw *the reflection of the light that approached (that we called lightning)*."[4]

With the spread of the news of the Apparitions, diverse people began to travel to the locale. From June to October, therefore, the seers were never again alone. Those first "pilgrims," at that point merely the curious, would they not also have seen lightning at Cova da Iria?

There is no testimony that speaks to us of that observation, except in one month – August! But it is interesting to verify that, on that day, the children were not present. The municipal president of the town of Nova de Ourém had earlier appeared in Aljustrel, and offered to take the young shepherds by car. His name was Artur de Oliveira Santos. He was president and founder of a Masonic lodge, a judge *pro tem* for the county seat, and a committed anticlerical republican. Acting, for this reason, politically, in defense of the "liberal Republic," he did not stop at Cova da Iria but took the children to his house.

When word of their detention reached the multitude of 15,000 to 18,000 Portuguese,[5] gathered near the oak tree, some among the throng became so outraged that they set out for the town of Nova de Ourém. The Being, however, even in the absence of the little shepherds, produced the "signal." And it was, in this way, that those people present observed for the first and last times the "lightning" or explosion of light.

A seminarian, later known by Father Joel de Deus Magno, related this from the Viscount of Montelo:

> We were there for only a short while, when some very happy men approached saying that Our Lady had appeared. I quickly bade farewell to the priests and went to the summit. The streets were already filling with those commenting on the tumultuous event. To each group, I asked what they had seen. Quicker than the flash of a match, many people surrounded me, who, amid great clamor, told me that they had heard thunder, and all the people had fled.... *Others said they had seen lightning....* [6]

But there were those who remained at the location that reported: "The people grew silent. The weather was clear. Then, suddenly, "*lightning took form in the sky over the altar*, and made a swirl of the round altar," we are told by João Pereira Novo, of the village of Famalicão near the town of Nazaré.[7]

The altar was comprised of a table of flowers and a semicircle of sticks with two lanterns. Maria Carreira had prepared it. Known also by the names "Maria dos Santos" and "Maria da Capelinha," this rustic neighborhood woman was the most important witness to the Apparitions and the greatest worker on behalf of Fátima. It was Maria Carreira who served as treasurer of the important amounts of money gathered in the early days, before the construction of the Chapel of the Apparitions, and who always worked toward the development of Fátima as a religious center.

In August, João de Marchi wrote that there arose "a hubbub, and I don't know what would have resulted in that, had there not been the sudden thunder... *[T]he thunder was followed by the lightning....*"[8]

PARALLELS IN UFOLOGY

Ufology is a consortium of scientific disciplines that studies the complex problem of unidentified flying objects, or UFOs. Formerly, all observations of this type were analyzed within the context of religious phenomenology. Supernatural entities benevolent or malevolent (according to the adopted religious patterns), angels or demons, gods or beings of light – these were the designations of the heavenly visitors of the past. The feminine figures have often been "recognized" as being Mary, mother of Jesus. They have been so ubiquitous, appearing under so many facets, formats, and aspects of the Catholic faith, that they may be tantamount to the most common polytheistic belief in history. Even an apologetic little book, written to celebrate the Virgin Mary, tells us: "How many 'Ladies' there may be on our Earth is something that no one can know, not even with electronic brains."[9]

In our time, an immense body of literature has been gathered that describes for us unusual observations made all over the planet. If we leaf through these copious volumes, we will certainly find testimony that speaks to us not only of lightning bolts, *but those occurring apart from stormy days*, hence supporting the range of manifestations that we speak of on the following pages.

Southeastern France, November 2, 1968

An eminent physician, who requested anonymity, told Michel that he was awakened by the screams of his 14-month-old son, who was pointing to a window through which he could see *lightning, which the doctor took as a sign of an oncoming storm.* Going to the terrace of the house, he saw outside, at a small distance, two identical objects in the shape of disks that, progressively, neared each other and ended up merging into one.[10]

Almonaster la Real, Spain, August 3, 1977

Within the phenomenology of UFOs, we also find accounts of "lighting" preceding a sighting of bizarre entities. Thus, Ceferina Vargas Martin of Spain was walking along a path when she suddenly received a reflection in her eyes. "It was a *dazzling light* that bothered her eyes. Some 15 or 20 meters further ahead, she received a new *flash of lightning* to her face. It was, like the first, a beam of white light the size of a bicycle light." Suddenly, as she noticed that her strength was beginning to falter, she saw that in the place where the light had been were two strange entities, one of which was the figure of a woman, very tall.[11]

Returning quickly back to 1917, it will be curious to establish a final synthesis of the data cited with Lúcia's description about their initial observation of the Being:

> Playing with Jacinta and Francisco, at the summit of the slope of Cova da Iria, while making a little wall around a thicket, *we suddenly saw, what seemed to be a flash of lightning.*
>
> "It's best that we go home," I said to my cousins, "lightning is flashing; a thunderstorm could come...."
>
> And we began descending the slope, touching the sheep, in the direction of the road.
>
> When we had more or less reached the middle of the slope, just close to a large oak that was there, we saw another flash of lightning and, after several more steps, we saw a Lady over the oak tree.[12]

The obfuscating luminosity emitted by UFOs is described in various ways according to the distance of the assembled witnesses. That idea, as a general rule, is present whenever one seeks to study the source of the emissions coming from UFOs. The American nuclear physicist James McCampbell has conducted an interesting and detailed series of experiments into the means by which to reproduce the brilliant light that emanates from UFOs. In his study, he exhaustively analyzed the effect of temperature on the ionization of atmospheric gases, so as to verify these flashes of white light. He concluded that they operate on the basis of pulsating emissions of microwaves, and with the help of an electromagnetic field created by these bursts, form a plasma field around the object.[13]

Fig. 5 – "Feminine" beings observed near Almonaster la Real, Spain, on August 3, 1977. Here, lightning also preceded the apparitional event (Courtesy of Stendek).

2. "THE BUZZING OF BEES"

And the Being spoke. To Lúcia, it was not strange at all. They understood each other in Portuguese, as if Mary, the Mother of Jesus, had become a polyglot, or as if 2000 years of history had not altered the language of the people. The news spread throughout the village, and on June 13th, part of the neighborhood came to the site of the Apparitions.

They were not many. "I counted the people and saw that only 40 were present," wrote Inácio António Marques.[1] And those people anxiously waited in that deserted place for the veritable Queen of Heaven to descend to the oak tree, in the hopes of contemplating her serene face, one popularly imagined being young, soft, and extraordinarily beautiful.

Stella, through the voice of writer Maria de Freitas (who behind the scenes wrote a great part of the book about Fátima attributed to Father João de Marchi), captured forever the impressions of that first day in which onlookers participated.[2] Among them was Maria Carreira, who, in the language of a simple countrywoman, later described for the journalist her memories of the event:

> At the same instant, Lúcia jumped up and exclaimed, 'O, Jacinta, *there she comes already, there was the lightning*," and then ran to kneel at the foot of the oak.'
>
> "And you did not see anything?" de Freitas asked.
>
> "Me? No, ma'am. And no one boasted about having seen the lightning. We would follow the children and kneel in the middle of the field. Lúcia would raise her hands and say, "You bade me come here, what do you wish of me?" *And then could be heard a buzzing that seemed to be that of a bee.* I took care to discern whether it was the Lady speaking."
>
> "And everyone heard it?" the reporter asked.
>
> "Well, it could be heard very well!" Carreira answered.

The buzzing of a bee – here is the voice attributed to Our Lady of Fátima by the miracle's greatest publicist. She, and the other onlookers, did not hear a voice speaking Hebrew, Aramaic, or even Portuguese, but a voice like that of an insect.

This same witness recounted this same episode to Father João de Marchi. In his work, entitled *Era uma Senhora Mais Brilhante que o Sol* [*It was a Lady*

More Brilliant than the Sun], we read[3]:

> I had been sick, and was feeling very weak. It must have been around midday, when Lúcia was asked: "Will Our Lady be long delayed?"
>
> "No, ma'am, she will not be long," she responded.
>
> The tiny child was watching for the signs.
>
> We prayed the Rosary and, when the girl from Boleiros was going to begin the Litany, Lúcia interrupted her, saying that there was no longer sufficient time. She immediately rose to her feet and shouted:
>
> "Jacinta, there comes Our Lady, the lightning has struck."
>
> All three children ran to the oak, as we ran behind them. We knelt upon the thickets and shrubs. Lúcia lifted her hands, as in prayer, and I heard her say:
>
> "You bade me to come here, please tell me what you want."
>
> Then we began to hear something like this, in the manner of a very fine voice, but what it said could not be comprehended or put into words, *for it was like the buzzing of a bee*!

But that buzzing did not disturb the silence of the mountain only in June. The following month, word spread throughout the entire region and nearly four to five thousand people found their way to Cova da Iria.[4] Jacinto de Almeida Lopes, proprietor of the site of the Shrine later established by the parish of Fátima, was among them. He would be one of the eyewitnesses chosen by the parish priest to testify during the *Inquiry*. The parish priest, writing in the third person, related the evidence given by Lopes:

> "Then what is it that you want of me?"
>
> After this question, she waited in silence for a short period of time, the time of a brief response. And during this silence, he heard, as if coming from the oak tree, a faint voice, *similar*, he says, *to the humming of a bee, but without distinguishing a single word.*

In July, Manuel Marto, the father of Jacinta and Francisco, made his way to the site for the first time. Questioned as to what he experienced, he told João de Marchi: "I heard *a sound, a din, such as a great fly makes inside an empty water pot,*" and wondered whether it was "far off or close by."[5]

Manuel Marto helped himself to odd comparisons. When interrogated about the same matter by the Italian priest Humberto Pasquale, he affirmed: "I heard something like *the buzzing of a fly inside an empty barrel*, but without articulation of words."[6] For his part, Pasquale added: "Mr. Manuel Marto explained to us that, during the entire duration of the appearance, those present heard an indefinable sound, *like that which is heard next to a hive, but altogether more harmonious, even though words were not heard.*"

In this same month, we find other testimony, however, which demonstrated that the buzzing must have been heard quite well, which, as a matter of fact, Maria Carreira stated. António Baptista, from Moita, in the parish of Fátima, was then 50 years old. When interviewed by the Viscount of Montelo on November 13, 1917, he declared, "on July 13th, I was at Cova da Iria. She (Lúcia) knelt. I thought I heard, at that moment, a little wind, *a zoa-zoa sound.* While Lúcia was listening to a response, *it seemed there was a buzzing sound like that of a cicada.*"[7]

"Many people say that when the Apparition was speaking, it could be heard," wrote J. de S. Bento, in a letter possibly penned on October 13th of that year.[8] "But they could not distinguish what She was saying." And another witness also made reference to the sounds of the "speech" of the Being. Manuel Gonçalves, Jr., a 30-year-old farmer from Montelo – the place name that the Canon Formigão adopted in his pseudonym – also declared on October 11th "some people have affirmed that they hear the sound of the answers."[9]

Herewith we arrive at 1978. In July 18th of that year, the authors interviewed the relatives of the seers and eyewitnesses then still living. One of the people with whom we spoke was Lúcia's sister, Maria dos Anjos. Sitting in an armchair, beside the house where she was born, living out the rest of her days, smiling to the daily visitors, she narrated for us once again the story that had forever altered the life of her family:

> "Did you know Maria Carreira?" we asked, on that hot summer afternoon.
>
> "I knew her as well as I knew my own mother."
>
> "She said that when Our Lady would speak, she would hear something like the humming of a bee ... *I also heard that little buzz.* I also got to hear it, but I know not what it was."
>
> "Was it as if there were many bees?" we asked.
>
> "No, only one," she responded, categorically.

"Do you recall what month that was?"

"At that time, I did not go there every month. It seemed as if a bee was around there whenever Lúcia was listening. But I have no idea what it was!"

"I have no idea what it was!" Her statement gives one pause to consider whether the event should have been given a Marian interpretation, if the sound that the Being made was not even understood. In truth, who can explain why her voice was comparable to the buzzing of a bee? Or yet to the buzz of a great fly inside a water pot, or of a fly inside an empty barrel? Have these sounds been heard solely in Fátima? Or have there been, in other parts of the world, other witnesses to identical sounds?

PARALLELS IN UFOLOGY

The Azores, Portugal, January 31, 1968

The Azores Air Station is in Cabrito, Cinco Picos, on the island of Terceira. On the night of January 31, 1968, Serafim Sebastião was working as a guard at the airbase. Thirty-six years old and married, Sebastião was a native of Ribeira Grande. The Setúbal sports competition was being broadcast on the radio that evening, and Sebastião was listening to the play-by-play. Suddenly, he could hear that his transistor apparatus was not transmitting properly. He went outside and observed a strange object hovering over the airfield. It was "the shape of an oval, with a metallic gleam that culminated in a tower of glass, with a small balustrade on which rested two beings." The noise and shape of the UFO were unlike those that habitually travel through the air. He was certain that it was not a plane, helicopter, or balloon.

Sebastião described his encounter with the UFO this way:

> I moved further back, and then saw that they were more accurately four men — two within and two without. They moved, and when I focused the beam of the flashlight on them, I saw nothing. I saw only a visor, and the color of the suit that was there, which was the color of lead....

But what does this well-known and widely publicized case have to do with the buzzing of bees heard in Fátima in 1917? It is that Sebastião also related the following: "When I drew near again to the face of the storage hangar and saw the two outside, *I only heard a buzzing, exactly as if it were a swarm of bees*."[10]

Pascagoula, Mississippi, USA, October 11, 1973

Two fishermen, Charles Hickson, age 45, and Calvin Parker, age 19, were near the banks of the Pascagoula River, when they saw an oblong-shaped UFO. It emitted a brilliant blue light *and made a sound similar to that of bees.* An aperture appeared in the object and three beings exited the craft by floating in the air through this opening. The men were taken into the interior of the UFO by two semi-transparent beings, approximately four and a half feet tall, *who emitted a faint buzzing, like that of bees.*[11]

Paravicino d'Erba, Italy, October 20, 1954

Renzo Pugina, age 37, had just put his automobile away in the garage, when he saw a strange, luminous being, almost 1.3 meters in height, close to a tree. The creature directed a luminous beam toward Pugina, and he felt paralyzed. When he attempted to attack the intruder, it elevated itself while making a noise in the nature of "*a faint buzz*."[12]

We recall that the visitor of Fátima was also, according to the seers, a luminous being, small in stature, which appeared over a tree and, at times, directed a light from its hands toward the seers. As one of the children stated: "[A]s it said these words... it opened its hands, causing the reflection that issued from them to penetrate our chests."[13]

As these examples suggest, sighting evidence involving "humming" or "the buzzing of bees" emanating from UFOs and their occupants is amply found in the UFO literature. It is sometimes reported by UFO percipients as having a somewhat lower pitch than that produced by a swarm of bees, but these cases can be correlated in the sense that all of them have as comparative terms the buzzing of insects. McCampbell studied this sound, and after locating its frequency, determined that its origin would ultimately be found to be an electrical system, which was consistent with witness testimony describing it as being "similar to a generator."

He wrote, however, that to the contrary of what would be supposed, "clinical experience demonstrates that certain people can 'hear' energy in a modulated radio frequency that they would interpret to be a type of *buzzing* sound. Apparently, this kind of pulsated energy short-circuits the structure of the ear and induces signals directly to the auditory regions of the brain. Thus, the buzzing emitted by the UFOs (or the entities themselves) could be stimulated directly in the head of the witnesses by a high frequency radiation in a low audible frequency."[14] McCampbell believed that the vocal modulation of the microwaves could be developed to communicate with deaf persons whose ear structure had been destroyed but whose auditory nerve remained intact. We shall see in our later discussion of the testimony of the individual whom we shall introduce as "the fourth seer" that she had the sensation of hearing inside her head the orders of the diminutive being. A similar process may have been involved in the projection of images. K. Gösta Rehn agrees with the notion that microwaves may have been applied to achieve these effects during the communication process by the entities in control of the phenomenon.[15]

Alternatively, the experimental verifications of the French physicist Jean-Pierre Petit would indicate that high frequency radiation associated with the discharge of current (comparable to the frequency at which radar operates) can directly stimulate the auditory nerve and create a sound hallucination of *the buzz* that would be audibly noticed in the range of 1,000 Hertz.[16]

These concurring hypotheses make plausible the dialogue at Cova da Iria, where a series of encounters occurred among beings of diverse natures. Later on this question will be amplified.

3. THUNDER

But the buzzing was not the only sound that resounded in Fátima. Other sounds accompanied the appearance of the strange Being of Light. The witnesses attempted to identify these by comparing them to others that they knew. They likened the sounds to *thunder*, to *rumors*, to *rumbling*, to *the clapping of hands*, to *the detonation of bombs*, to *the hiss of rockets*... Lúcia would catch sight of the lightning and then inform those present of the arrival of the Being. These saw no lightning (except when the seers themselves were not present), but they did hear a sound similar to thunder, that identified the moment when the Apparition would appear over the oak tree. At the instant of her departure, this sound resembled a "hiss" identical to the roar of a rocket.

The thunder echoed in the arid mountain from June to August. Did it come from above? Let us see what the eyewitnesses left us in their accounts of the Fátima incident.

THUNDER AT THE ARRIVAL OF THE BEING

JULY

Although a June 1917 statement about this phenomenon exists, it does not clearly specify whether thunder was manifest at the arrival of the Apparition or at her departure, or perhaps was even mixed with other phenomena observed at the end of her appearance. An unequivocal statement by a witness divulging that thunder was, in fact, heard at the arrival of the Being was published in the July 23, 1917 edition of *O Seculo*. "In this," the newspaper recounted, "*a sound similar to the rumble of thunder can be heard*."

The Viscount of Montelo declared that Manuel Gonçalves, Jr.[1] said that one could hear "a *rumor* in July and in August," by which he meant a sound like thunder.

AUGUST

In August, it seems that the "thunder" was either more notorious or took onlookers by greater surprise.

Gonçalves told the *Parish Inquiry* that in that month, he "noticed that there was *a strong and inexplicable rumbling* beside the oak tree that frightened the crowd, who began to flee, and to scream movingly, and to even have fainting spells." Many eyewitness accounts suggest that such panic was provoked by the thunder.

According to another man who was there, João Perreira Novo, "*[T]he ground shook*, very, very strongly.... When the ground shook, some fell, while others were aghast. I, as well, became so disturbed that, as much as I wanted to see what was happening, I saw little." His statement, the first one written by an eyewitness, was made in a letter to a friend authored on the day after the August visitation, but was published fully 22 months later in the Leiria newspaper *O Mensageiro*. Its chronology cannot be established with certainty, for Perreira Novo shows himself to be quite imaginative.

Manuel Pedro Marto gave this account during *The Official Interrogations of 1923*:

> At Cova da Iria, after having spoken to several people, I clearly heard a *rumbling, followed by dust and fog*. The crowd fled. Almost everyone took off their hats, screamed for Our Lady, and was very happy, saying that they had robbed the children, it is true, but that Our Lady had manifested.

In the *Parish Inquiry*, the priest reported the testimony of Joaquim Inácio Vicente as follows: "I heard two *strong detonations*, similar to *the bang of bombs or shots*, coming from the side of the oak tree."

Still other witnesses refer to the fear provoked by that sound. Joaquim Xavier Tuna told the Viscount of Montelo:

> The crowd, hearing the *noise* at the foot of the oak tree, fled. Some men, who were atop a tree, fell, without any harm befalling them. When I saw what was happening, I told the crowd not to flee, because it was Our Lady who was appearing. The crowd then ceased fleeing, and almost everyone found himself falling to his knees.[2]

In the newspaper *Concelho de Mação* [*Mação County*], Joaquim Gregório Tavares also captured this popular attitude of reverence: "On August 13th, the mayor of Ourem detained them and took them to Ourém. The crowd did not keep from going to the site. At the moment of the appearance, they felt *a strong tremor, and they fell to their knees*."[3]

There were even those who called this thunder a "miracle." Maria dos Anjos, Lúcia's sister, recalled for Antunes de Paiva:

> In the month of August, we were at Cova da Iria when, suddenly, we began to hear *a din that seemed to be coming from the palm trees*. Thinking this clapping had worked the imprisonment of the little shepherds, we became alarmed, and began to flee. At this, I heard a voice that said: "O, people of little faith, do you not see that this is a miracle?"[4]

Lastly, journalist Avelino de Almeida noted: "Others hear *subterranean noises* that indicate the presence of the Lady…."[5]

"THE ROAR OF ROCKETS" AT THE DEPARTURE OF THE BEING

"Then you want nothing more of me," ended Lúcia.

"I want nothing more of you."

The Being then walked confidently in the direction of the clouds. Those present merely saw *a cloud* rise up and again began to hear a hum.

JUNE

"[W]hen Our Lady withdrew from the tree, it was like the distant gust from a rocket when it lifts off," Maria Carreira told João de Marchi, about the June visitation.[6] And in *The Official Interrogations of 1923*, she stated that during this apparition, one could hear "the same whistle when she spoke" and one could see "the same *hissing of rockets* at her departure."

Notwithstanding her account, Inácio António Marques, a postal employee at the time he wrote his statement in 1922, confirmed Avelino de Almeida's words: "It seemed to me that I was hearing subterranean thunder."[7]

JULY

Relative to this month, Maria Carreira testified, in *The Official Interrogations of 1923*, that "the same buzzing" could be heard, "when She spoke and *the same hissing of rockets at her departure*."

Still, the father of the two seers told of the sound of thunder, at the moment in which the Being departed. "At this time, something could be heard," he told Father João de Marchi, "like a large clap of *thunder*, and the little arch upon which the two little lanterns had been placed shook completely, *as it would have in an earthquake*; Lúcia, who was still kneeling, got up and turned around so quickly that even her little handbag ballooned."[8]

And pointing to the sky, Lúcia shouted: "There! There She goes!" And a few moments later: "She can no longer be seen!"

Humberto Pasquale also stated that, "Mr. Manuel Marto explained to us that... at the end, a small, white cloud became visible... at the same time that *the far off boom of thunder* could be heard."[9] This witness stated, however, that in August that sound was heard at the beginning of the apparition, not at the Being's departure.

Nevertheless, with the flight of the crowd, the panic, the fainting spells, the screams, no one tells, in August, of any sound at the moment of departure.

But in this month of July, we find yet another statement about the strange noise. J. de S. Bento, in a letter that he wrote and which is in the Formigão Archives, tell us that, "When Lúcia said, 'There She goes,' I heard a roaring in the air that seemed like *the beginning of thunder*."

AUGUST 19th

The rocket's roar seems to have been heard on another occasion – August 19th. At the time of this apparition, in addition to the seers, João, the brother of Jacinta and Francisco, was present at the Valinhos site. That night, his mother questioned him and he confessed that although he opened his eyes as widely as he could, he had not seen anything. He had heard something *like the sound a rocket makes when it lifts off* when Lúcia, after the conversation with the Being, had said:

"Look, Jacinta, the Lady is going away."[10]

Excluding the "rocket's roar," where do the witnesses say the strange thunder comes from? It was "subterranean," said Inácio António Marques, Manuel Marto (in July), the newspapers *O Seculo* and *Concelho de Mação*, and even João Pereira Novo.

"It came from the oak tree," confirmed Manuel Goncalves, Jr., Manuel Marto (in August), Joaquim Xavier Tuna, and Joaquim Inácio Vicente.

But Maria Carreira furnished us interesting evidence, relative to the month of August: "The thunder was more or less like the other time (in July); some say it came from the street, others from the oak tree. It seemed to me that it came from far off...."[11]

THE THUNDER AND THE GODS

Curiously, different mythologies connect "thunder" to the activity of the Gods, to their functions, or to their names. Erich von Daniken, in his work, *O Ouro dos Deuses* [*The Gold of the Gods*], briefly summarized the divinities associated with this phenomenon: "In the writings of Homer (circa 800 B.C.), Zeus is "the hurler of lightning bolts and the master of the most tumultuous thunder" – the supreme god of the skies.[12] The Nordic god Thor is also "the owner of the thunder." In Hindu civilization, Rama and Bhima climb into the mountains of the clouds "with enormous rumbles, astride an immense ray." In Aztec legend, Mixcouatl, "the thunderous serpent of the clouds," descends to Earth. Even today, native Canadians speak of a "Thunderbird" that came directly from the sky. Tane, the god of the legends of the Maori of New Zealand, is a "thunder god."

PARALLELS IN UFOLOGY

In Fátima, the sounds of thunder were heard at the moment that the Being appeared and at the moment that she departed. We find also in Ufological accounts that sound, heard at the moment when the UFO appears and when it instantaneously "disappears." Once again the Gods–Fátima–UFO triangle establishes itself.

a) At the beginning of the observation

Itenham, Brazil, summer of 1952, 3:00 AM

"A woman was awakened by a *thunder* and by a dazzling bluish light.

Leaving home, she saw various objects in the shape of flying disks at a distance of 200 meters and one meter from the ground...."[13]

Coimbra and Figueira da Foz, Portugal, January 24, 1952

At times, the thunder is detected at both instances – when it arrives and when it disappears. It is that effect which this news told us of:

> Something strange happened yesterday in the early hours, which gravely alarmed residents of the city and surrounding areas, seen as far away as Figueira da Foz [the news is given from Coimbra.]
>
> It was the case that, a little after 5:00 AM, those people who were awake heard a singular noise, *similar to that of thunder*, which lasted merely a few seconds. Others, who were already afoot, *not only heard it* but maintain that they saw it, at that moment, cross the sky in the direction of the ocean, a large, luminous disk which at a certain height *seems to have exploded, causing the sound* which many people claim reached their ears....[14]

But the greatest number of records of sounds identical to thunder has been noted at the moment in which the UFOs disappear before our astonished eyes.

b) At the end of the observation

Santiago de Riba-Ul, Oliveira de Azeméis, Portugal, January 3, 1977

Sixty years after the Fátima incident, from Portugal came this report:

> António Carlos Perreira, among hundreds of people attending a show in that town, near midnight, observed a cigar-like object, emitting a very strong beam. The UFO seemed to be of a steel-gray coloring, with some illuminated apertures. Nearly 10 minutes later, the object disappeared as it had appeared – instantaneously – *accompanying itself by a loud bang.*[15]

Southeastern France, November 2, 1968

The French doctor previously mentioned who awoke one night to the crying of his infant son, also observed that two luminous disks were merging into one. At a certain height, there could be heard *a sound like an explosion*, and the disk "immediately disappeared from the place where it was, *leaving a whitish cloud in its place*."[16]

"There was a noise as if from an explosion... leaving a whitish cloud," declared the French doctor in 1968. Manuel Marto, illiterate, in 1917, stated that, in July, "*a small white cloud became visible at the same time that the faraway boom of thunder could be heard.*" Despite the difference in time, space, and circumstances, could these two men be describing different phenomena?

*

Investigating only the ten-year period from 1958 to 1968, McCampbell gathered 103 cases of noises in the course of approximate observations of UFOs and those in which the witnesses were understood to have given identical characteristics. In the work we have been following,[17] this scientist divided the sounds produced by the phenomenon into five categories: *violent, low tone, blowing, high tone, and ringing*.

In the detected violent sounds, two sub-groups are defined with certainty: the shockwave-type explosions and the continuous deafening sound. The expression "thunder"belongs to this last group, as is evident. Thus, McCampbell's findings suggest that these sounds are directly linked to the application of force for a rapid acceleration or deceleration of a UFO, although they should not be confused with the normally silent maneuvers of take-off or landing.

The physicist points to a case that occurred in Baden, Pennsylvania on August 12, 1965 as a paradigm in support of his thesis. The witness observed a disk-shaped object that suddenly emitted an intense blue light and about three seconds afterward heard a shockwave.[18] McCampbell theorized: "If the light generated a shockwave, this would travel at nearly 1,100 feet per second approximately, reaching the witness in close to two seconds." This internal consistency reinforces a probable association between the blue light and the shockwave, in the mind of this investigator, who integrated it into his analysis about UFO propulsion.

The "thunder" heard at the arrival and departure of the Being at Fátima *satisfies all of the categories of sound* systematized by McCampbell. We have: a violent sound (described as "*thunder*"); a low tone (described as "*humming*" or "*buzzing*"); turbulence (described as "*agitation of the air*"); a high tone (described as a "*rumble*" or "*boom*"); and a ringing sound (described as "*the hiss of a rocket*"). A perfect collection.

4. BIZARRE CLOUDS

At Cova da Iria, two types of clouds were observed:

1. A light, vaporous cloud that appeared above a tree, seemingly enveloping and hiding the Apparition, and commonly known by the designation "the miraculous cloud of smoke."
2. Colored clouds that glided through space, at a constant height, moving in strange directions.

1) Clouds of smoke

In each month, from June to October, this phenomenon was observed.

JUNE

Maria Carreira left us diverse descriptions of that strange little cloud.

Relating to June, we have three of her statements. "As for us, we saw nothing," Maria declared to Father João de Marchi: "Only *a little cloud*, a hand's length away from the branch, *that was rising slowly*, moving toward the East, until it vanished. Some people were saying: 'There it is. I see it!' until, at last, no one claimed to see it."[1]

To *Stella*, she stated:

> When Lúcia was saying, "Look! There she goes... There it goes..." *we were only seeing a cloud*, and when I saw her she was about an inch away from the little oak. We followed it with our gaze, as it proceeded slowly toward the East, until it disappeared. But it was apparent that Lúcia was still seeing something, because she paid no attention to us, until, at last, she said: "There! Now it can't be seen. *It has just now entered the sky and the doors have closed.*"[2]

A sky with doors! Isn't that strange?

In *The Official Interrogations of 1923*, the Viscount of Montelo wrote about the testimony given by the witness: "She looked and saw *a cloud of smoke, rising up from the oak and directing itself as it lifted, moving toward the East,* as the child pointed toward it. It appeared to be very high up and very far away. At last it disappeared from view. The cloud was a very light fog. It was sunny and hot, and the day was not overcast."

JULY

Manuel Goncalves, Jr., a married business owner who resided in Montelo, testified before the *Parish Inquiry*: "On this occasion, it was also noted that at a certain height from the oak tree, a *type of mist or cloud* formed that rose in an eastward direction, causing the brilliance of the Sun to pale in comparison, and disappear."

Manuel Pedro Marto also observed the cloud of smoke. "No matter how much I looked, I could not see a thing," he recounted. "Then I could confirm myself that I saw a type of little *grayish cloud* that hovered over the oak."[3]

AUGUST

"In August, *a cloud descended upon the oak tree*. In July, the same thing was observed. There was no dust in the area. *The cloud powdered the air, such that it appeared hazy*, Manuel Gonçalves, Jr. declared to the Viscount of Montelo on October 11, 1917.[4]

It is for this month, during which the number of visitors to Fátima was greater, that several different written testimonies are available. In 1960, José Joaquim de Assunção told the American writer John Mathias Haffert:

> It was close to the tree, and when it reached a certain height, everyone began to flee. I was astonished, and someone told me they had heard thunder. But I allowed myself to stay. Then *a very light little smoke passed right by my head* and I was so moved and so certain that it had been Our Lady… I was as happy as if I had seen her.[5]

There were those who reported that this cloud formed after a noise compared to thunder was heard. One can read in Manuel Pedro Marto's testimony to *The Official Interrogations of 1923*: "*There appeared to be a fog around the oak tree, after the rumble.*"

When she was questioned, Maria da Capelinha, said: "The thunder was followed by a flash of lightning and, soon after, *we all began to notice a little cloud* – very pretty, very white, very small – that hovered a few minutes over the oak tree, rising, afterwards, to the sky, and disappearing in the air."[6]

But there were those who detected a bit of blue in that "white" cloud. Joel de Deus Magno, at the time, still in the seminary, confirmed: "…[T]hey saw a blue and white cloud descend, which shortly thereafter rose up and disappeared."[7]

"Could it have been a natural cloud?" So questioned a woman in the magazine

Raios de Luz [*Rays of Light*] on September 1st, identifying herself only by the initials L.S. She elaborated: "I looked toward the oak tree, and saw it surrounded by the fog that is reported to have been observed. Was it from dust raised by the crowd? Perhaps, but it did not raise up anywhere else, and, I repeat, there was no wind...."

SEPTEMBER

On September 13th, the mothers of the seers secretly attended the Apparitions. Olímpia de Jesus described for *The Official Interrogations of 1923* what she witnessed: "... [W]hen the crowd showed that it saw the signs, they did not notice what he was saying, but it seemed to them they saw a little smoke rise up from the midst of the crowd at the foot of the oak."

Journalist Avelino de Almeida reported about the phenomena surrounding the Apparitions seen from May to October for the October 13th edition of *O Seculo*. Before going to observe "The Miracle of the Sun" with his own atheistic eyes, he wrote of the white cloud: "It is over a gentlewoman that the figure of the Virgin, like the promise of a child's confession, manifests itself, and something like a cloud, that could be said was dust, wraps all around her, if the wind is blowing at the time."

OCTOBER

Different accounts of the observation of the cloud over the oak tree in the final month survive. The most complete is that of the lawyer Almeida Garrett, son of Dr. Gonçalo Xavier de Almeida Garrett, dean of the University of Coimbra. Garrett, the elder, who was in attendance at "The Miracle of the Sun," published a circular entitled *A Miraculosa Nuvem de Fumo* [*The Miraculous Cloud of Smoke*], in which he defended the thesis that the phenomenon was not natural.

Two months later, at the request of the Viscount of Montelo, his son related everything that he witnessed on that 13th day, in a document that can be found today in the *Arquivos Formigão* [*Formigão Archives*]. The young barrister wrote:

> It must have been 1:30 in the afternoon, when, in the precise location where the children were, a slender, tenuous, bluish column of smoke rose up perhaps two meters in height over their heads, and at this height vanished. This phenomenon, clearly visible to the naked eye, lasted several seconds. Not having noted its duration, I cannot confirm whether it took more than one minute or less. The smoke dissipated brusquely and, after some time passed, the phenomenon occurred a second and a third time. Every time, and

> particularly during the last time, the slender wisps of smoke could clearly be seen in the ashen atmosphere. I pointed the binoculars in that direction. I could see nothing beside the columns of smoke, but I remained convinced that they were produced by some stationary incense burner in which incense was being burned. Afterwards, people worthy of belief told me that it has produced a similar effect on the 13th day of the month each of the five months previously, and that on those days, as had been the case on this, nothing was ever burned there, nor was a fire ever lit.[8]

Another witness, Manuel da Costa Pereira, also referred to a white cloud that appeared and disappeared. In a letter she wrote to the Viscount of Montelo, she declared "*a column of smoke*, that looked much like a cloud, *hovered over said locality, rising three to four meters above the ground.* The phenomenon repeated itself more than three times, I believe."[9]

In addition to this account, two statements were made to the *Parish Inquiry* about the cloud of smoke. Jacinto de Almeida Lopes told the parish priest that he saw:

> [A]t times, above the crowd that surrounds the oak tree, rising from the ground one after another, *small clouds of smoke*, or what seemed like smoke, similar to the smoke that wafts from an incense burner at the time of burning or to the whirl of smoke produced by a cigarette. At first I judged – because I was set apart some distance from the oak tree where he saw the smoke – that it must have been someone there smoking or building a bonfire to keep warm. But later I verified that there was no flame there of any type.

The parish priest also recorded his account of what Manuel Goncalves, Jr. told him:

> [A]fter the rain had ceased, several times he saw *a type of smoke* issuing from the oak tree, which was similar to incense smoke at the time of incense burning, and heard the people near him say that it was cigarette smoke or a bonfire, but to him it only appeared to be smoke like that when incense is burning, not aware that on this occasion there were neither smokers nor bonfires of any kind.

Manuel António Paula, who usually lived in Lisbon, but who had come to spend an autumn holiday in his village of Fátima, stated that he saw:

> [A] fog, a little, very dense smoke, which he did not find odd, as he believed it to be incense burned in honor of Our Lady, but was later astonished when he was told that there had not been any smoke at all, that a fire had not been made, nor had even a match been lit.

But there was one who did not think that what was seen was a "little smoke." The Viscount of Montelo wrote: "Just as I could, so too could other people, who were out in the street, perfectly detect with binoculars, and even with the naked eye, in the area of the Apparitions, above the sacred oak, *a large cloud, that completely wrapped that place*."[10]

In 1978, we had the opportunity to speak with Lúcia's sister, Maria dos Anjos. During the course of the conversation, we asked her:

> "And near the oak tree, you saw nothing?"
>
> "*I saw a small, moving cloud*," she responded. "The people saw a small cloud approaching, but the people couldn't even say what it was."
>
> "Was it like those?," we asked, pointing toward white clouds in the sky.
>
> "It was not like those," she stated. "It was a small, little cloud, a small...."
>
> "...Round cloud?"
>
> "It was very small. I don't know if it was round, since it was so many years ago! It was in October. In the other months, I don't know."

The day before this conversation took place, on July 17, 1978 to be exact, we spoke with two female witnesses in Leiria. One of them, 76 years old, told us that, in September 1917, "*there were those who said that retreating within the cloud was the form of a silhouette.*" She herself, however, only remembered a white cloud, just as the others had, which rose, little by little, until it disappeared in the air.

Another of Lúcia's sisters, Glória, told Radio Fátima in 1957, that in October she saw "a sort of little cloud of smoke that moved directly, parallel to the Earth, from the location of the Seminary of Consolation (which was located to the East) to the site of the Apparitions."[11]

It would appear that that cloud was seen beyond Fátima. *Stella* related one curious account of a nurse from the Hospital de Dona Estefânia in Lisbon, where Jacinta was interned and later died.[12] As a matter of fact, Jacinta had already declared in the *Parish Inquiry* that she had seen other visions of the Lady.

In 1958 or early 1959, Sister Maria do Carmo da Fonseca, an aide to the Canon Formigão, went to Lisbon to speak with those who knew Jacinta when she was at the hospital. One of the nurses, Leonor Assunção de Almeida, was 20 years old at the time the young seer was admitted. She shared with the Sister an incident that surprised her. Little Jacinta's bed was located in front of a window that faced east. The nursing staff did not know, at first, who the little girl was. One day, however, Jacinta began to say that the Virgin Mary had begun to visit her. On one occasion, Jacinta even called to the nurses during one of the visitations.

> "*When she called to us, we saw that, in the white clouds which looked like smoke, a figure had really taken shape,*" Leonor recalled.
>
> "But that was inside the Infirmary?" asked Sister Maria do Carmo.
>
> "*No, in front of the window, on the outside,*" she explained.

The Sister published her interviews in *Stella* under the pseudonym "Ancilla." She spoke with other nurses, but none described having witnessed the same phenomenon. Hence, we are left to speculate as to whether this fanciful account was fact or fiction.

2) Clouds in space

In Fátima, other types of clouds were observed. These were seen not over the oak tree, but in the atmosphere, mixing with the natural cloud formations.

AUGUST

It is in this month that we find the first references. Inácio António Marques said:

> The time has already passed, and the children have not appeared. The crowd is waiting impatiently, when suddenly a voice carries over the crowd, saying that Ourem, the administrator, has taken them. Protests are heard. When the crowd is about to disperse, shouting is heard, and a wave of heads turns towards the sky, and everyone exclaims at once what they are seeing. I then look to the sky, and *I see the clouds changing colors and see them moving in different directions.* [13]

"Some white clouds could be observed in the sky,"Manuel Gonçalves, Jr. related to the Viscount of Montelo, on October 11th. "Near the Sun, *which turned successively blood red, rose-colored, and yellow*. The crowd turned this last color."

A stonemason from Chainça in the parish of Santa Catarina, named Joaquim Inácio Vicente, testified before the *Parish Inquiry* that he had observed what he described as "*amazing colors, which successively took over the clouds,* obscuring the Sun's rays behind mist, colors of brilliant scarlet turned to shades of pale rose, and from this to the bluest indigo." This description "was declared to me minutes afterward in my home by several people," the priest concluded.

"Many people, among them my maids, said that they saw *a pretty cloud at the base of the Sun, which moments later disappeared,*" Mr. L. De S. wrote. "I saw nothing, but I felt a shiver and an extraordinary commotion...."

Lastly, as for the month of August, Joaquim Vieira de Assentiz, an advisor from Torres Novas, told the Viscount of Montelo: "A little, white cloud appeared that made its way from south to north, in an eastward direction, taking on very pretty colors."[14]

SEPTEMBER

In this month, on a lovely sunny day, there were also those who witnessed strange clouds. Joaquim Vieira, continuing his earlier statement, added that, in September, he saw "*a blue mark in a dark-colored cloud*, moving away from the Sun."

Certainly, those people who saw such unusual clouds shared their stories with their associates. In *O Mensageiro* for December 27th, a woman from Alcobaça known only by the initials M.C.S.P. stated, "[T]here were people who were saying that they had seen rose-colored clouds here and there. Not all of them were believed."

OCTOBER

Strange clouds in the rainy sky were also observed before "The Miracle of the Sun." In the following chapter we shall discuss them.

PARALLELS IN UFOLOGY

The bizarre, colored clouds, moving contrary to the wind, are not exclusive to Fátima. They have been observed in various epochs. Many times, sheltered and hidden within these clouds are varied and colorful objects that remain unidentified.

Lisbon, Elvas, Campo Maior, Évora, Portugal, November 2, 1730, night

The citizens of 18th century Portugal witnessed just such a spectacle. One among them described what they saw when he wrote:

> It has been confirmed, by means of notices from several parts of the kingdom, that in our hemisphere have appeared a notable phenomenon that began as *a small, rose-colored cloud* and kept growing in size and color until it grew to the size of a large flag the color of fire....[15]

Japan, in the year 1847

Japanese scribes recorded later, in the 19th century, that "*clouds of fog*" (luminescent clouds) were observed over the central part of Japan, near what is today Matsushito. "*[T]hey move through the sky and then disappear*."[16]

In modern times, since Fátima, clouds of an unusual nature have continued to be seen. Here we cite two examples from modern history.

Mont-de-Marsan, France, October 17, 1952

Henry Durrant wrote that on this date, the radar technicians at an air base 150 kilometers from Oloron noticed, "the radar suddenly started acting crazy." One of them, who went outside to see what was happening, saw "*an ashen cloud turning over itself at about a height of 200 meters*." This 'cloud' was proceeding from west to east very quickly... "*and looked like flakes of smoke*."[17]

Parr, Britain, July 22, 1969, 8:30 PM

William Holland and two others saw a silvery object that glided at a height of 20 meters in England in 1969. *The object rose up and entered a cloud of uncommon color, which was moving against the wind.*[18]

Clouds that hide beings, clouds that hide objects. "I spotted a *luminous cloud in all the colors of the rainbow*," stated Australian motorist Ronald Sullivan, in 1966.[19] In August 1917, Manuel Gonçalves, Jr. also observed forming "near the Sun *a cloud in all the colors of the rainbow*."[20] Two time periods, two countries, two different situations! Just as in Mont-de-Marsan "*an ashen cloud*" altered the functioning of radar, so too had Manuel Marto been startled to see "*a little, grayish cloud* that hovered over the oak...."

*

We find ourselves confronting two types of "clouds" and many hypotheses. In the case of the nebulosity that fell and rose over the oak at the apex of the Apparitions at Fátima, a finding made by McCampbell while studying similar cases in Ufology may be germane to our investigation. He observed that observations of this type suggest that while it is suspended over a site (in this case the oak), a UFO overcharges the dynamic state of oxygen in the atmosphere, and afterward, its departure allows it to fall gradually with the production of light.[21]

Among those cases cited in McCampbell's study is that of a UFO resembling Saturn suspended near the ground for 15 minutes. A short while later, the observers noticed "a singular, luminous fog fluctuating in the air beneath the area where the object had been, and witnessed it slowly dissipate." The same detail was observed in a sighting case in Argentina, in which "clouds of white smoke" were left in the area from which six UFOs disappeared. Similar traces are perhaps clearly visible in some photos of objects with a trail, of which the most evident might be the one taken by American astronaut James McDivitt.[22]

The Frenchman Jean Plantier justifies the "cloud-objects" as:

> [O]ne of the consequences of the models of propulsion by direct action over an atom. As the column of air produced by the object does not "weigh" more or as much as [the object itself], it would produce a current of ascending air sufficiently strong so as to eventually neutralize the inversion caused by the purity of the sky. And if there were no inversion, the ascendancy would not be but stronger. It would have to be then mere luck to see surging, suddenly, a small cloud (*cumulus)* capable of moving itself, if necessary, against the wind. [23]

From his point-of-view, McCampbell maintains "the UFOs frequently take refuge in the interior of clouds, whose humidity content is substantially more elevated than the surrounding air." From the eyewitness accounts, it can be deduced that the clouds involved become luminous when intercepted by a UFO, and their color is defined as "uncommon." The scientist thinks that hydrogen probably is at the base of these colored emissions.[24]

5. EFFECTS ON THE ENVIRONMENT

"On the 13th of each month," Dr. Pereira Gens wrote, "[I]t was, without any doubt, the noticeable diminishment of sunlight that was most often referred to by the pilgrims."[1] But it was not only the diminishment of sunlight that made itself felt on the horizon beyond Cova da Iria. Different witnesses pointed simultaneously to the reduction in the temperature of the air and the prism effects involving the Sun's rays that spread throughout the environment where the Apparition appeared.

JUNE

Already in this month, we are told by Inácio António Marques: "I, as a non-believer, would like to deny everything that I am seeing, but contemplating the atmosphere I see that everything is *overcast... the day darkens...* I feel that *the temperature is almost supernatural* and I am afraid to be there."

JULY

Manuel Pedro Marto was most impressed with the reduction in temperature also. In *The Official Interrogations of 1923*, he stated, "it was very pleasant, but soon thereafter, *the weather grew cool*." He offered still more details to *Stella: "And while she was speaking to the Lady*, a cooling could be felt as though the crowd had suddenly been placed in the shade, and I could see a cloud of smoke.... And as soon as the Being departed, the agreeable weather once again became so strong, that when I grabbed my Jacinta to lift her up, I put my hat on her head to shade her."[2]

But it wasn't only Manuel Marto who was surprised by the momentary cooling. Manuel Gonçalves, Jr. also reported, in the *Parish Inquiry*, that "on July 13, 1917, he went to the site at the time appointed by the child seers to see the Apparition, and he noted that at the hour the heat was great, *it began to diminish*."

J. de S. Bento stated that on that day, he arrived at the hour the Apparition appeared, and saw that a thin fog caused the Sun to lose its strength, and with it, the heat ceased which until then had been great.[3]

Pereira Gens observed that the Sun "suddenly lost a lot of its brilliance, such that it could be stared at at-will."

AUGUST

Whereas the day of the Apparition had been full of sunlight in the month of July, in August the 13th day of the month dawned with a blue sky and stifling heat. The seers did not appear, but the onlookers felt the arrival of the Being. "...At exactly two o'clock, by my watch, and without the aid of the wind, there was a steep drop in [air] temperature, like one experiences during a solar eclipse," Mrs. L. de S. declared in the September 1st edition of the magazine *Raios de Luz*.

Other effects were cited. João Pereira Novo described how "*the rocks changed color* and many people began screaming."[4]

"[T]he light of the Sun lost much of its intensity," Manuel Gonçalvez, Jr. [5] thought. "All of the objects surrounding me turned yellow," Joaquim Xavier Tuna perceived.[6] But mostly it was Maria Carreira who could truly best describe for us the "strange thing" that she saw, a spectacle of unreal colors: "The trees seemed not to have branches or leaves, but only flowers; they seemed loaded with flowers, each leaf appeared to be a flower. *The ground was divided into squares*, each one a different color; the clothes were also the color of the blue arc. The two lamps imprisoned in the arc appeared to be of gold."[7] A picture that is not far from the realm of science fiction.

AUGUST 19th

It would seem that this kaleidoscope did not only alight on a small area around the oak. Six days later, on August 19th, the Being also appeared in the Valinhos, two kilometers from Cova da Iria. At this moment, without knowing anything of this unscheduled visit, one of Lúcia's sisters, Teresa, was indifferently returning home with her husband:

> We were going to enter Fátima," she remembered,[8] when we began to notice that *the air was cooling*; the Sun took on a yellowish color and cast many colors on everything — the same kind of things that were seen on the 13th at Cova da Iria.
>
> "What is this? … Some mystery is afoot here!" I said to my husband. It was there, on his white shirt, that I began to see the colors.
>
> "Oh my, but we are all deluded!"
>
> "By what?" my husband asked.
>
> "*Well, don't things look the same as on the 13th?*"
>
> When we arrived at the church, everything had changed again. Later on, we learned that, at that exact hour, Our Lady returned to appear to the kids in the Valinhos.

SEPTEMBER

In this month, precisely at noon, the Sun began to lose its brilliance. There was no one who failed to notice this fact, for this pattern had repeated itself on the 13th day of every month since May, and at the same time of the day. When it did so, "the atmosphere took on a yellow color, maybe because of the reduction of sunlight," wrote Joel de Deus Magno.[9]

But Inácio António Marques believed that this was verified at the end: "Lúcia prayed the Rosary at the appointed hour. Next came the conversation with the Lady, and [Lúcia] said, "There she goes." The Sun darkened, such that the Moon and the stars that surround the firmament could be observed. *The heat diminished,* and a tender breeze came to cool our brows."

It is possible, however, that this witness exaggerated somewhat as to the extent of the darkening. The Viscount of Montelo provides a far less dramatic account of the same event. "I did not approach the site of the Apparitions. I spoke to almost no one, but remained in the street at a distance of nearly 300 meters. I barely *noticed the diminishment of sunlight* that seemed to me a phenomenon of little importance, perhaps attributable to the high altitude of the mountain."[10]

Others associated the reduced light with a reduction in temperature. "Those present on September 13th state that from noon to one PM, it being a most beautiful day with a burning Sun, the temperature suddenly dropped, giving the day a small eclipse in that star," one observed.[11] Avelino de Almeida refers to some [who] "say that the *temperature cools* and some compare the impressions of the moment with those that are received when there is a solar eclipse."

Yet it also seems that during this month, the environment was tinged with colors. Lawyer António Rodrigues da Silva linked this coloration to the fall of filaments.[12] "Meanwhile, from the heights came off or unfastened something like flakes of snow or cotton on the branch, the size of ancient cents," he wrote. These "descended upon the oak, and the *air became tinged with the colors of the rainbow*."

Curiously, a description identical to this one was made during the apparitions at Baião in 1938. Maria Amélia was at work one day, when she noticed particles of snow falling to the ground and disappearing. "The trees were enchanting," she remembered. "*As many colors as there were appeared there*!" The fall of these snowflakes "*was on the same day and at the same time that everything became colored.*" On the day that these snowflakes and colors fell upon Baião, there, at the top of the mountain range, another apparition of the Virgin was taking place.[13]

PARALLELS IN UFOLOGY

Guadalajara, Spain, July 25, 1938

In the same year as the Baião apparitions, during the time of the Spanish Civil War, two military men, one a lieutenant, came face-to-face with a potent, white light that they first judged to be an enemy searchlight. At a distance of

60 meters, however, they saw a dark object in the shape of a lentil. A circle of blue light reached them, illuminating them *and causing them a feeling of cold,* such that they were unable to determine if it was an effect of the light or of the fear that they felt.[14]

Grande Canária, Las Rosas, Canary Islands, June 22, 1976

Shortly after 9:00 PM, Dr. Padron Leon was following a car that was leading him to a critically sick patient when, toward the north of the island, he perceived an enormous sphere at a distance of about 60 meters. The doctor, among other things, felt *a type of intense cold* that, according to him, was "different from physical cold."[15]

*

The phenomenon of diminished sunlight associated with the phenomenon of diminished ambient temperature arises frequently in the Fátimist literature. We can consider the two effects separately or as one.

On the one hand, their interdependency can lead us to conclude that a "solar eclipse" caused the sensations that were felt. Some of the witnesses at Fátima described a hiding of the Sun, possibly a concealment of the Sun's rays partial in nature. Such an "eclipse," provoked by the interposition of something in the sky vertically above the affected zone, would have brought with it a diminishment of temperature.

On the other hand, if the two phenomena were not related, we confront the possibility that the event involved an "artificial eclipse" of some kind, an eclipse confined to the area of Cova da Iria. Seeking to confirm the existence of an object capable of obstructing the Sun's brilliance, we find that no evidence exists prior to October 13th. Yet jumping ahead to "The Miracle of the Sun," a curious description leaps to our attention. It is an important description, one that we shall dedicate an entire chapter to. This description was made following the observation, through binoculars, of "a ladder near the Sun." If we assume that this object was also present on the 13th day of the previous months (when those present did not have binoculars), then sunlight may have been absorbed by fixing the "ladder" in a horizontal position in the sky, at approximately six kilometers high.

Why situate a ladder-like device at an altitude of six kilometers? If we consider that it drives itself within the interior of (or manufactures) the bizarre clouds so often insisted upon as having been seen by witnesses, and define them as medium-sized clouds, we might not be far from the truth.

We propose the hypothesis that in order for such an object at the stated height to have produced an "eclipse" over the stated area of land adjacent to

Cova da Iria that was in shadows, the object would have to have been 600 to 1,000 meters in diameter.[16] In light of that fact, we accept the possibility that the "ladder" may have served the important function to artificially cloak the solar disk (in some way as it absorbed or re-converted radiant energy?).

In support of this hypothesis, we offer the following points:

First, modern apocrypha furnishes us with numerous accounts of circular, fusiform objects of great dimensions. Even if it were "only" 600 meters across, the ladder seen above Cova da Iria could have produced a shadow that enveloped the area. Are such dimensions possible? Soviet investigator Z.S. Kadikov says that they are. They have been seen in recent UFO sightings in the Caucasus.[17] Moreover, we have no evidence that these dimensions demarcate the limits of something that is unidentified.

Second, beyond the possibility of direct interposition, we can theorize that the "ladder" itself assumed the function of controlling the various bodies described as "colorful clouds," in its to-and-fro movements in front of the Sun. Auguste Meessen, professor of theoretical physics at the Catholic University of Louvain in Belgium, imagines that "it would be conceivable that a group of UFOs could produce a type of semi-transparent film, absorbing a part of the visible light, except for [the] infrared."[18]

Third, in regard to the "ladder" itself as distinguished from the membrane imagined by Professor Meessen, let us not neglect to consider the existence of cases in which demonstrations of visibility/invisibility were performed by the UFO craft of our day.

As far as the diminishment of temperature is concerned, whether it is associated with the "solar eclipse" or not, it is of interest in the sense that it stresses the importance of verifying the quandary associated with the "ladder," described by one percipient as a "luminous ramp." A principle of refrigeration may have been at work, wherein the compression of the air surrounding the object by heat may have led to the inverse result of cooling it, which is a reciprocal effect that has been observed in many UFO cases.

6. ODORS

On the 19th of August, the seers appeared radiant announcing in Aljustrel that Our Lady had once again appeared to them. Not at Cova da Iria, as usual, but this time in Valinhos, a property that was also deserted and with small, vegetating oaks in the midst of a large amount of crags.

> "Aunt," Jacinta said, excitedly, "[W]e have seen Our Lady once again."[1]
>
> Lúcia's mother smiled, with condescension.
>
> Jacinta insisted: "We saw, Auntie! Look, she had one foot here and the other here – and she showed her two grass shoots, which appeared bent in almost a right angle."
>
> "Liars!," her mother responded. "Let me see that."
>
> Scarcely had Maria Rosa taken the sprig of flowers in her hands, when all those present perceived that from the flowers emanated *a delicious perfume*, as if containing *unknown essences*.

Let us consider the statement that was made by Lúcia's mother herself that can be found in *The Official Interrogations of 1923*.

> Lúcia arrived home at night bringing in her hand a bouquet from the oak and saying that Our Lady had appeared to her a little before sunset, at around four o'clock in the afternoon, she having returned home with the flock at noon.[2] Her mother took the bouquet and noticed that it smelled very good. *The smell could not be compared to any other smell.* In October, Lúcia said: "She is here now." She spoke loudly. Her mother saw nothing. When her daughter said, "She is here now," Lúcia's mother only noticed the same smell as that of the bouquet from Valinhos.

Humberto Pasquale, who supposedly lived with the family of the seers, gives us several other facts about that smell in the work *Eu Vi Nascer Fátima* [*I Saw the Birth of Fátima*].[3]

Maria Rosa related:

> At this moment, I was disappointed. Suddenly, from those leaves an indefinable perfume was given off. *It was not the perfume of incense, or of rosemary, or of violet, or of soap....* [It was] a perfume I know not how to define... *that was emitted in waves, and which, when sought, could no longer be sensed!* This strange phenomenon was very shocking to me.

Manuel Marto also spoke of the perfume:

At this moment, I saw Jacinta in the street, jumping for joy, with a branch of flowers from the oak tree in her hand. At the same time that she was entering the house, a perfume reached me that was *more refined than any I had ever smelled in my life.*

"Hey, Jacinta, what is it you are bringing there?" I asked her.

"It is a bouquet from the oak tree of Valinhos, where Our Lady appeared. It still has a piece from a short time ago.

"Well, let me see it!" I took the branch, smelled it, but there was nothing. The perfume had disappeared.[4]

Could this odd fragrance, which, "when sought could no longer be sensed," be a "little invention" of the seers' parents, fabricated by them to emphasize the supernatural dimension of the Apparitions? Probably not, if we take into account the fact that we also find references to smells at the time of UFO sightings.

PARALLELS IN UFOLOGY

Jonestown, Pennsylvania, USA, April 5, 1967, 7:45 PM

John H. Demler, a justice of the peace, was heading northbound on 72nd Street, when the motor of his car stopped abruptly and his headlights turned off. He then saw an object about 10meters in diameter gliding low to the ground above his automobile. The object emitted the sound of an electric motor, spewed flames, and gave off a smell of sulfur and *camphor oil....*[5]

Camphor, as we know, is an aromatic substance.
But in Brazil, we find a description that more closely resembles what Lúcia's mother described.

São Paolo State, Mogy-Guaçu, Brazil, October 18 or 19, 1965

"Mrs. Lúcia Anhaia saw an orange light approach her residence at the height of the tree-tops. She did not hear a sound, but as the light grew closer, she *smelled a pleasant aroma* which she attributed to an emanation of the local flora."[6]

*

The pulsing emission of microwaves continues to serve as a hypothesis to explain the odors reported, in this case, at Fátima. Countless descriptions of odors exist in UFO history, the most numerous of which are references to the smell of sulfur dioxide. Other odors, similar to benzene and its derivatives, are also frequently described. McCampbell theorizes that these olfactory effects are related to an electrical discharge on the surface of the UFO, one undoubtedly associated with its luminosity. "A pulsing discharge of microwaves in the air would be enough," he writes, "to generate nitric acid and, as a byproduct, benzene, noted in the proximity of the UFOs." In a similar manner, other substances are formed via chemical reaction. Note that, among other things, "power," "strangeness," and "balsamic fluid" have been described by witnesses in different UFO cases.[7]

7. LUMINOUS OBJECTS

The documents surrounding the Fátima incident describe diverse objects and attribute to them various designations. For the purpose of this exposition, we may classify these objects into three categories:

1. Objects inside of clouds
2. Classical UFOs
3. "Flying eyes" or *"foo-fighters"*

OBJECTS INSIDE OF CLOUDS

AUGUST

Eyewitnesses described the first category of objects in the month of August. In *The Official Interrogations of 1923*, we find one of the most beautiful and characteristic observations – "a type of luminous globe gyrating within the clouds." It was Manuel Marto who furnished this observation. Alas, he undoubtedly passed away without ever having heard anyone speak of UFOs.

Maria Carreira also bequeathed to us a poetic observation: "The leaves of the trees appeared to be flowers and the celestial objects were also very pretty: *large rose-colored and silver clouds – something that reflected a lot....*"[1]

OCTOBER

Before "The Miracle of the Sun," similar objects were also observed. There was a witness, whom we shall call "Mrs. J.," who wrote a beautiful account on the 30th of October. This took the form of a letter to the managing editor of the newspaper *Correio da Beira* [*The Beira Mail*], which published her letter in its November 10th edition. She ended the letter by identifying herself as "a subscriber to your paper" and then signing the letter simply "J." History would prove that hers would be one of the best accounts of "The Miracle of the Sun":

> At one o'clock, *where the cloud separated*, the sky cleared; and such was our fright when *a silver globe appeared, making a small circuit and appearing to cut, here and there, through the clouds*! This it did three times, in three or four minute intervals. At this time, to our rear, the scene involving the little shepherds was taking place beside the oaks; we were located about six or seven meters from the site in order to escape the mob. The eldest of the two shepherd girls imposed silence at this time and the rest of the scene was played out involving the three of them." The "silver globe making a small circuit" this witness called "a rehearsal or prelude to the Sun."

CLASSICAL UFOs

It is interesting to note that within the documents of Fátima, classical Ufological descriptions arise, despite the regressive timeframe of the incident relative to 1947, the year widely accepted as the time that modern UFO activity, and public interest in their origin and study, began.

AUGUST

In this month, Joaquim Xavier Tuna contributed to the historical record a description that is very different from the other statements: "In August, on the 13th day, I saw the Sun come down in the sky at the hour of the apparition. It never descended quite as much as it did on that day, not even on the 13th of October. Every object which surrounded me turned yellow."[2]

SEPTEMBER

Yet it seems that it was in September that objects abounded in the skies over Cova da Iria. Let us begin with the intriguing description by Joel de Deus Magno:

> I shall never forget the violent impression I felt to see so many thousands of the faithful falling to their knees, which, crying, prayed aloud and implored, full of confidence, the protection of the maternal Queen of Heaven. It was then that many onlookers *saw an oval, only slightly less voluminous than an egg, white in color, bright and brilliant, with its largest part turned downward,* inscribe in the firmament a long, straight line. Some observed this phenomenon for a long while, and others for a shorter time.[3]

But there were those who did not see, as seminarian Magno did, "the largest part turned downward." Rather, these witnesses perceived that the strange craft moving slowly over the multitude was, in fact, taller than it was wide. José Maria Pereira Gens, a medical doctor, was one of those witnesses. We are told by Dr. Gens:

> At one time, the voices began to say, 'It can no longer be seen… it can no longer be seen…' and they quieted. I deduced then that something had happened, and the Lady, poised over the oak, would already be conversing with Lúcia.
>
> Thus it was, in fact: and, in the end, when Lúcia said 'There She goes…' and pointed towards the heights, all those people once again looked, and again could be heard the joyful voicing of 'There She goes… there She goes....'
>
> I confess that at the height I did not resist; I raised my eyes and, in the direction that had been signaled, *I distinctly saw a luminous object that was retreating towards the East.*[4]

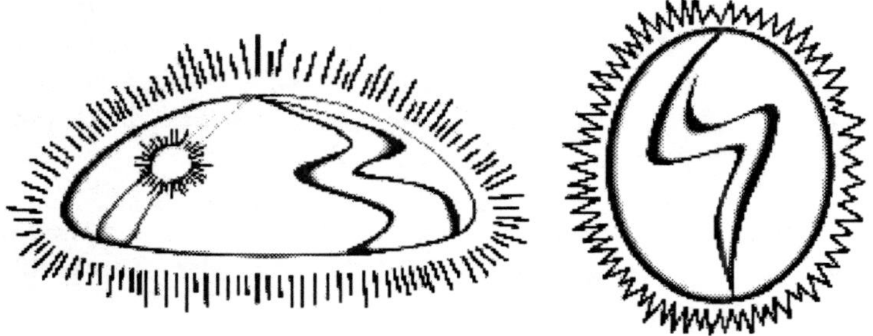

Fig. 6 – Object (or objects) observed on September 13, 1917 by Joel de Deus Magno (left) and Dr. Pereira Gens (right).

The physician continued:

> My eyes did not see a luminous globe, but an *object that was taller than it was wide, in fact, luminous, moving serenely and with certain speed*, until, I lost sight of it, completely, on the horizon.
>
> The sky was clear and clean; in that direction there could not be seen a hint of a cloud, nothing, in fact, that could stain the blue and pure surface of the firmament.
>
> I noticed that luminous object high in the sky, in front of me, moving with deliberate speed, serenely, toward the East… and it disappeared....
>
> In truth, in July, I merely noticed a reduction in the intensity of the Sun's light; now I saw more, I saw, moving in the firmament *that luminous object, where today my faith says the glorious body of the Queen of Heaven was hidden.*

But Monsignor João Quaresma, vicar-general of the Leiria diocese, who was one of the ecclesiastical authorities named by the bishop to the *Commission of Canonical Inquiry*, considered it natural and admissible that the Virgin would utilize a means of transport, as would any other mortal. He wrote:

> At noon, it became completely silent. The murmuring of prayers could be heard. All at once shouts of jubilation arose.... Voices could be heard praising the Virgin. *Arms were raised pointing toward anything in the heights*. 'Look everyone, can't you see?' – 'Yes, I already see!' Satisfaction shined in the eyes of those who could see. In the blue sky, there wasn't a single cloud. I, too, raised my eyes, and began to scrutinize the vastness of the sky, to see what other happier eyes, before I looked, had contemplated 'There, you can see it as well!'
>
> With great admiration, I clearly and distinctly saw a *luminous globe that was moving from east to west*, slowly and majestically gliding through space. My friend looked too and had the happy chance to enjoy the same unexpected and enchanting apparition… when, suddenly, *the globe, with its extraordinary light, disappeared from our sight.*
>
> Near us was a young girl dressed like Lúcia and of more or less the same age. Full of glee, she cried continuously, 'I can still see Her! I can still see Her! Now she is descending!'
>
> *Only minutes later, the exact time these Apparitions usually lasted*, the young girl began exclaiming again and pointing toward the sky, 'There, She is

> rising again!,' and she continued to follow the globe with her eyes, until it disappeared in the direction of the Sun.
>
> 'What do you think of that globe?' I asked my friend, who appeared enthusiastic about everything we had seen.
>
> 'That it was Our Lady,' he responded without hesitation.
>
> This was also my conviction. The young shepherds had beheld the very Mother of God; to us was granted the grace to see *the carriage*[5] *that had transported her from Heaven to the inhospitable moor of the Mount of the Winds.*[6]

How difficult it is to conceive of abstract realms. The French canon Barthas, in his work *Fátima*, also speculated that Paradise is a place located somewhere in the Cosmos, far from Cova da Iria: "Several narratives add that the luminous globe was oval-shaped, with the largest side turned downward. All who saw it had the impression, as did the two priests cited earlier, that it was *a question of a shape similar to that of an airplane*, that brought the Mother of God to her promised encounter with the young shepherds and that transported her again, afterwards, to Paradise."[7]

Another ecclesiastical authority, well versed in matters of Fátima, is Canon Galamba de Oliveira. He also observed a UFO in September, which he described as follows:

> I saw nothing close to the site, but, after the apparition, I can't indicate the precise moment, I looked toward the sky, perhaps because someone invited me to do so, and *I saw, at what appeared to be one meter from the Sun, some sort of luminous-type globe* that shortly began to descend towards the West and, from the line of the horizon, began climbing again in the direction of the Sun.
>
> A justifiable distress overtook us. We prayed earnestly for I know not what. All of those present could see the same globe, with the exception of a Catholic brother of mine, today a priest himself, a native of Torres Novas. I took him by the arm to show him, but, at that moment, *I lost site of the globe* without him managing to see it, which lead him to tearfully say: 'Why is it that I cannot see? Who knows if I am in mortal sin!'[8]

However, there were those who witnessed objects that were neither circular nor oval in shape. Precisely, what they saw was cross-shaped. And that observation was not limited to the local religious. "On the 13th day of September," related Joaquim Xavier Tuna to the Canon Formigão on November 13th, "I saw *a cross of great size exit the Sun* and direct itself toward the horizon

Fig. 7 – Cruciform object "coming out of" the Sun on September 13, 1917, as described by Joaquim Xavier Tuna.

on the East. Its pace was not hurried. *Sometimes it appeared, other times it hid itself*, until it jumped out of sight. *I saw still other things that I am incapable of explaining*. In the Lapas parish, there were others who saw the cross at the same time."

A globe... a cross... but there appears to have been more than one object crossing the blue space of the area. Inácio António Marques, the postal employee, speaks to us of several strange "white cups." "Then they could be seen way overhead," he wrote, "cutting through the eastern sky toward the West, *some small, white bodies that were white as snow.* There were those who claimed that they were doves, but one could see perfectly that they were not birds."

Understandably, the less well educated identified the "cups" that they saw with simpler, more possible things, like birds and stars.

Thus, in a letter from J. de S. Bento that is part of the *Arquivos Formigão*, we find this picturesque description: "The Sun and stars did the same thing, made the same movements, that they made in previous months. The crowd enthused as they looked to the sky, some saying *that they saw stars, others that they saw doves, others that they saw colored stars with accompanying swallows*. There was an enthusiasm in everyone...."

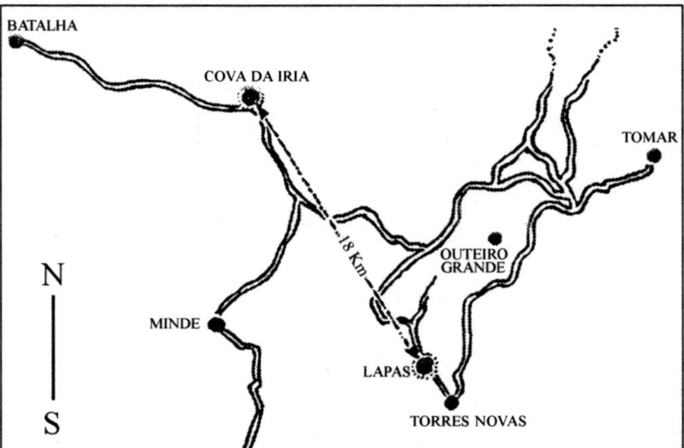

Fig. 8 – On September 13, 1917, a cruciform object was observed above Cova da Iria and the village of Lapas at the same time.

The Baron of Alvaiázare, a lawyer and notary in Vila Nova de Ourém, tells us: "Speaking with several people who had been there on September 13th, some declared to me that they saw nothing, *others that they had seen a star,* [while still] *others made fantastical descriptions*."[9]

What could those fantastical descriptions have been like? Perhaps today they would no longer be regarded as fantastic and would add important details to the phenomenology of Fátima.

A professor from the Seminary at Santarém, the Reverend António Maria de Figueiredo, gave one of those "fantastical" statements to the local parish priest which made up part of his *Inquiry*: "I take advantage of this occasion in order to say that on that 13th day, at around 3:00 PM, the Rev. António Maria de Figueiredo came to fetch me from the presbytery... and declared to me that he *had seen stars in a zone inferior to the stellar zone* and that he had sought me out simply to make this declaration."

OCTOBER

But the stars shone once more through the light of day before "The Miracle of the Sun." This time, it was Mrs. L. de S. who furnished a telling observation in the magazine *Raio de Luz* for November 1st. "Many persons who are deemed highly credible saw a *pretty star* moving with a *flash* toward the little oak tree of the 'contact'."

"FLYING EYES" OR "FOO-FIGHTERS"

In addition to the objects described by some witnesses, observations of small craft were also recorded. They appeared above the oak, before disintegrating like soap bubbles. They were only detected during the last two months of the Apparitions.

SEPTEMBER

"On September 13th, I was in the same location, with my back turned towards the North. I was a bit crestfallen, not having seen anything extraordinary the month before. *Suddenly, I saw something that resembled a bubble of soapsuds,* such as children usually make by blowing through a little straw." This beautiful description of what we believe to be a "flying eye" was made to the Viscount of Montelo by Joaquim Vieira de Assentiz.[10] He added: "The first time that I saw it go past, I fell silent. I saw it a second time, and asked aloud: 'What is this?' I could not explain what it was. *I lost sight of it about one dozen meters above the oak*. My wife didn't see it, because she was looking in a different direction."

The *Parish Inquiry*, relaying the observation of Manuel Gonçalves, Jr., informed us that "at the time [of the Apparition], an extraordinary I-know-not-what was passing over the oak, which appeared to be white flowers, and that other people also noticed this phenomenon, saying they were stars."

At times, these "flying eyes" were described in a more positive way, such as in this account given by a domestic, Emília Alves:

> In September, I was at the foot of the children, but could not see them because of the many people. At Cova da Iria, I heard them to speak in this way: 'Kneel down, kneel down, because Our Lady is coming!' And afterward, a *very white, little ball* that looked like cotton on the branch came directly, directly, slowly to where the children were. *And there it disappeared right where they were!* It was still a ball, big like this: like a fist or no bigger. There were many people who saw, but many others, also, who did not see.[11]

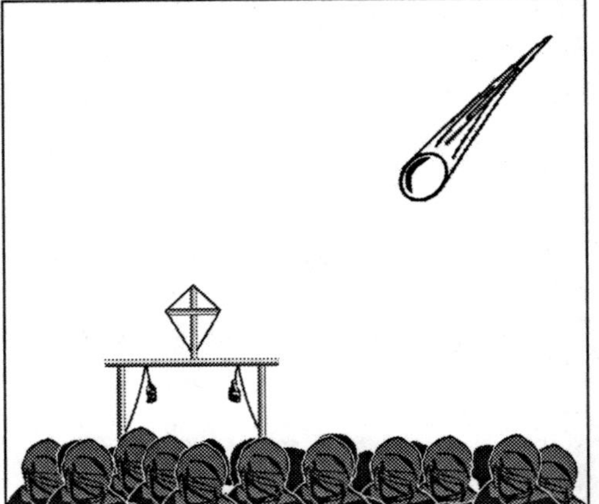

Fig. 9 – A "foo-fighter" sighted by Maria Carreira on October 13, 1917.

OCTOBER

Maria Carreira, with her extraordinary capacity for observation, left us this unusual description in *The Official Interrogations of 1923*:

> When Lúcia said 'There comes Our Lady,' one of this witness' daughter, also named Maria, was present atop a rock, one meter east of the oaks, to protect the arch so the crowd would not damage it. *The girl felt a blow to the face. She saw a very pretty light at her feet and she screamed: 'There! Our Lady!'*
>
> The witness looked and *saw a star, a ball, not entirely round, like an egg, very pretty, in the colors of the rainbow, but much more vivid, with a tail a meter-and-a-half-long, in brilliant colors*. It passed by very quickly and close to the oaks and disappeared a handbreadth above the Earth.

PARALLELS IN UFOLOGY

It would almost be unnecessary to present analogies, since the observation of luminous flying objects, which appear and disappear, constitute a verity of Ufology. Still, let us look at some cases that are most similar to those observed by the witnesses of 1917.

1. Objects inside of clouds

a) In Fátima, Manuel Marto saw "some type of luminous globe spinning in the clouds." His observation must not have been much different than that which A. Rosado saw over Lisbon on December 10, 1954. He saw "*a silver ball that shone intensely among the high clouds*."[12] If Maria Carreira had been Rosado's side, she would certainly have said that the cloud was "a silver color" and that it was "something which reflected a lot."

b) "Mrs. J." said that "a silver globe making a small turn appeared to cut through the clouds here and there...."

In orbit around Earth, as seen from Skylab II

A frequent observation that has been made pertinent to our investigation is that of objects spinning around their own axes. Although it makes no reference to clouds, it is worth citing the following case that involved American astronauts who witnessed an unknown object, far above our blue planet, in space.

> During this shift aboard Skylab II, close to 450 kilometers from Earth, astronauts Jack Lousma, Owen Garriott, and Alan Bean observed and photographed a green UFO for over 10 minutes. Secondly, they declared that the object, which was at a distance of between 50 and 80 kilometers, in an orbit very close to their own, *spun every 10 seconds*.[13]

Above Castelo do Bode, Portugal, June 17, 1977

A pilot for the Portuguese Air Force, José Francisco Rodrigues, observed a UFO enveloped within a cloud while flying over a dam at Castelo do Bode. "I decided then to fly by instruments and enter the clouds," he would later recall. "I was deciding which cloud I would enter, when *I saw something dark, in the middle of a cloud*, that contrasted with the rest, which were

Fig. 10 – The reconstruction of a flying object, surrounded by clouds, seen near Nimes-Courbesac, France, in October 1952. Within the object were observed "silhouettes" of humanoid forms.

whitish."[14] The UFO seemed to be camouflaging itself inside the cloudbank or emitting a vapor in which it concealed itself.

The truth is that many times diverse, strange objects have been seen surrounded by clouds, round or not round, gyrating or using some other type of movement. Above the Nîmes-Courbesac airdrome in October 1952, something like the design presented in Fig. 10 was seen.[15] Not even in this obscure detail does Fátima stand alone.

2. Classical UFOs

a) At Fátima, seminarian Joel de Deus Magno reported, "…they saw an oval, a bit more voluminous than an egg, a vivid and brilliant white in color, with the widest part turned downward…."

In our time, American astronauts also observed something similar in space. Over Hawaii, NASA astronauts James McDivitt and Edward White suddenly observed "a brilliant craft, oval in shape, followed by a luminous trail."[16]

b) But Dr. Gens seems to contradict the statement of de Deus Magno. He affirms that the object was, in fact, luminous, but much taller than broad. It is possible that the UFO moved – as is usual – first on its minor axis, and then on its major axis.

Paço de Arcos, Portugal, October 17, 1954, 5:30 PM

Mariana Campos, in a letter to the newspaper *Diario de Lisboa,* wrote that she saw "*a whitened strip* as though it were a tube of florescent light (João Vieira also saw a mark in a cloud) which moved very slowly.[17] There was a height at which we saw something like a little dish in front that turned frenetically, but merely for a moment. We were watching for 10 minutes, at the end of which we began to verify that *it assumed a vertical position, because up to that point it had been moving horizontally.*"

c) There were witnesses at Fátima, however, who did not refer to the oval aspect and other details, but limited themselves to calling the Lady's vehicle a "luminous globe." To this end, it seems interesting to us to remember a French sighting observed 12 years before Fátima.

Cherbourg, France, March 30, 1905

The newspaper *Cherbourg Éclair* reported that "Saturday night, *a luminous globe*, coming from the North, was seen to describe a large curve over the city and disappear, around 11 o'clock, in the direction from which it came.[18] Officials and persons of certain competence clearly saw this luminous phenomenon, which gave the impression of an electrical steel lamp that was strolling through space, seemingly following a determined course."

Oddly, the newspaper *Jornal de Leiria*, in an edition dated October 21, 1917, related this phenomenon to "The Miracle of the Sun," saying however that, in Cherbourg, the planet Venus was observed, there being some who described "*an oval disk which traced sinuous patterns in the sky.*"

Oval objects, and luminous globes, appear; therefore, in Fátima and in Cherbourg, it would seem, were recorded different descriptions of one phenomenon.

d) Joaquim Xavier Tuna, an eyewitness to the aerial phenomena seen at Fátima, stated: "I saw a cross of great size come out of the Sun and direct itself toward the East. Its progress was not hurried. Sometimes it appeared, other times it disappeared.... In Lapas Parish there were people who saw the cross at the same time."

In a *prima facie* sense, it might be presumed that the cruciform nature of the object that this witness perceived could be attributed to the religiosity of the witness. Not so. In other parts of the world, and in other eras, luminous objects in the shape of a cross have appeared.

United States of America, January 20, 1951

Two control tower operators saw a luminous object that had the appearance of an airplane, "with a body the shape of a cigar and with straight wings which were larger than those of a B-29."[19]

In short, a cross.

Fig. 11 – An object in the form of a cross observed in the skies above the United States on January 20, 1951 (Cited by Project Blue Book).

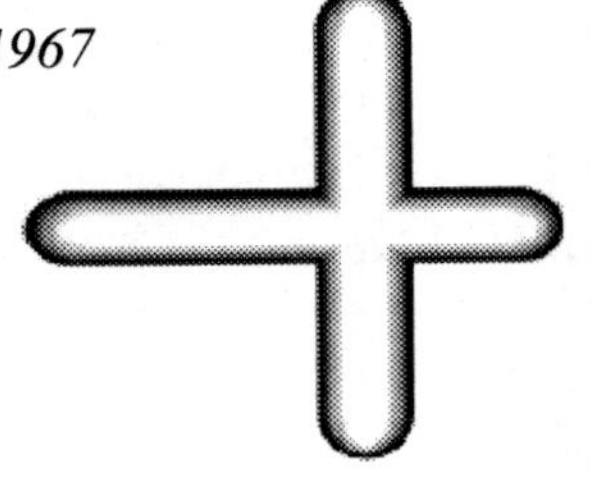

Holsworthy, Brandis Corner, Britain, October 24, 1967

This time, a police brigadier and another officer followed at great speed an object that appeared, he said, "quite large, quite brilliant, and *cross-shaped*." In a press conference, the brigadier stated "*it was like a type of flying cross,* much larger than any star, irradiating luminous points from every angle, much like when one looks through a glass with condensation on it. Before disappearing in the distance, it was picked up by a second object. This was also large, *cross-shaped*, extremely brilliant, and silent."[20]

e) In Fátima, a witness observed a "cross" that appeared and then disappeared. The British policemen saw their "cross" disappear suddenly at 4:16 AM and reappear at 4:23 AM just as abruptly as it had disappeared.

Arada, Romania, June 1969

In a clear sky, the painter Nicolas Dimitras once saw a *white and luminous* object, which propelled itself in a straight line, at a constant speed, *like a bird* in level flight, flying level with the treetops, disappearing behind these.[21]

f) A Fátima witness, Inácio Marques, provided an almost identical account. "Then they could be seen way overhead," he wrote, "cutting through the eastern sky toward the West, *some small white bodies which were white as snow.* There were those who claimed that they were doves, but one could see perfectly that they were not birds."

3. "Flying Eyes" or "Foo-Fighters"

Ota, Portugal, September 4, 1957

This sighting was made in Portugal 40 years after the Fátima incident: "When, at around 9:15 at night, Lieutenant Álvaro Vicente assisted a night flight in Ota," the account reads, "an intense light appeared to the east of the landing strip; it was 20 centimeters in diameter, and moved in a vertical manner, up and down, and *ended up disappearing* some 40 meters from the ground."[22]

Lastly, we would include among this survey of physical descriptions of classical UFOs certain declarations made by witnesses at Fátima about "the doors of the sky," as if this were, in fact, a portal of some kind to the craft that bore the Being. "The children were silent," Maria Carreira remembered, "with their eyes always on that site, until, a little later, Lúcia said: 'That's that! Now She can't be seen; she has entered the sky. *The doors have now been closed.*'"

Jacinta confessed to her mother: "When she entered into the sky, it seems the doors closed with such speed that *even Her feet seemed wedged....* The sky was so pretty! There were so many albardeira roses!"[23]

What might Jacinta actually have seen? "Albardeira roses" are small, wild roses, from white to vivid-pink in color, which beautify the streets of Portugal.

*

UFOs immersed in clouds, disks, spheres, globes, "foo-fighters"– these constitute the basic gallery of aeroforms, seen everywhere and in all times, which to this day defy identification. We speculate that the majority of these machines are craft designed to fly in the lower atmosphere.

A generic classification attributes to UFOs of a spherical or globular shape an average diameter of five meters. The discoid form and its variations – for example, lenticular – in which the perspective of each witness always seems to exert an influence, span various dimensions. McCampbell differentiates between a *standard* type of disk-shaped UFO of about eight meters and a larger type, seen more frequently, that reaches nearly 30 meters. The object sighted at Fátima on October 13th, which we shall examine later, can be placed in this latter group. The spheres or disks of a much smaller size, whose diameter, according to the Dutch physicist Jan Heering, might reach merely 10 centimeters, this scientist supposes to be "intelligent" in nature.[24] They are apparently remotely controlled vehicles, perhaps with remote sensing functions that are pre-programmed.

This scientist thinks that they are intelligently piloted. The peculiar structure of the smaller crafts is intriguing. The *foo-fighters* seem in a fundamental sense to be constructed of light. They are generally spherical in form, with a diameter varying between 10 centimeters, or less, and up to five meters, or more. They move intelligently, showing themselves to be at times authentically living beings. They appear to be made from some type of gas or plasma substrate. They maneuver slowly. They can appear suddenly, and then disappear just as suddenly, as if they have been switched on and then switched off, like a light. "This structured light," Heering thinks, "seems to indicate the existence of other types of rarified or volatile matter."

Independent of these morphological considerations, we believe that the more or less diffused objects seen in clouds at Fátima involved situations of mimicry or camouflage, and that some of the objects seen, whether discoid or not, including "the Sun" that "danced" on October 13th, were, in fact, bearers of other, smaller craft (the spheres or *foo-fighters*). When evaluated together with the bizarre geometric forms sighted, like "stars" and "crosses," they constitute evidence that the Fátima incident should not be viewed within a religious framework, but rather within a Ufological one.

8. RAMPS OF LIGHT

The seer wrote in her *Memórias*: "The lighting was not truly lightning, but the reflection of a light which drew near. It was because we saw this light that we would say, at times, that we saw Our Lady coming; but we could only properly distinguish Our Lady when that light was directly over the oaks."[1]

On October 13th, the Viscount of Montelo asked her: "Was she wrapped up in a gleam?" *"She came in the midst of a splendor," Lúcia answered. "This time it was also blinding. From time to time, I had to wipe my eyes."*

This splendor wrapped up not only the Being – it also wrapped up the Seers themselves. "We were so close," continued Lúcia, "that *we were within the light that surrounded Her or that She gave off. Maybe a meter and a half away, more or less.*"[2]

We know that only the children saw the Being. As far as the crowd was concerned, the rest were only aware of a cloud of smoke. Is it possible that no one else, among the many thousands of people present, observed the light that surrounded the Apparition?

Our search has led us to discover that there was, in fact, another witness who also detected it – Gilberto dos Santos. In his narrative, he does not describe, however, merely seeing a gleam. Gilberto saw more – *a ramp of light, extending downward from the Apparition to the oak.* This thing appeared so substantial to him that he even called it a "street." *The Being, descended, therefore, a luminous "street," a ramp of light.* Here is his description of the kaleidoscopic scene that unfolded before him:

> While the three little shepherds were piously kneeling, gazing at the Apparition, *I saw that they, and the small oak, were within a luminous-colorful-transparent circle of colors similar to the rainbow.* The colors were not in stripes like in a rainbow, but in an amalgam, wherein the tones mixed together. The circle was the limit of a street of colored light *coming from the sky – from somewhere between the Sun and the East.*
>
> When the children stood up, the street of colored light *disappeared a bit at a time, from the ground up*, and, in a few seconds, disappeared completely. At that moment, I was aware that the three little shepherds had directed their gaze to the side of the street of colorful light.
>
> I could distinctly observe that lovely phenomenon; and as I supposed that everyone present had witnessed the same thing, I became surprised to hear from some of the others that they had seen nothing.

A month later, on October 13th, Gilberto returned to the same site. He was already there when the three Seers arrived in the arms of people he judged to be family members. What happened during this visit he would later describe as follows:

> Also, on this occasion I observed, once again, that the three Seers, the small oak, and several people who were close to the Seers, were located *within the luminous-transparent-colorful circle,* as I had also seen in the month of September. *The luminous circle measured between two to three meters in diameter, approximately.* When the three Seers rose, I saw the colorful street of light disappear a little at a time, from bottom to top, and in a few seconds disappear completely, like the month before.

And he added in a note: "When Lúcia was in Torres Novas, for a few days' visit in the home of my parents, she told me that when I observed the phenomenon of *the street of colored light disappear from bottom to top, it was really the occasion in which Our Lady rose to the sky.*"[3]

The Seer corroborated this in her *Memórias:* "*[She] immediately began rising serenely, lifting toward the East, until disappearing in the immensity of the distance. The light that surrounded Her proceeded to open, as if a street enclosed in the stars....*" [4]

PARALLELS IN UFOLOGY

But would the Lady of Fátima have been the only celestial being to descend and ascend again on a ramp of light? Let us examine a few more cases from UFO history.

130 kilometers from Helsinki, Finland, January 7, 1970, 4:45 PM

Two skiers saw a haloed object descend from a luminous, ashen mist, which manifested in pulses. Through the haze, "they perceived an object of metallic appearance, which was three meters in diameter." "*A ray of light exited from the bottom of the craft, and a small and strange creature appeared* in its interior. Afterward, *the light re-entered the craft,* and everything disappeared.[5]

Nicanor-Olivera, Argentina, August 31, 1978

The Arias family was awakened by an intense luminosity outside their residence. An egg-like object hovered over a nearby eucalyptus tree. They observed that *a circular light was emitted from one of the edges of the craft. At the end of that light, they saw two bulky beings that brought forward with them, at chest height, a red light that "seemed to run as if falling from a small waterfall."* The movements of the entities were rigid, and the witnesses described them as "floating travelers, seated on something."[6]

*

There are cases in which UFOs emit beams of light of unusually slow propagation. These define themselves, in the case of nocturnal sightings, by the way in which the luminous beams contrast with their surrounding environmental darkness, giving the impression of being a sort of solid light.

A beam of "solid" light is apparently constituted by a tubular area in the interior of the light source, in which a very particular phenomenon is produced, which we still do not understand, in which each point in the interior of the light is a producer of light. The UFOs modulate the form and duration of the beam. The beams are susceptible to being deflected. Heering thinks that a relationship must exist between these luminous beams of light and the effects associated with them, such as the immobilization of witnesses bathed in this type of radiation.[7] This solid light progresses silently and slowly, taking on the shape of a cylinder that is hollow or full, or in the form of a conical-tubular shape. They can be convergent or divergent. There are cases in which they are illuminated from relatively high altitudes, as witnessed in the Ellezelles case [see *Inforespace*, no. *6*] and the Trancas case [see LDLN, no. 121, and

Fig. 12 – The reconstruction of a sighting of a little humanoid carried by a beam of light in Heinola, Finland, on January 7, 1970 (Courtesy of Jacques Lob and Robert Gigi).

Phénomènes Spatiaux, no. 33]. In Villiers-en-Morvan and in Trancas, the blue beams were seen extending the amazing distances of 2,200 and 3,200 meters, respectively. The velocity of the propagation varied between 13 and 26 kilometers per hour. A cross-section of a beam of this type can vary between five centimeters and three meters. The "ramp" observed at Fátima would not need to be, then, more than one or two kilometers, and its diameter less than the area of the small oak, to fall perfectly within these dimensions.

To stress another important point with some particularity: *In several cases, the source of the beam can clearly be seen through an aperture that appears on the UFO.* Compare this with Lúcia's description regarding the way in which the lady from the heavens disappeared.

In most cases, the focused beams that have been seen projected from UFOs have also been seen to reintegrate into their source, the UFO, following the same pattern in which they appeared, but in reverse, retracting, until they completely disappear within the craft. In numerous accounts, there are indications of some form of condensation or a luminous fog at the moment that the beam reintegrates with the

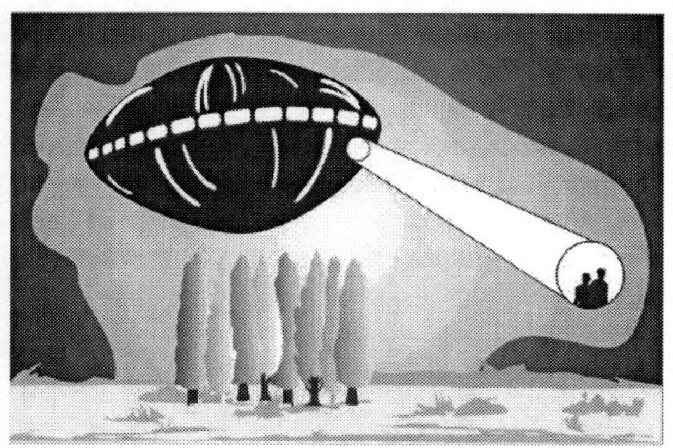

Fig. 13 – Nicanor-Olivera, Argentina, August 31, 1978: two human forms carried on the end of a beam of light emitted by a UFO (Noted by Alejandro E. Chionetti).

craft. This was true in the case of the UFO spotted flying above the dam at Gabriel and Gallan in Spain.[8]

As we have already seen, beyond the external effects of UFOs and whatever the intentions of their occupants might be, both of which belong to the realm of speculation, we can say, unequivocally, that these beams serve to transport alien beings. This, indeed, seems to be one of the most disturbing constants of the Fátima incident.

Physically, this light would be similar to the type of laser energy that is produced by a magneto-hydrodynamic propulsion model and carried out in a strong magnetic field, theorizes Petit.[9] Another hypothesis is presented by Meessen: "One can think of a beam of protons, provoking a luminescence of the air resulting from a sequence of interactions of protons with the electrons of air molecules, as it passes through these on its trajectory."[10] This investigator cites the possibility that beams of this type might cover considerable distances. He calculates that 500 Me V protons might cover 1.3 kilometers in the open air before stopping, while those of 1,000 Me V might cover three kilometers.[11]

A propos of these potentialities, physicist Heering cites the November 1976 edition of *Physics Today*, wherein James F. Ziegler published a photograph of a proton beam focused into a perfectly cylindrical shape. This laboratory feat corroborates what the witnesses saw at Fátima and illustrates what is possible to achieve with an emission of this type, the physicist concludes. Still, he poses some quandaries, like the differences in color among light beams emitted by the same UFO, the slow progression of the beams, the means by which the color and luminosity of the beams are preserved, the forces exerted by the beams (whether, as revealed by their behavior over the oak at Fátima, they involve repulsion or attraction), and the nature of the pulsating beams.[12]

Despite these questions, according to the current state of UFO investigation and the majority opinion of investigators, the Fátima witnesses could have been in the presence of a variable type of energy, which, for engineer Jean Goupil, is comprised of particles modulated by means of interaction with an "agent" or "wave" from their previous rates of acceleration, such that they all have the same velocity.[13] The transport of alien beings, the inspection of Earth environs, and the neutralization of potential threats would constitute the principal functions of these beams.

9. BREEZES

We find, in some Fatimist statements, references to breezes, whirlwinds, and clouds of dust. Inácio António Marques experienced them in June and September. Curiously, he placed them at the end of the time period of the Apparitions, as if the Being were carried aloft, away from Fátima, in a craft, provoking a displacement of air.

JUNE

In June, the newspaper *A Voz de Fátima* published this first person account by an eyewitness: "Lúcia once again looks through space, as though following with her gaze someone who was rising from the ground, and as if, in ecstasy, indicating the direction that She takes until lost in the infinite. I, as a non-believer, want to negate everything I am seeing, but, contemplating the atmosphere, I see that everything has become turbulent. It seems as if *two opposing currents of air have met there, lifting a cloud of dust*. The day grows dark…."[1]

Other witnesses called the "cloud of dust" a "cloud of smoke," and stated that they saw the Lady moving in its interior. They did not speak of any air current, only a diminishment of light and temperature.

Despite this fact, other references to "soft breezes" were made on the other 13th days of the month during the time of the Apparitions.

JULY

Manuel Marto noticed that the Sun clouded, and "a fresh, little, consoling breeze began to blow. We no longer seemed to be at the height of summer," he observed, suggesting that whatever was unfolding above had dampened the heat of July. "The crowd was so quiet that it was impressive."[2]

AUGUST

João Perreira Novo recalled that in August, "the crowd was silent. The day was clear. Then, suddenly, a lightning bolt from the sky formed over the altar, and it made a circle, *a whirlwind that covered more than 300 people in dirt.* Everyone fled, falling and crying."

In its totality, Novo's statement could have been exaggerated or apocryphal.

Among the nearly 18,000 people present, no one else later told of this strong whirlwind. It could have been a "cloud of smoke" and not a whirlwind of dust. A reader of *Raio de Luz* was probably closer to the truth when she wrote:

> There was a sudden drop in temperature, without wind, producing the sensation that one has when there is an eclipse of the Sun. I looked toward the oak, and saw it enveloped in this fog that they say was always noticed.... Was it dust lifted by the movement of the crowd? Perhaps, but at no other point did it occur and, I repeat, there was no wind. It was cool.[3]

SEPTEMBER

Despite the fact that this witness referred to the fact that there was no wind, Inácio António Marques said that a breeze was also felt in September, contemporaneous with an aerial sighting that could easily be drawn from today's close encounter literature. "The conversation continued with [the] Lady, and at the moment Lúcia said 'There She goes,' the Sun darkened.... [T]he heat diminished and a breeze came to caress our foreheads. Then way up, above our heads, could be seen... very small bodies...."

PARALLELS IN UFOLOGY

In our everyday lives, when an automobile passes, or an airplane rises, a dislocation of air is provoked that we can immediately feel. In Ufology as well, cases have been reported where there are sudden breezes that agitate the dust below and trees nearby.

South Table Mountain, Colorado, USA, January 29, 1950

A Denver man named Quintana saw an egg-like object, silver-green in color, flying at about 15 meters, which poised delicately in a ravine. "A light shone on the top of the object," the annals of Ufology inform us. "[A]nd the witness *felt a breeze* and [smelled] an acrid odor."[4]

Ávila, Muñotello, Spain, September 19, 1967

A young man, 24, was returning from a fishing trip riding his bicycle. As he rode, he turned his head, and discerned in the sky a black dot. He could sense *a breeze strong enough to make him feel cold.* "The sensation was repeated, and then he saw a very close object, in the shape of a disk, which advanced with incredible speed."[5]

At Fátima, Manuel Marto had felt "such a fresh, little breeze blowing." And Inácio António Marques, too, stated, "the breeze came to caress our foreheads." Intriguingly, the Spanish citizen cited above also felt "a breeze," and attributed to it a "sensation!"

*

Based on the model proposed by Meessen, the propulsion of UFOs in the lower atmosphere would imply the following:

First, that it is a matter of propulsion by reaction;

Second, that a dislocation of ambient air causes it;

Third, that it is possible without mechanical means, rather, through a direct electromagnetic action upon the conjoined charged particles supplied by the ionization of air surrounding the craft. Hence, logic would support "the observation that the dislocations of air [result] from the charged particles dragging the neutral particles that are the consequence of collisions."[6]

The data observed in Fátima relative to this aspect of the physical manifestations (e.g., "The Miracle of the Sun") correspond to the framework provided by other references about the effects associated with suction.

10. ANGEL HAIR ["THE RAIN OF FLOWERS"]

In 1917, the people of Portugal witnessed another unusual phenomenon, known in the Fatimist literature as "The Rain of Flowers," a poetic and mystical term that undoubtedly resulted from the charged atmosphere created by the paranormal events of that year.

This phenomenon was observed once at the time of the Apparitions, but also at various times in later years. We can confirm, without equivocation, that "flowers" rained over Cova da Iria on September 13, 1917; May 13, 1918; May 13, 1923; May 13 1924; between 1923 and 1925; and on October 17, 1957.

September 13, 1917

This day dawned clear, full of light and with a blue sky. At the time of the Apparition, witnesses saw an unknown substance fall from space. One witness described what he saw this way: "Before or after seeing the luminous globe, but certainly on the same day, myself and some others... began to see something fall, as if *the petals of roses or flowers of snow* were coming from the heights and disappearing just a little over our heads, without us being able to touch them." It was the Fatimist writer, Canon José Galamba de Oliveira, who furnished us with this statement. At the time, he was only a 14-year old seminarian.[1]

But there were those who gave the substance that fell other names. António Rodrigues da Silva, a lawyer, remembered what he saw in these words:

> At the time that had been indicated by the little shepherds – midday – a cry went up to 'Look to the Sun!' I verified that the Sun had turned opaque – a dull color which is not easy to describe. However, something like little flakes of snow or balls of cotton fell on the branches, in the size of old coins, after they were unfastened from the heights and fell upon the oak.[2]

In 1961, Maria do Carmo Marques da Cruz Meneses, who lived near Leiria, told Haffert: "I saw 'The Miracle of the Petals' a month before 'The Miracle of the Sun.' White *balls* had fallen from the sky, which, when I went to catch them, turned to nothing."[3]

Among the multitude present in September 1917 were several Catholic priests in disguise. Barthas, the French canon, wrote that one of them was the priest of Santa Catarina da Serra, who was observing, at a distance, from the cliffs: "Upon seeing the rain of flowers, he became so troubled, that he forgot his intentions to remain discrete and began to pray the Rosary, along with the crowd."[4]

May 13, 1918

When the appearances began, both fervent believers and curious onlookers started to gather at the site, recognized, by 1918, as "sacred." Thus, on May 13th of that year, the people who found themselves there observed with stupefaction the mysterious rain of petals. One of those present was Maria do Carmos Meneses, who, in a letter written to her brother, the poet Marques da Cruz, wrote: "I observed, on May 13th of the following year, some *white balls* which fell from the sky."[5]

Dr. Pereira Gens also knew people who had seen the phenomenon on this date. And Canon Barthas added:

> We knew from the Canon Formigão that Monsignor Sabino Pereira of the Church of São Salvador in Santarém had maintained his incredulity relative to the Apparitions. In 1918, however, he consented to accompany a group of his parishioners to Fátima. When they arrived at Cova da Iria, they saw the phenomenon of *the rain of flowers,* which completely changed the attitudes of Monsignor Pereira.[6]

But this "rain" did not stay around after it fell.

May 13, 1923

By May 1923, Fátima was already attracting great devotion from believers. A grand pilgrimage took place, and, curiously, an identical "rain of flowers" fell over the area and its pilgrims. The Viscount of Montelo in the June 13, 1923 edition of *A Voz de Fátima* described this phenomenon. Under the title "The Pilgrimage of Santarém," the renowned Canon Formigão wrote:

> Precisely at the moment the pilgrims arrived at the site, an atmospheric phenomenon was produced, the cause of which is completely unknown, and which was witnessed by thousands of people of all categories, many of who were unsuspecting and absolutely inaccessible to suggestion.
>
> Innumerable *blocks,*[7] *white as snow, of different sizes,* were seen to fall over a group of The Daughters of Mary, which excited the admiration of those present. [The blocks] fell apart, as if by an enchantment, at a low height, above their heads. The pilgrims of Santarém took part in the collective prayers and canticles, associating themselves with the heart and soul of the intentions of the grand, national pilgrimage.

Naturally, various persons read this news published in *A Voz de Fátima.* One of them, Father Benevenute, of Carrascos, did not agree with the account, and so he wrote the newspaper on June 23rd. His letter is found today in the *Arquivos Formigão*:

> It is good to forewarn the chronicler of the *A Voz de Fátima* so that he may rectify the news that he gave on number 9, page 4, col. 1. The flakes did not fall solely over the group of the Daughters of Mary of Santarém, but *over all who were in the area and near the Parochial Church.* I must say that that atmospheric phenomenon took place here in *Outeiro* as well. I witnessed it,

> attentively and relaxed, *on the following Monday.* Outeiro Grande is at least three leagues from Fátima.

But we possess the testimony of yet another eyewitness. It is the very descriptive statement of Dr. Enrique Vieira Lima, a surgeon at the Civil Hospital of Lisbon:

> Having stopped next to a group, and looked fixedly at the Sun, taking care to shield my eyes from staring directly at the solar body, and having seen nothing, later it was recommended to me that if I persisted, I would see something. A daring insistence was necessary in order to be able to see at last what amazed everyone and caused so much fright to look at. And I saw, twice so, with precise clarity, what very aptly the people of the town, in their imaginative language, likened to "*petals of almond flowers.*" They fell from a great height, but were *not seen to be coming off of the Sun*, as observed by the people who surrounded me. And rapidly and smoothly, at the same time, when they *drew near to the ground, they would disappear*. They were very white and brilliant, like an ardent Sun in a very limpid and serene atmosphere. Not wanting to admit what I was seeing, even to myself, I ended up, at last, and after quite some time, concluding that they were no known or described natural phenomenon. This inclined me, therefore, towards a supernatural explanation. Today, I firmly believe that it must have happened this way, because I had witnesses who helped me reconstruct the phenomenon....

First, we could fixate upon the Sun, and taking a long time with impunity, see within it a *magnificent phenomenon of beauty and color*. Afterwards, an abundant rain of the aforementioned petals began. And when I arrived there, it was no longer possible to see the Sun, and it was at the end of the phenomenon, which took quite a long time....[8]

May 13, 1924

One year later, the Cova de Iria was once again the scene of another mysterious "rainfall." The crowd which brought itself there was numerous, and among them was to be found another medical doctor, José Pereira Gens, at that time already in possession of his medical diploma, which he received in 1922. In his work *Fátima, Como eu a Vi e como a Sinto*, Gens described in great detail the observation that he made shortly after eating his lunch beneath the olive trees beside an ancient road near the Cova:

> At a given time, we noticed that there were some people standing, staring insistently at the sky, and pointing with their hands on high, who said with

> enthusiasm, 'There comes more… there comes more….'
>
> Intrigued, we rose to investigate. They told us, then, that they saw small white rags, that looked like the petals of marigolds, falling, but were unable, however, to follow them with their gaze to the ground....
>
> Looking with attention, we could see, distinctly, *the small white rags*, descending from the heights, but were unable, however, to accompany them with our gaze until they touched the ground. They appeared to be, in fact, marigold petals, or, perhaps… *orange flowers*, which, by their major consistency, best explains the speed at which they fell. Turning our gaze to the highest part of the olive trees, the small bodies, which could be noted perfectly, approached the tops of the dark green trees, and became lost there. We confess that we were unable to see any up close. *It was a very white substance, coming from above, in flakes....*[9]

But on this day, another person, who much later would come to ponder the perplexities of Fátima, observed these flakes fall. P.O. Faria, who, in his works *Perguntas sobre Fátima* [*Questions about Fátima*] and "*Fátima Desmascarada*" ["*Fátima Unmasked*"], made this statement:

> I, too, witnessed this phenomenon on May 13, 1924, having seen it from below, in the midst of the crowd. I remember it perfectly. I was 10 years old. I left early for school; but, arriving near there, instead of continuing on to class, which was in Atouguia, I turned toward Cova da Iria, and when walking uphill there with my "school sack" slung over my shoulder, was drawn there by my curiosity.
>
> I saw everything, and later resumed on my way to Atouguia in fear of receiving a beating for having missed school.
>
> When I entered the room, I worked everybody into [a] frenzy. The teacher was going to scold me for having been late, but I quieted her with a heated narration of the events that I had just witnessed in Fátima. And I told it in the same way that Doctor Gens described it. *A rain of white petals* (or something similar) fell softly over the crowd, disappearing before they reached the ground.[10]

Between 1923 and 1925

Gilberto Fernandes dos Santos also observed a "rain of flowers" at Cova da Iria, but we do not know the exact date. He had hired a photographer named Joaquim Baptista Freitas to re-enact the first day of the Apparitions, with other children portraying the seers. The photographs would serve to illustrate a brochure about the events of 1917. Consequently, on some day between 1923 and 1925 [we cannot determine which one], dos Santos, by sheer serendipity, almost captured visual evidence of "the rain of flowers." He would later write:

> On the occasion during which, for the third time, the photograph was taken of the reconstruction of the Apparition, for maybe 15 minutes, I observed that, over the image, in perhaps a 20 meter area, there fell, from the sky, many little, white flowers (very white) – like petals from an almond tree or small flakes of snow, in the shape of such petals – but which, when they were about three to five meters from the ground, all suddenly disappeared – like bubbles from soapy water children play with. I looked at them in the hopes of catching some, but I couldn't manage to catch a single one, because not a single one fell to the ground. They all mysteriously disappeared.[11]

On other 13th days of the month in various, subsequent years

When we spoke with Lúcia's sister, Maria dos Anjos, in June 1978, she confirmed for us that she, too, had seen this phenomenon, not only at the time of the Apparitions, but possibly in later, undetermined years. She could remember much:

> "I saw the same little rain of flowers after that; it *seemed like a small swarm of bees, enraged*" – she said, gesturing with her hands – "at the site of Cova da Iria. They appeared to be small flowers, passing one over the other. None fell to the ground."
>
> "Muddled up, one on the other?" we asked.
>
> "*Muddled up.*"
>
> "At the height of the Apparitions?" (The previous conversation had been about the sound effect resembling the buzzing of bees.)
>
> "Yes, yes," Maria insisted. "And those ladies who had umbrellas opened them to keep us out of the rain, but none fell."
>
> "They fell, and afterward muddled themselves?"
>
> "Yes. There were many people who also saw this. Many people. I had no umbrella. But those ladies who did have them opened them, and did like

this" – Maria made the gesture of the rising and falling of an umbrella – "but they couldn't catch any."

"Then you never managed to have one in your hand."

"Not me. They didn't fall!"

Other people refer to the falling of "flowers," during forgotten years, although possibly in the decade of the 1920s. "I saw on May 13th many rose petals falling," Maria do Carmo Meneses told her brother the poet: "*They came out of the Sun, but in large quantities. Far above, they were large, but at our feet, they were small and disappeared.* Even the men opened their hats to catch them, but they would see nothing. One fell on my left shoulder. I went to catch it, but saw nothing."

Angélica Maria Pitta Morais also wrote:

> Since then – October 13, 1917 – and until now, I have gone to Cova da Iria several times on the 13th day of the month. I have witnessed another *miraculous sign*, which was the fall, from the sky, of some *luminous "drops" or "pearls,"* which everyone wanted to catch, but which would disappear at about the height of our hands. I arrived at the judgment that I had captured one of these luminous "balls" in my hand, but upon opening my hand, there was nothing. *This happened at the hour of Mass*, and lasted maybe five minutes.[12]

In July 1978, we, too, asked Amélia de Jesus da Silva about "the rain of flowers":

"Do you not recall, after 1917, having seen a rain of flowers fall there?"

"I never saw that. But my mother and many people saw it."

"After 1917, or in the same year?"

"It was later. It was at the time of the blessing of the sick. There were many sick people there...."

"At the time of the blessing of the sick?"

"*It was always during the blessing of the sick that the tiny, little rain fell.*"

"And what did it look like?"

"Some said that they were *tiny flowers* and other *larger roses*. My mother, one

> 13th, saw such flowers fall. She said: 'Look, it appears to be *olive flowers, tiny*, small, which fell, that seemed to be falling from a sieve, like flour from a sieve."
>
> "And did you see where they fell?"
>
> "*It was falling from above.* Some stopped it with their hands; others stopped it with their hats. My mother stopped to think: 'They say that flowers fall here. It is certainly this.' Afterward, she heard people who surrounded her, who were close by, say: 'Ah, today such few charms fell! Sometimes, it is for a longer time. Today, fewer charms fell. They called them 'the graces of Our Lady!' "

October 17, 1957

On October 17th, 40 years after the Fátima incident, white substances again fell from the sky over Cova da Iria. They were different from those we have discussed, because they did not become undone when they hit the ground. They remained in the electrical wires and transformed the bushes in the area into beautiful Christmas trees. They were even transported to Lisbon to be analyzed. Curiously, the news at the time told of a sound, a buzzing like that that the seer's sister had reported in 1917.

The news of the falling of these flakes was broadcast by Rádio Fátima (which no longer exists) and published by the newspapers *A Voz* [*The Voice*] and *Diário de Notícias* [*News Daily*].

For this reason, the following could be read, as transcribed from radio news, in the next day's edition of *A Voz*:

> THOUSANDS OF WHITE FLAKES
> RAIN DOWN ON COVA DA IRIA
>
> Cova da Iria, 17 – Today, since this morning and until midday, from out of the skies of Fátima and its neighboring areas thousands of white flakes rained down, of what seemed to be a material much like silk.
>
> The flakes could be seen at a height of 15 meters. Some descended vertically and others began to move in a north-south direction.
>
> The public, with great expectation, looked at them, suggesting hypotheses with respect to the phenomenon. Few flakes were caught, because the movement of hands, in the attempt to grab them, caused them to separate, due to disturbance of the air.

> There were flakes that were so big that, clinging to electrical wires, they reached the ground. Once bound, they clung with a certain viscosity.
>
> The flakes were not transparent, and could be photographed. Apart from a certain resistance, when the flakes were broken apart they made a light sound, and one could easily rub them in one's hands.

In its turn, the *Diário de Notícias* of October 19th explained:

> METEOROLOGICAL PHENOMENON?
>
> From a cloudless sky and with a radiant Sun, over Cova da Iria fell a shower of white flakes, of unknown substance.
>
> Cova da Iria, 18 (Special for *Diário de Notícias*) – It was at nine o'clock AM yesterday morning.
>
> Suddenly, from the northern end, out of the same direction from which one day the three little shepherds saw that intense light appear which was "more brilliant than the Sun," from which proceeded the apparition of Our Lady, *came a shower of transparent, white flakes, shining a brilliant light*, which descended over Cova da Iria. Because almost everyone was gathered in prayer, few perceived the phenomenon.
>
> Very light, almost unreal, the flakes fluttered in space, and the very act of grabbing them impressed on them, with the slight dislocation of the air, rapid and disordered movement.
>
> *The flakes made a slight sound, like a buzzing*, when they were stretched between the hands, and they came apart as if by magic.
>
> A similar phenomenon does not exist in memory. Ecclesiastical authorities offered no opinion on the subject.
>
> Meanwhile, a sample of the flakes was sent for analysis from the sanctuary to a laboratory in Lisbon.
>
> The news ran swiftly, from mouth to mouth. Many speak of a supernatural phenomenon.

Dr. Gens referred to this observation in *Fátima – Como Eu a vi e como a Sinto*. According to Gens, "it greatly intrigued everyone, as the nature of such a phenomenon could not be easily understood." He asked: "Could this event have any similarity or any relation to what was observed on May 13th of 1918 and 1924? On the first two occasions, the flakes were small, like orange blossom petals, and came undone before they landed. This time, however, they fell in an appreciable quantity and formed a pile… which lasted a long time, and which could be observed, whether on the ground, or over the tree branches and bushes, and on the electrical and telephone wires."[13]

PARALLELS IN UFOLOGY

Ponte de Lima, Portugal, October 12 and 13, 1857, 1:30 PM

The fall of white flowers in Portugal was not confined to the years after the Fátima incident. Indeed, there was news of such enigmatic blossoms falling from the sky and touching the ground in the mid-19th century. In the October 15, 1857 edition of the Valença do Minho newspaper *A Razão* [*Reason*], we can read:

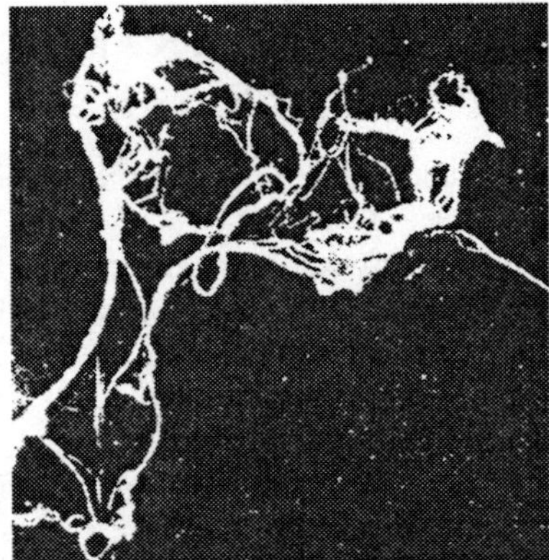

Fig. 14– A sample of "angel hair" photographed on October 17, 1957, in Cova da Iria. "Angel hair" is also called "fibralvina," a term coined by the Portuguese researcher Raul F. Berenguel (Courtesy of *A Voz*).

> At one o'clock PM on the 12th and 13th, in Ponte de Lima and its immediate vicinity, one or more people in the shade looked toward the brilliant Sun on those days (as much as human sight allows), and saw *many flakes or strands which were rarely to be found on Earth.* Although it may be said that in many years this phenomenon has been observed, we maintain that a rain of strands never fell as they did on those two days. Someone was able to catch a few. Mr. Francisco de Salles e Brito, a very enlightened person, who was quite impressed by this never-before-seen event, obtained one of the so-called flakes after it fell on a pine tree. It is a little more rigid than a spider web because, far from breaking, it has elasticity, and is similar to cotton, whiter, and can be made, in the same manner, into a thread. It seems that it isn't only here below where this is being turned against.

As common sense would indicate, no religious connotation was given to this news. The 1857 event was reported as a matter of natural science. But 100 years later, the Being who appeared at Cova da Iria was greeted as a Christian deity.

Moving a century forward once again, to 1957, we find that those threads first detected in 1857 did not fall merely over Fátima. On the same day, the Dorothea Sisters clearly saw at their Colégio de Nossa Senhora do Carmo, in Évora, the same downpour of white flakes that fell at Cova da Iria.[14]

Évora, Portugal, November 2, 1959

Two years later, Évora again became the stage of a similar phenomenon. On November 2nd, the passage of various unidentified objects over Évora was noted. They were "round in shape and had a very brilliant sphere on top. Coinciding with the passage of the objects, an intense rain of whitened filaments, which lasted nearly four hours, fell over the city."[15]

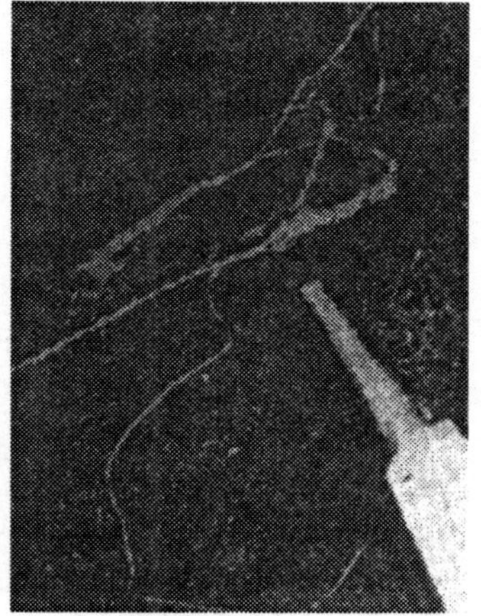

Fig. 15 – A sample of "angel hair" collected in Oloron, France, on October 17, 1952 (Courtesy of Jacques Lob and Robert Gigi).

Florence, Italy, October 27, 1954

On the outskirts of Florence, "two witnesses, on the terrace of a café, noticed two luminous objects in the sky which were moving in a straight line, at high speed and close to one another. Then they made a 45-degree turn, and departed in the direction of Florence. Later, the soccer teams from Fiorentina and Pistoia interrupted the game in which they were embattled so that 10 thousand spectators could watch the maneuvers of the two luminous balls, which passed three times over the city stadium, while whitened threads descended over the area."[16] Following this particular event, the threads were taken to a laboratory.

Oloron, France, October 17, 1952

"It was a splendid day," one may read in the book *The Discovery of UFOs*, by Jacques Scornaux and Christiane Piens.[17] "The sky was blue and cloudless." Suddenly, a man named Prigent, his wife, and their three children saw that, "to the North, upon the blue background of the sky, an odd, flake-shaped cloud fluctuated.... The object was whitish, not luminous, of distinct design."

According to the Prigent family, at a certain distance from the front of the cylindrical object, some 30 other objects followed its trajectory. All of the crafts left behind them some type of white matter, much like filaments known in Ufology as "angel hair," which fell upon the trees, electrical wires, and the roofs of houses, before dissolving after several hours. When one tried to catch them, they quickly disintegrated.

"ANGEL HAIR" DOSSIER – THE *FIBRALVINA* OF THE UFOS

a) A strange substance and its symbolism

If, per chance, doubt remains as to the intimate tie between the apparition phenomenon and the UFO phenomenon, the appearance of the popularly designated "angel hair" or "Virgin threads" during the events at Fátima should eliminate such doubt. So consistent the relationship appears to us – take note of the number of Fátima witnesses who testified about "angel hair" – that we view it as one of the most substantial proofs that the Fátima incident was of a Ufological nature rather than a religious one.

Nearly two dozen mystical or poetic terms portrayed the force of the environment around the Apparitions. Some of these symbolic expressions included: "rose petals," "rain of flowers," "marigold petals," "orange blossoms," "graces of Our Lady," *et cetera*. Beside these, we find other, more prosaic descriptions, such as "flakes as white as snow, of different sizes," "small white rags," "a very white substance, coming from above in flakes," "cotton on the branch," "like a swarm of bees jumbled one upon another…."

Of the definitions that were left to us relative to the observations at Fátima, we can classify three types of substances in respect to their morphology and behavior:

1st type: "flakes" of different dimensions, which faded before reaching the ground (1917, 1918, 1923, 1924);

2nd type: "flakes" which were present for several hours on the ground before fading (1957);

3rd type: "flakes" which produced a buzzing sound and fell in spiral movements, fading rapidly or gradually (seen in various undetermined years and in 1957.)

These minor differences do not disprove so much as they serve to establish a common origin. To investigator Raul Berenguel, the *fibrous* aspect of the substance, together with its white coloration, suggested a definition less poetic and more consistent with "angel hair," which was the finding he presented at the Congress of Iberian Ufology held in Porto, Portugal on October 7th and 8th, 1978:

> *Fibralvina* – a substance that falls from the atmosphere after the passage of UFOs or apparently without visible cause. During the fall, they rain down in brilliant balls of thread and, according to the height of the fall, scatter themselves, forming a veil of great extension. It is a question of an organic substance, with an accentuated tendency towards sublimation, of reduced density, whose lightness can make it fall in points distant to the initial site of the fall.
>
> Different types of "fibralvina" appear to exist; therefore, chemical analyses oftentimes differ. The physical characteristics do, however, remain constant, these being, namely, an extraordinary mechanical resistance to traction and torque, an extremely small thickness, which confers upon it a very great tenuousness. In a group, the fibers distribute themselves randomly in an intricate tangle whose gaps are filled in by a translucent and viscous gelatin. The filaments burn rapidly when exposed to a hot flame, leaving an imperceptible trace. They are attracted by electrostatic charges and adhere notably to wood. The elements found in the different types of "fibralvina" that seem to exist are: sodium, carbon, hydrogen, oxygen, tin, boron, calcium, and magnesium. The presence of silicone is also indicated. The decomposition temperature is approximately 280 degrees when analyzed.[18]

Thus, from the word *fiber* and the Latin stem *alvis* was crafted the more reasonable and palpable term to apply to the substance that fell in Fátima during and after the Apparitions of 1917. The fact that this substance continued to fall in the region is a sign that the cause of the first falls did not permanently abandon the locality where its marvelous effects first attracted multitudes.

b) The nature of the "fibralvina"

We have already examined some of the previous historical falls of this substance. Charles Fort, compiler of the "damned facts" known today as Fortean phenomena, included some examples of "fibralvina" in his *magnum opus*, *The Book of the Damned*.[19] We saw also how a great majority of the witnesses describe to us the dissipation of the "flakes" in unequal increments of time. There are cases in which reference is made to the existence of a nebulous formation wrapped around a UFO in the shape of a cigar, from which falls filaments or strips a few centimeters or several meters in length. But as we shall see, the description of the causal object associated with the fall of the "fibralvina" (when one can be visually identified) is not always uniform.

In 1957, Craig Phillips, a biologist for the U.S. Fish and Wildlife Service, took a research trip on behalf of the Miami Aquarium aboard the ship *Sea Horse*. Nearly three miles out from Florida, the sky was clear, when the crew began to see something akin to "spider webs" falling from the sky. The downfall lasted for two hours. Phillips collected some samples to view later under a microscope in his laboratory, where he was convinced that he would observe the fine drops that adorn many spider webs. When he opened the place in which he had kept the samples, he found not a trace of the "webs." "This fact is inexplicable," Phillips later remarked. "I never saw anything like it."[20]

The January 1970 issue of *Spacelink* magazine told the case of Marius Maguan, a farmer from Saint Ann, Manitoba, Canada, who saw two UFOs on his property on September 18, 1968. He saw a floating substance "like popcorn falling from a machine." Samples were examined and infrared spectroscopy revealed the substance to be cellulose, with fibers .02 millimeters in diameter. Previous investigations showed the fiber to be "*rayon* covered by a viscous substance."[21]

Unlike the benign results in these cases, a downpour of this same material in Tennessee caused one witness to vomit, others to experience itching sensations, and strange effects to be felt by other people who entered the area on subsequent days. Even animals in the area would not leave their shelters.[22]

As for the previously mentioned case in Florence, Italy, in 1954, beyond the observation of a strange object, a long rain of "cotton" was seen to fall, very luminous, shining in the rays of the Sun. A young student, Alfredo Jacopozzi, managed to catch some of the substance, and took it to the chemistry department of a local university. A chemical analysis performed there found that the "snow" was principally composed of boron, silicon, calcium, and magnesium in a macromolecular structure. The witnesses interrogated remembered the passage of strange objects immediately before the fall of the "flakes of cotton." The objects, they said, were convex above and concave below.[23]

c) "Fibralvina" and UFO propulsion

Some authors, upon studying the relation between the fall of "fibralvina" and the presence of UFOs, have proposed that the filaments referred to could be "spider webs" produced by small arachnids. Ascending currents of air to altitudes as high as 1000 meters would carry these, forming actual clouds, aloft. According to this theory, the downpour of these webs would be evident at the beginning of each season, chiefly in the spring. The engineer, Jean Senelier, critically analyzed this hypothesis, showing that the entomological explanation – segregation of the "webs" by the small spiders in flight – only coincides in part with the range of altitude at which the phenomenon has been verified and, still, outside a comfortable margin of certainty.

Senelier, highlighting the number of falls of "fibralvina" that have been observed in the month of October, asserted that the substance cannot be attributed to a "normal" reaction to the mechanism of UFO propulsion. Rather, it might be an unexpected manifestation in the atmosphere in response to the ejection of "debris" from the craft.[24]

French investigator Fernand Lagarde revived this idea. The UFOs, he surmised, upon arriving at that layer of our atmosphere where they crowd together, hovering, attracting human observers below, and being carried by an electrostatic charge, redress the cockpit of the craft. M.R. Eraud, writing in *LDLN* magazine in support of Lagarde's thesis,[25] put forth the following sequence explaining the phenomenon of the "fall": (1) the spacecraft is limited by its force field; (2) the pilot wants to unload the filamentous shield; (3) he reduces the velocity of his craft and for an instant cuts off its force field; (4) its protection discontinued, the craft moves; (5) the UFO finds itself suddenly in contact with the air; and (6) immediately emits a shockwave, (7) leaving behind itself a dislocated mass trapped by atmospheric resistance.[26]

It is possible that some analyses might have identified authentic spider webs, despite scientific knowledge establishing the actual habits of the arachnids supposedly involved and their biological processes. What is important to underscore, however, is the outlining of a cause-and-effect relationship attributed to the propulsion model of UFOs. The "arachnid" hypothesis is merely one decorative element in these particular models, in the sense that if spider webs can be caught in the magnetic field of the object, *other materials can also be*. What is attempted to be proven here, beyond the question of what the "fibralvina" is made of, is its simultaneous association with the UFO phenomenon, more appropriately, with overflights by unidentified crafts.

Jean Plantier, one of the first French authors to propose a model of explanation for the propulsion of UFOs, suggests that the "filaments" could be a trace left behind the objects by positive particles, that combine themselves chemically with neighboring particles or with the constituents of air surrounding the objects, chiefly water vapor. The shine of that "heavenly cotton" would result from its exceptional absorbency, making one think of any kind of salt, disintegrating upon contact with the ground as it loses ionization, caused by its temporary instability.[27]

The Belgian Maurice de San theorizes that UFO propulsion produces white "filaments" and the "fibralvina" are equivalent to the "crystallites" studied by L.B. Loeb in 1963.[28] Loeb attempted to identify the fundamental characteristics of "angel hair" from cases in which it was possible to gather samples. Maurice de San postulates that the formation of these filaments could directly result from a very intense electrical field surrounding the UFOs. As they travel through the atmosphere saturated with water vapor, the molecules existing there are affected by the electrical field produced by the craft, and deposit themselves on the surface of the object.[29]

In a similar way, Yvan Bozzonetti of the OURANOS Commission speculates that the electrical field of the UFO could repel this filamentous material. The ionization potential of the craft would permit deposition of an unstable compound, a type of plastic substance, which would disaggregate itself spontaneously under the influence of atmospheric light, water vapor, temperature, or yet still, oxygen.[30]

Elaborating upon the idea exposed by Jean Senelier – that of the rejection of something useless on the part of the UFO – the Frenchman François Gardes proposes that this detritus could be a support for unknown energies, a bit like the water vapor and ashes left behind by the old steam locomotives. This investigator compares the "filaments" to the luminous orbs, which, left behind by certain UFOs, fall apart or evaporate when touched, just as "angel hair" does.[31]

d) Visibility and invisibility of UFOs in the fall of "fibralvina" at Fátima

We already know that during the course of the penultimate Apparition, the one in September 1917, it was noted that a luminous globe appeared and "rose petals or flowers of snow" fell from the heights and disappeared just over the heads of the crowd. In subsequent years, the formula for this plot became permanent. Those present would point to the Sun as the direct origin of the falling "flakes." It is during the fall of these filaments that the witnesses were able, fully and at length, to look at the Sun. In fact, an object aligned vertically with the Sun would not provoke any other effect but the hiding of the solar disk by interposition. It would also cause the multitude to point to the Sun as the fount of the "filaments" – a fact that, we know, could not exist in nature. It is said that in a 1923 occurrence, onlookers could stare at the Sun and see in it "a magnificent phenomenon of beauty and color." After such events, it would once again become impossible to openly stare at the Sun. The concealment of the Sun simply ceased, and "our" object removed itself.

In odd years, the presence of "the pseudo-Sun" seems to have become a constant. The words speak for themselves: "They"– the filaments – "came out of the Sun in great quantity." And there, above, the strands seemed larger than at the feet of the witnesses. As the "filaments" fell to the Earth, the "miracle" of the progressive sublimation resulted, and the filaments would decrease in volume in proportion to their proximity to the ground and to levels of elevated temperature. There exists, nonetheless, at least one observation of "fibralvina" at Fátima that is not accompanied, at least visibly, by a "pseudo-Sun," or beforehand, circular or spherical objects placing themselves in the vertical of the location. The case from 1957 is one example which is, otherwise, extremely significant in every aspect. The landfalls of "fibralvina" at Oloron and Gaillac, in France, or yet, in Graullet, Tarn, on October 13, 1954, are others. October, or Autumn, is always a constant in these cases. And the descriptions always conform. What are seen are flakes, either on the ground, or in the trees, or on telephone wires, which remain there for several hours.

But returning to what Fatimists call the "falha solar" (or "missing Sun") of that date, we believe in not deceiving those who are looking to this detail for an argument to separate the UFO phenomenon from its true path. The truth is that the fall of "fibralvina" does not depend on the visible presence or *de facto* confirmation of an aerial object, such as in September 1917, or in the remaining cases previously described which took place around the world. That is, the unidentified cause of the production of "fibralvina" may occur outside of our range of visual perception. It was this type of observation that was made by officers of the Portuguese Air Force at its base in Sintra, near Lisbon, in the late 1950s or early 1960s. General Conceição e Silva described the event:

> On a clear, sunny morning under a totally clear sky, we thought odd the appearance of fine filaments, like spider webs, which came undone upon contact with the hands. The fact was not associated with the appearance of any objects, since the same were not seen, at least not in Sintra.[32]

e) Fátima, 1957 - an analysis and various photographs of "fibralvina"

When, at almost nine o'clock in the morning of October 17, 1957, there fell an intense rain of white flakes over the Sanctuary at Fátima, producing a discrete buzzing, still many spoke of "a miracle"– "a supernatural phenomenon." The samples that were taken of the substance were more stable than usual and hence could be subjected to laboratory analysis, albeit limited.

The specimens were collected by a group of people from Radio Fátima, who sent them to the Catholic newspaper *A Voz*. The newspaper delivered them to Cândido Ançã, a former editor who once edited a science page for that publication. On October 18th, already that "knowledgeable chemist, very different and studious, whose laboratory is a truly noteworthy center of work," was handing over to the newspaper his report, which was published on the

19th. Here is Ançã's analysis:

> The substance presents itself, on the whole, with the aspect of "flakes" constituted by aggregates of very white filaments, disposed of randomly, as with felt.
>
> The first conclusion that can be drawn from the microscopic examination is that we are dealing with natural fibers, and not artificial fibers.... They form a type of felt-like material, as I said, constituted by undulating fibers, at times knotty, formed by very tenuous aggregates of fibers which are more tenuous still, which only mechanical action manages to ruffle. Compared to that of cotton, the fiber of the examined "flake" is considerably thinner, undulating, and felt-like in its texture.
>
> The second conclusion that is possible to draw from the micro-combustion carried out under the microscope is one that has to do with the vegetable and not animal product, since the combustion takes place rapidly and with the formation of almost imperceptible residue of white ash, and not with the spherical formation at the extremity of the fiber, as can be generally observed in the combustion of filaments of animal origin....

Note that the diversity of scientific conclusions such as this one might not result from the diversity of the origins of the "fibralvina" examined, but from the diversity of the means and processes utilized in the various analyses performed in different years. What Cândido Ançã gleans from his analysis, the reader can compare to the long report cited previously. His analysis may also verify the similarity of the phenomenon seen in Fátima with that of Oloron, as depicted in photos published in the media of the time. Similarly, the substance that fell in Fátima in 1957 conformed to the generality. However, a finding that the substance was very light could not be made in this instance.

f) Organic origins?

We have already seen that on the same day that "angel hair" fell in Fátima, it also fell in Évora. Two years later, precisely on November 2, 1959, this city was overflown, around midday, by two discoid objects, light ash in color, with a darkened periphery. One of them, in its movements over the city, made abrupt stops, which were soon followed by dislocations at great velocities.[33]

While not having many thousands of witnesses as at Cova da Iria, the celestial dance appearing above Évora was nonetheless contemplated for a long time by numerous people, especially by the students and professors of the Commercial and Industrial School that then existed in Évora. There as well, people saw our well-known "fibralvina" fall from above in the shape of flakes and filaments. As in other points of the globe, its fall was not considered a "miracle." But let us continue to follow the constant description of the original report:

> Coinciding with the passage of the unidentified aerial objects, they began to notice in the sky, a little after midday, numerous filaments that fell almost from a great height and almost vertically. Those filaments disaggregated themselves from true balls of thread, that descended in the atmosphere with a curious circular movement, and their whiteness was so great and so intense in its brilliance that they appeared to possess their own inner light. The phenomenon lasted almost four hours and the filaments deposited themselves over the trees, telephone wires, roofs, *et cetera*. It was not easy to recover the filaments because many were disintegrating and would disappear before reaching the ground. Of the material gathered, it was possible to conduct a spectral analysis, in which a double line of sodium could be detected.[34]

Under a microscope, the strange substance was found to be "a weaving of numerous and very fine filaments sometimes crossing each other in disorder, similar to capillary tubes wrapped by a substance of gelatinous aspect, transparent, colorless, and lightly yellowed." The author of the analysis, who at the time was director of the above-mentioned school, refers to the purpose that those filaments served as weaving and hovering at a great altitude where they stood out. It was light and resistant, simultaneously.

The idea that emerges from this report is that the objects observed over Évora would transport with them a "biological" body of great dimensions, medusa-like, under the bottom of the "technological" object carrying it. Such an impression was, at least, the conclusion drawn by the author of the report, who used a telescope on the day of the sighting to follow the transformations of the UFO.

As a matter of fact, that conjecture would be supported by the aforementioned author, who found, in one of the "fibralvina" preparations gathered by his students on the day in question, a strange creature, endowed with a rounded central body, from which, with perfect symmetry, 10 tentacles radiated, each one trifurcated at the end, forming three, finger-like extensions. This discovery was broadly debated during the First Iberian Ufological Congress, the report of which, from which we have taken several passages, can be found reproduced in the previously cited book by Raul Berenguel.

The question of the "unknown organism" found in a preparation of the celebrated filaments came to focus with greater clarity the hypothesis of the organic origin of the "fibralvina," that, varying as to its cause was not then recent. Still, during the course of the subsequent investigation sponsored by the CEAFI in Évora, together with eyewitnesses to the fall of flakes on November 2nd, the idea that the substance might be part of a colony of aerial organisms dragged along by a UFO was once again suggested.

In addition, the similarity of the filaments that fell in Évora in 1959 with those observed in Fátima in 1957 was confirmed when the investigators showed the witnesses a photograph of the "angel hairs" gathered in Cova da Iria, and got the response: "They are identical." The only exception was that those of Évora had a more ashen cast than those of Fátima. As far as the rest were concerned, they were the same "flakes of cotton, as if on the branch, some larger than others, and which, when in contact with our fingers, began to disappear at different rates of speed."[35]

Yet, as we previously stated, the notion that the "fibralvina" had an organic origin is not a new one within the bibliography dedicated to this theme. It is evident that some authors, such as A. Maurras, Assistant at the Toulouse Faculty of Science, share the perspective we have identified as to the hypothesis that arachnids might have been involved.[36] Several analyses carried out by that investigator, for instance, the gathering of that substance that fell November 7, 1965 between Auch and Revel, convinced him that organic matter was involved. The same idea has surfaced again much more recently, during the course of analyses that have been possible to perform in the United States.

A fall of "fibralvina" that took place on October 12, 1976 in Sonora, USA, provided some samples for an analysis conducted by Dr. David J. Miletich, Director of the Anesthesia Research Laboratory of the University of Chicago. The first results of this analysis were published in the *International Reporter*, vol. 2, no. 8, August 1977, a publication of Professor J. Allen Hynek's Center for UFO Studies.[37] Noteworthy, of course, were the classical characteristics of "angel hair" – its fibrous texture, thread-like structure, the high dose of static electricity, its tendency to remain attached to even smooth surfaces, and its involvement of a lightly viscous substance.

The report concluded that the substance had an organic origin, but when they decided to test its radioactive index, they found to their great surprise that the sample was contaminated by the radioactive hydrogen isotope *tritium*. The report forcefully concluded, "Save for accidental contamination, this level of tritium seems to indicate that the sample was exposed to some form of nuclear fission or fusion."

The other important observation was verified in the Michael Reese Hospital Microbiology Laboratory: an incubation of the "fibralvina" in a *standard* and neutral nutritive medium revealed no bacterial growth. *The fibers are sterile.*

The report concluded that the fibers could have originated from a *living organism*. In accordance with that hypothesis, even though it would be banal, the origin of the "fibralvina" could be attributed to insect secretions. Nonetheless, the properties referred to – radioactivity and sterility – are unexpected. When one starts from those properties, does the "arachnid" idea remain plausible?

We shall maintain, for the time being, that the association of downfalls of "fibralvina" with the presence of UFOs seems to be confirmed all the way down the line. The intermittent production of this substance, as already suggested by Jean Senelier, seems to indicate that it may be synthesized by the occasional interference of a random electrical field with the controlled ejection of the strange matter that, in the case of Évora, possessed a corpuscle that protected itself.[38]

It does not cease in its curiousness to compare several consistent physical characteristics of the descriptions from Fátima at various times with passages taken from the report of the fall of "fibralvina" in Évora in 1959:

FÁTIMA – VARIOUS	**ÉVORA – 1959**
"Very white and brilliant...."	"Its whiteness was so great and its brilliance so intense...."
"Like small swarms of bees, muddled up one upon another...."	"They descended in the atmosphere with a curious circular movement...."
"Up above, they were large, and at our feet, they were tiny, and they disappeared...."	"Those filaments were part of a weaving hovering at great height and where they stood out...."
"The movement of the hands, when wanting to grab them, provoked their removal by the agitation of the air...."	"Their extreme levity originated a rapid removal and raising in the atmosphere at the slightest dislocation of air provoked by the approximation of any person...."

We suppose the analogies speak for themselves. The "graces," the "petals" belong to a religious language in the very framework of the Apparitions interpreted as such. It was not only in Fátima that the fall of the enigmatic filaments frightened the believers. In Baião (Alto Douro), for example, during several apparitions of the same type of being, the phenomenon repeated itself as a fatal effect of that type of manifestation, such as in the UFOs: "They seemed like flakes of snow when falling. They disappeared when they reached the ground. When that happened, the Lady had already appeared the first time. The trees were all covered with those things. Lovely!"

For the inhabitants of Baião, a mountainous area, even though these events took place in 1938, they continue to be "a very great miracle." Testimony from that time provides us with details: "At that time at which he agreed to appear to Bonifácio… the little things fell at that height." The chapel guard, standing, praising the Being, also provided this description:

> It was falling, as tinsel falls.[39] It came to fall in this manner. The wind pushed it and it ran with the wind. It looked like snow. The crowd went to catch it, but did not catch any of it. It fell apart. It was some kind of flowers. In those days, the little boy would say that Our Lady was coming….[40]

The symbolic charge of the "angel hairs" or flakes – their association with a range of related religious and mythical references – is, by definition, purely secondary. Their manifestation, however, as products of "ejection" by UFOs, yes, this is essential and significant.

11. EFFECTS ON ANIMALS

Although we may have, essentially, leaned over towards the observation of phenomena as performed by the multitude, we should not miss the fact that the seers pointed to an interesting element, on May 13th, that has been established in contacts of this type – the control of animals.

Lúcia, for her part, shared nothing with us about this subject in her *Memórias*. Interestingly, however, Jacinta's mother furnished the following testimony when she appeared before *The Official Interrogations of 1923*: "At the onset of the Apparition, when Lúcia was saying that she could see Our Lady, Francisco, seeing nothing, advised his cousin to throw a rock at her, and Lúcia said to the lady: 'Then you are Our Lady from heaven and Francisco cannot see you?' "

The Lady had already told her that she was from the sky. But the Lady said to Lúcia: "Tell him to pray the rosary and he will see me." The little boy said that he put his hand into the pocket of his jacket where he had the contents from Mass. And when he prayed six or seven Hail Marys, he could see the Lady and could pray no more.

On the occasion when he could already see her, he noticed that the sheep began moving toward a wheat field that was in the lowest part of Cova da Iria, and said that he was going to fetch them. He was about to set out to do so, when Lúcia told him: "O, Francisco, don't go, because Our Lady says the flock won't eat the wheat." Then he observed: "Then the sheep are already in the wheat and aren't eating it?" And he came back. His mother then asked him: "After Our Lady went away, the sheep ate the wheat?" He responded: "Ah, if you let them, they'll eat it all!"

This episode of the sheep not eating the wheat at the time of an Apparition is also referred to in the November 18, 1917 edition of the publication *O Conçelho de Mação*, although placed in a previous epoch:

> At the site of Aljustrel, one kilometer from Fátima, in Ourém County, reside three little shepherds.... They claim that for 18 months, near their home, a very pretty lady has appeared to them. She said nothing to them then. *The flock stayed; but once the Apparition disappeared, it ran to the wheat field.*

The editor of the journal *O Mensageiro* questioned the seers, as we know, in October. In the November 29th edition of his paper, he published the following:

> We only had Francisco left to speak with, who arrived home from school, on the occasion when I spoke to Lúcia. He is the only one who has fulfilled what the Lady said the second time she appeared – that they learn to read. He is nine years old. He could not hear the Lady speak, but could see her dressed in white. When the Lady would speak, the sheep, *although they wandered in the corn and beans, caused no damage. They neither knocked them down nor ate them.* He did not know how to respond to the rest of the questions we posed to him.

In 1978, we spoke to Amélia de Jesus da Silva, who was born the same year as Jacinta. She told us about several episodes in the seers' lives and other details from the time of the events. One of the facts that she narrated to us concerned the strange effect over the animals on the first day of the Apparitions.

She expressly told us about someone who had attended the encounter on the 13th of May – specifically, the enigmatic Maria Carreira.

> That woman was a softy. She was the first to begin caring for the little

chapel. She watched over the little chapel until she died. That "little woman" is the one who began to see from the start. She passed by there and saw the kids staring toward the oak. "Shameless brats! You're standing there while the sheep are here eating the beans." They paid no attention. She returned to say: "Keep it up, and I'll go over the road and I'll tell your parents. You, standing there playing, and the sheep here." When they thought it right, I think they told her: "Not even one bean is eaten. We were watching Our Lady, and *she said we should let the sheep wander that they would only eat the grass." And the little woman verified then and there and saw none had been stepped on nor eaten.* She is the one who soon began to follow that.

*

The pre-detection of UFOs and their humanoid occupants by animals is well known. The British investigator, Gordon Creighton, gathered 200 cases of this type, in which birds, ducks, chickens, sheep, horses, dogs, and other animals were affected by the presence of something unidentified.[1]

We think that in Fátima inhibiting effects were registered on the flock led by the little shepherds that can be identified with some of the classic symptoms noted in Ufology: "*The flock stayed*, but once the Apparition disappeared, it ran to the wheat field," a journal explained. And Francisco revealed: "Although the sheep wandered in the corn and beans, they caused no harm, *they neither knocked them down nor ate them*." This was when the "Lady" was present. Curiously, no doubt, this was uncommon behavior for the animals when everyone was afraid that these would make a ruckus in the crops....

But what do contemporary narratives tell us? That in El Castanuelo, Huelva, Spain, in December 1970, a shepherd, named Juanito, who followed after his sheep on the road, became "paralyzed" along with the animals when confronted by a strange craft with four feet.[2] In Denmark, when a UFO landed in a meadow, witnesses verified that the cows that were nearest to the craft were immobilized and the birds stopped singing.[3] On another continent, in Trancas, in Argentina, on October 21, 1963, three dogs and a dozen hens were caught within an annex by a beam of light emitted by a UFO hovering on the outskirts of the city. The animals became apathetic and silent, and recovered slowly in the intervals of the luminous emissions.[4]

The radiation proposed by McCampbell – microwaves emitted by the phenomenon – could be at the heart of this symptomology of fear, expectation, and silence. On the other hand, we can take into account the presence of gases seeping from the ground, such as ozone, or even the possibility that witnesses were affected by high frequency sounds. In either case, despite the global diversity of symptoms, animal psychophysiology seems to mirror that of humans, exceeding mere passivity before the UFO phenomenon, to include such common features as complete immobilization, and other characteristics experienced by eyewitnesses.

12. THE TESTIMONY OF THE "FOURTH SEER"– THE SMALL, "TELEPATHIC" HUMANOID

"O, Conception, do you not hear a voice within you? He represents himself, Him whom I hear within me saying that I go there and pray three Hail Marys."
– "Fourth Seer"

We can read in the book *Mensagem de Fátima* [*Message from Fátima*], authored by Father Dr. Luciano Guerra, actual rector of the Fátima Sanctuary:

> *1917: angelic apparition (according to explanation by Our Lady during the fourth Apparition) to one said* [*to be*] *Carolina, 12 years old, and to a child of Espite.*[1]

Now, Lúcia never refers to said dialogue with the Being. In 1947, the future bishop of Viseu, D. José Pedro da Silva, perhaps surprised by that inexplicable silence, affirmatively asked the seer:

> Aunt Maria da Capelhina, so-called, said, in the official statement, and still today confirms it, that her daughter, Carolina, had seen an angel taking a walk at Cova da Iria, asking that three Hail Marys be prayed.... And, afterward, had asked her sister to ask Our Lady what "that" was; and that the sister, at Valinhos, had asked Our Lady but received no response that it was an angel.... Is there any truth in this?
>
> I don't know. I don't remember anything.[2]

This response by the seer is strange. She can't remember a thing? Yet she remembers long discourses and interminable secrets with terms that in that era were unknown? Or was that detail about which the future bishop suggestively designated as "that" eliminated from Lúcia's mind?

The official statement referred to by da Silva can be found in the document known by the title *The Official Interrogations of 1923*. It was redacted by the Viscount of Montelo and consists of the following, in full:

> In Valinhos, Lúcia asked the Lady, at the request of the witness, if Our Lady had appeared to anyone else at Cova da Iria, and the Lady responded that it was not Her, but that the pretty, blonde figure of small stature seen by Carolina, youngest daughter of the witness, age 12, and the young girl of seven, of Espite, on July 28th, beside the oak, had been an angel, which Carolina later saw over the oak.[3]

Lastly, the official documentation of Fátima points us to visits by other beings to Cova da Iria, beyond the Lady, and speaks to us of other seers, beyond the three most well known. Because of this fact, we designate Carolina Carreira as *the "fourth seer" of Fátima*.

The "fourth seer" of Fátima lived in complete oblivion and anonymity. She declared to us that she remembers no one, not even any priest, having questioned her before we did. She only told her mother and siblings at home. Had it not been for the Canon Formigáo having invited the mother to testify, her evidence would have been completely lost.

This anonymity, in the meantime, brought her advantages. If they had included her narrative, she would have been bothered by the veneration of the believers, and it is possible that they would also have sent her to a convent. Instead, Carolina was able to marry (her husband was still alive when we spoke with her), and while she had no children, she had sisters and nieces who treated her with affection. Her life was normal, without the need to make sacrifices of the type exaggerated by sinners like the other seers (such as Lúcia). And in order to speak with us it was not necessary to solicit the authorization of the bishop of the diocese.

Naturally, we recorded all of her statement, given on July 22, 1978, on a sunny Saturday morning. It is fully published here, except for repetitions that have been deleted. Here is, therefore, what we were told by the "fourth seer" of Fátima:

> "I was far way. I was watching the livestock on behalf of a landlord. The owner of the livestock asked my mother's permission to allow me to go to his house until he could procure a maid to watch the livestock. My mother let me go there until the master, the owner of the livestock, got a maid. He

got someone, a maid from Coimbra! The young girl went there for me to show her the farms, the nearby village of Valados, and such. One day, we sat to watch the livestock (they were sheep) and the livestock soothed from the heat.[4] A truck of mules passed in the road headed north. It was a feast day in the North, in Santa Catarina. Since the livestock was calm, I spoke thus to the girl: "O, Conception, let's go up there, to the road (because the livestock had stayed below, in a cave), let's go up there to see if that car continues on above Cova da Iria." We went to the road, and we watched the car continue its climb. Afterwards, I said: "O, Conception, let's go, if not, the livestock will misbehave and the boss will be very angry." We came up here and toward the oak, and the oak [she indicated] was about from this wall here to that other there]. They formed a corner. There were some small walls that my mother (God rest her) had made to enclose the oak. We began to look thus below where a child, maybe 10 to 11 years old, no more than that, was walking. She was walking within the rectilinear enclosure of stones that my mother had made to protect the oak. She went from here to there, and from this side to that, and went in that way, like this. She was a child of eight, nine, or 10 years of age. She wore a white dress. And it seems to me that I heard within myself: "Go there and pray three Hail Marys; go there and pray three Hail Marys." Several times. I said to the girl: "O, Conception, don't you hear a voice inside yourself? It seems to me that I heard within myself a voice saying for me to go there and pray three Hail Marys. Don't you hear anything inside yourself?" "Not me, I hear nothing." "Well, we need to go or else the livestock will stray and we'll be in a scrape with the boss." (He was a nice guy, but had quite a temper. For that reason, if the livestock strayed we'd hear about it!) Afterwards, we went to the foot of the livestock. We got there and the livestock were still soothed. I said: "O, Conception, the livestock are so peaceful; let's go there again to see if we see the same thing. It appears to me that I hear the same thing. Let's go there and see." We went again to the same place we had come from and an image was then already above the oak."

"An image?" we asked. "Then it was not the same image you had seen below?"

"I don't know if it was the same. Naturally, it was the same, because Our Lady told Lúcia that it had not been Her who had come there, that it had been an angel! It was then an image above the oak...."

"In the same place where the Lady usually appeared?" we wanted to know.

"Yes, the same. It appeared then to me: "Come here and pray three Hail Marys; come here and pray three Hail Marys." I turned to ask the girl: "O, Conception, you hear nothing, no voice inside yourself?" "Not I." I said, "Look, there's a mouthful, it seemed to me that they said to me: "Go there and pray three Hail Marys." And now it seems that I hear inside myself: "Come hear and pray three Hail Marys." But I, always with the same fear, being afraid that the livestock would stray, that's all."

"You never went, then, to pray the three Hail Marys?"

"I never did. Only, if it was afterwards. I can no longer remember if I prayed them. I only know that I returned again with the girl to the foot of the livestock."

"That angel, how was its hair?"

"It was blonde."

"What was its height?"

"Since I was a bit removed, it seems to be that it would have come up to your neck."

"Did it seem to be a transparent being like the angels?"

"It seemed to me to be a child from hereabouts with a little white dress and blonde hair."

"It had nothing about its waist?"

"No, but we were a bit far off, here above, at the top of the road."

"You don't remember, therefore, any details about its feet, if it was shod?"

"I don't know. It wandered within that little wall, that's why I never learned if it was barefoot or shod."

"Did it seem to you man or woman? Boy or girl?"

"It seemed to me to be a child…."

"But a boy or a girl?"

"Are you serious!" she laughed. "I had no desire to speculate."

"Was it luminous?" we asked.

"No. It was simply strolling from one side to another."

"And it went in a commonplace manner, like any other child?"

"Such as any other child. It went from one corner to the other within the stones.... Such that from the stones downward one could see the dress. The walls hid it."

We showed her, following, an illustrated color postcard with the statue of the Angel of Valinhos, and asked her if the angel she saw was similar.

"I don't know how to answer," she replied. "The hair seemed longer." She gestured. "Maybe it was to there. It must have been this way."

"And when you saw it over the oak? You saw it better there already...."

"Above the oak I saw that image...."

"The dress was also white?"

"The dress was almost exactly as that of an image we have in a church in Fátima Parish, a red cloak and a crown on the head – that we have for Our Lady of Sorrows in our church in Fátima. It was similar to this."

"You saw that over the oak?"

"Above the oak."

"And what was the dress like?"

"The dress was as I say, like that of the Lady of Sorrows, from top to bottom, long."

"Floor length?"

"That, I don't know, it couldn't be seen well and we didn't get that close, we still stayed away off. We stayed at the bottom of the tarred road."

"Did you see anything on its head?"

"Well, Our Lady of Sorrows had a crown on her head." Then she asked her sister, who was present: "Didn't Our Lady of Sorrows in the church of Fátima have a blue cloak and a crown on her head?" The sister answered in the affirmative, but noted that many works had been done in the Church.

"And did the image you saw have that crown? Don't you remember its form?"

Fig. 16 – A reconstruction of a sighting of the little being reported by the "fourth seer," Carolina Carreira, on July 28, 1917, in Cova da Iria.

"I don't remember," she sighed. "It has already been so many years!"

"And you don't remember what the little crown was like?"

"It had no light. It was a little, round crown."

We pursued the matter of the size of the crown insistently, even plying her with drawings, but Carolina could provide no further details.

"Didn't you see its hair?"

"It had a cloak about its head. It looked like a dark robe. I don't know if it was wearing a dress, I only saw the cloak. But it could well have been like this." She gestured again. "It is best that you not say that I saw Our Lady of Sorrows. Our Lady says that I saw an angel! That night, I came to sleep at my mother's house. I arrived home and said: "O mother of mine, today I saw this… and this… at Cova da Iria. I don't know what it was, it looked like a little child of nine or ten." "You are a blunderer, you are only lying, and you're this or that." "O mother, I am not lying, I saw, I saw and Conception also saw."

"This Conception is still alive?" we interrupted. "What was her family name?"

"Oh, I don't know. She was from far away, up over there, from the North, from Espite. I came home to my mother's house and she stayed at the boss' home. I never saw her again. Neither do I know another name for her other than Conception. Well, that night my mother told my older brother, who died of pneumonia, during the great fevers: "Listen, Carolina, the kid, is saying that she saw a little, ten-year old child at Cova da Iria, on the little fence that surrounds the oak. I don't know if she's lying or not." My brother began to scold me: "You are an idiot, a dummy, you saw what there?" "I saw, I saw...." I always affirmed that I had seen something. Afterwards, my mother said this: "Leave it be, because on the 13th I will tell Lúcia to ask Our Lady if She came here on this day...."

"July 28th," we interrupted. "It is written that you saw this angel on July 28th."

"Maybe. I only remember that it was a holiday to the North. Afterwards, my mother told Lúcia, and she said that Our Lady had said that it was not Her, but that it was an angel."

"The second time, as well, in which it seemed to you that you had seen Our Lady of Sorrows, you never got closer?"

"No. I never drew closer."

"Did you feel something strange that day? Didn't you feel ill-disposed?"

"No. I was only worried about the livestock."

"And you didn't feel any drowsiness?"

"Nothing. It only seemed to me that I heard the voice of the angel. "Come here and pray three Hail Marys; come here and pray three Hail Marys." It was the only strange thing I felt."

"And do you remember at what time that Apparition took place?"

"It must have been nine or 10:00 AM."

ONE IGNORED –"CLOSE ENCOUNTERS OF THE THIRD KIND"

Sixty-one years were needed to uncover this lead, which confirms the existence of a living witness with testimony fundamental to our thesis – the presence in Fátima of anthropomorphic beings, reasonably linked to the UFOs, as their operators or pilots. That witness, ignored, perhaps purposely, becomes a source of additional clues. These clues help to outline with increasing clarity the true environment of the Apparitions as they were experienced, isolating Fátima from the religious sphere, and allowing the investigation of what actually happened there to be driven to its inevitable conclusion.

Because of its revelatory nature, the experience of Carolina and the young woman from Espite would have to remain in the musty, quasi-anonymity of a simple evidentiary statement, far from everything and everyone, neutralized by its "incongruence." Fortunately, we were able to pass from that discrete clue provided in the verbal statement of the "fourth seer," to the entire, universal body of observations regarding these types of beings of small stature. In the process, it brings us an anticipated confirmation – here also the "unusual" could not have been invented – of one of the constants found in "Operation Fátima": the mental manipulation experienced by the principal witness of July 28, 1917.

That form of manipulation, involving "remote control," is a participative element in many of the cases currently catalogued as "Close Encounters of the Third Kind."

a) Biotypology of the being that was seen

The "child" that Carolina and her friend saw strolling near the oak, fulcrum of the Apparitions of the Lady on the series of 13ths, is not so unusual in the annals of Ufology, as it was, at that time, for the priests in charge of registering the important testimony. A "little boy" with blonde, shoulder-length hair, dressed in white and seeming to be around 10 years old. A "little girl" whose fundamental property is that of controlling the behavior of the young Carolina.

"*It represented itself to me [it seemed to her] that I could hear inside of me:* "Go there and pray three Hail Marys…" – an insistent phrase, pretending to guide the steps of the witness to the small oak. What for – "A voice inside of me"– was this absurd sensation, repeatedly felt and underscored by our interviewee?

The perception of an order or command, experienced internally, is not unheard of. It is, in fact, an authentic mental manipulation that is understood to occur during contacts with beings associated with UFOs. It is from there that the significance of the rarity of the described experience is almost lost.

The investigator Jader Pereira summarized, with regard to the behavior of the extraterrestrial beings, six cases of *telepathy* and seven of *mental manipulation* of the human witnesses.[5] These phenomena have verified themselves during the course of time: from Teheran, Iran, on October 13, 1954, through Indian Head, USA, on September 19, 1961, to San Lorenzo, Argentina, on June 30, 1968. That investigator is still considering other cases of "mental pressure," even though with recourse to other means.[6]

But, beyond that, not even the designation "angel" is exclusively used in the religious context of Fátima. Oddly, in another case typical of mental communication, which took place in Garganta la Olla, in the Cáceres Zone of Spain, in 1934, an old woman employed identical expressions to define a being of small stature, dressed in a brilliant garment. The woman was working in field when, upon seeing the being by a cliff near to her, *thought she heard immediately a voice in her mind, telling her to go home, as her granddaughter had been born*. When she approached the being, it began running and disappeared. When she arrived home, the old woman was able to verify that she had heard correctly. They then named the newborn "Angel," *for they thought that someone sent by God had announced the news*.[7]

The actions of the being, as we see it, "drove the remotely controlled witness to movements and attitudes that were contrary to her own will."[8] And what constituted Carolina's "internal voice" if not a translation of that extrasensory manipulation? The "order" of the "blonde child" of Fátima was in contradiction to the will of the witness. What, then, were the true designs of the small being?

b) The "blonde children" of "Magonia"

Before 1917 and after, small beings endowed with supernormal powers frequent the memory of the localities that, at every step, record them in popular mythology, in folklore, where the rational abates itself and becomes a coded message.

From there it becomes, necessarily, strenuous to establish similarities between the beings of small stature that converge in, more or less, technological details, with those of the creatures which make up part of that which Jacques Vallée denominated as "Magonia," a universe as unattainable as the various possible universes responsible for the UFOs of our day. At least, for now, returning to Vallée, we see that he divides his dwarves into two categories: Negroid creatures identical to mediaeval gnomes, and those creatures who correspond to the descriptions of sylphs and elves of the Middle Ages and of the "fairy tales" present in the folklore of every latitude.[9]

But this biotype, blonde and telepathic, reminds us of yet another mythological creature of the Middle Ages – Oberon. It was a similar creature, sung by Alfred de Vigny, who "...was beautiful as the Summer Sun," telepathic, since he read minds, appears and disappears instantly, and never grows old. Also Lutino, being short in stature, is described in legends as having "abundant blonde hair."[10]

Even archeology itself reinforces this evidence in South American ruins, more precisely in Cuzco, Peru – an area preferred by UFOs. In that area on August 20, 1965, dwarves were observed coming out of a discoid object. In his turn, the governor of Santa Barbara, in the same country, solemnly declared that he saw two small beings walking in the snow, in September 1965. They emitted a deafening noise while disappearing.[11]

The biotype "blonde child," be it folkloric gnome, type one occupant or type three humanoid, variant two (consonant with the classifications), prolongs itself through the ages, without age. Fátima is not unusual therein, and we need not even require leaving our continental rectangle. It is enough to hear what the people of the village of Malcata say, in the county of Sabugal. There, instead of "Blonde Children," they are the enchanted "little munchkins," playing on the banks of the Côa River – creatures of short stature who, according to local expressions, were "charming" and whose presence was considered to be a sign of riches in the subsoil.[12]

From this scattered report, perhaps more apparent than real, a permanent link remains between Oberon, the "little munchkin" of Malcata, and the blonde "child" of Fátima. Beings of another nature perhaps, but quite concrete in their diversity. Non-humans, para-humans? We don't know. But more like us than we could suppose. In this way, Carolina's "child" (or the "angel") in the version of the "Lady" described, for this reason, cease to represent a piece of conviction in the universalities of the UFOs and of their presence in the lands of Fátima.

c) Classification of the "celestial beings" observed in Fátima

The morphology of the aliens, in particular their respective height relative to human beings, has been the focus of percent-based studies. It will be interesting to examine some data referred to by Spanish investigator Vicente-Juan Ballester Olmos, which Henry Durrant reproduced in his previously mentioned work.[13] In over 15 cases, with a view to the height of the humanoids observed on the Iberian Peninsula, Ballester Olmos estimated that in ten, or in other words, two-thirds of the cases, witnesses have observed that the beings were shorter than normal in stature, about 1.5 meters in height.

McCampbell, author of one of the most complete scientific compendiums about UFOs, analyzed the biometric data from 217 cases of alien contact found in the "Magonia" catalogue of Jacques Vallée, verifying that, in 119 cases, the beings observed are defined, quantitatively and qualitatively, as "dwarves."[14] Many of the alien beings of short stature, however, are calculated between 70 cm and 1.3 meters, at the limit of normal for humans.

We also note here the analysis of the wave of landings in South America in 1960 done by Gordon Creighton, the British expert. He found that in 51 cases, 10 referred to "small men" and 12 to beings of nearly 90 cm.[15] Ballester Olmos, comparing the textbook cases by Jader Pereira and those from Jacques Vallée's catalogue, established the following portrait.[16]

Table 2: Height of Aliens Relative to Humans

Investigator	Sample	Interval	Percent
Jader Pereira	230 cases	shorter than 1.60 m	63%
James McCampbell	217 cases	shorter than 1.60 m	55%

The special characteristics of a certain number of beings defined as being present in the phenomenology of "apparitions" are also found when we contemplate the nature of various groups of beings detected in modern UFO observations. This dichotomy is revealed when we systematically compare the attributes of Lúcia's so-called "angel" with that of the "angel" seen by the "fourth seer."

LÚCIA'S ANGEL[17]	**THE FOURTH SEER'S ANGEL**
– young, 14 years old	– young, 10 years old
– 1.30/1.40 meters in height[18]	– 1.10/1.20 meters in height
– gown, full-length and luminous	– gown, full-length and white
– white complexion	– white complexion
– shoulder-length hair	– blonde, shoulder-length hair
– transparent, "perfectly defined" contours[19]	– well-defined body
– in one case, evanescent	
– aerial movement	– terrestrial movement

Returning to Jader Pereira's classification and to the three types and respective variants which we selected, we see that the integration of these "celestial beings" from Cova da Iria is admissible in any of these, even though, to our understanding, the "angel" of the "fourth seer" could best be seen in type 3, variant 2, the same occurring in type 1, variant 3, which may best adjust itself to Lúcia's "angel." The reader can verify the validity of our assertions if they give themselves over to the work of consulting the bibliography where the presence of *beings luminous, headless, evanescent, paralyzing, angelic, translucent*, and so on, are established in the context of the UFO phenomenon.

13. EXPERIMENTAL OBSERVATIONS OF THE EFFECTS OF MICROWAVES

One working hypothesis, subject to experimental verification, attributes some of the physical phenomena occurring at the time of the Apparitions to the eventual effect of microwave radiation (that falling in the electromagnetic spectrum between 30 and 300,000 MHz). We refer, namely, to the following:

a) the declaration of the "fourth seer," Carolina Carreira, when she alluded, in the course of contact with an "angelic being" of small height, to the non-auditory reception, inside her mind, of a repetitive order: "Come and pray three Hail Marys. Come and pray three Hail Marys";

b) the various indications by witnesses near to the site of the "contact" by the three young shepherds with a communicating "being," who heard a "humming of bees," which is, as we have seen, one of the characteristics of modern Ufological phenomenology that appears with some frequency;

c) the properties of microwave radiation, discussed by McCampbell,[1] among others, and [which] would justify the triple effect registered by the testifying masses of Fátima during the solar phenomenon of October 13, 1917: intense heat, rapid drying of clothes, physiological effects.

The most suggestive fact to retain is furnished to us by the witnesses when they refer that the "buzzing of bees" cited was always produced when the "luminous lady" spoke with the three seers, *"but without moving her lips."*

Since McCampbell, other labs have reproduced the experiences that confer a coherent principle to the totality of witnesses in regard to this question of "communication/reception of messages," and, particularly, as regards the hearing of sounds identified as the "buzzing of bees."

We refer, for example, to the experiences of investigators from the Canadian Institute of Electrical and Electronic Engineering, specifically, to the works of James C. Lin, Sergio Sales-Cunha, Joseph Battocletti and Anthony Sances, published under the title, "The Auditory Microwave Phenomenon."[2] These investigations could prove to be promising for the gradual comprehension of this problem and, in a general way, for the elaboration of explicative models of certain secondary effects, of a physical and physiological nature, registered in human beings and lesser animals, in the presence of unidentified aerospace phenomena.

Scientific exploration of the auditory "phenomenon" of microwaves may help to explain, in a rational and coherent way, what type of reception/communication is involved in cases of "contact with messages," whether they occur in a secular context (i.e., UFOs) or a religious one (i.e., "Marian apparitions"). This may be especially true in situations like Fátima, where the contact includes altered states of consciousness.

The Canadian case cited above gives an account of the effects of small discharges of microwave radiation reverberating in the crania of human subjects. The heads of the individuals subjected to these emissions were placed outside the reach of a conical antenna. The experiments took place in an appropriate compartment. The perceptions that resulted consisted of a combination of audible sounds.

The studies showed that the individuals perceived buzzing types of noises or pops within the head, when subjected to microwave radiation between 200 and 300 MHz.

Generally, these sounds were perceived as something produced in the interior of the head or in the posterior part of the cranium. Remember, once again, that the "fourth seer" of Fátima would hear the commanding words of the "little angel" inside her head.

A new contribution, virtually contemporaneous with the cited experiments, was communicated to us by Petit, director of research at the French CNRS, and Assistant Director of the Calculus Center of the University of Provence, which came to reinforce the plausibility of this working hypothesis. Certainly, according to Petit, in the course of the experiments carried out in 1979, in the ambient area of the Department of Microwave Studies and Investigations annexed to the National Center for Space Studies of Toulouse, its director, Professor Thourel, personally confirmed accidental reception by non-auditory means of modulated, low frequency microwaves when exposed to the active rays of a transmitter.[3]

Returning to the Fátima case, we verify that the "buzzing" or "humming" was not exclusive to the three small seers. In fact, others who were in the vicinity of the "contact" site gave various accounts of those impressions. They

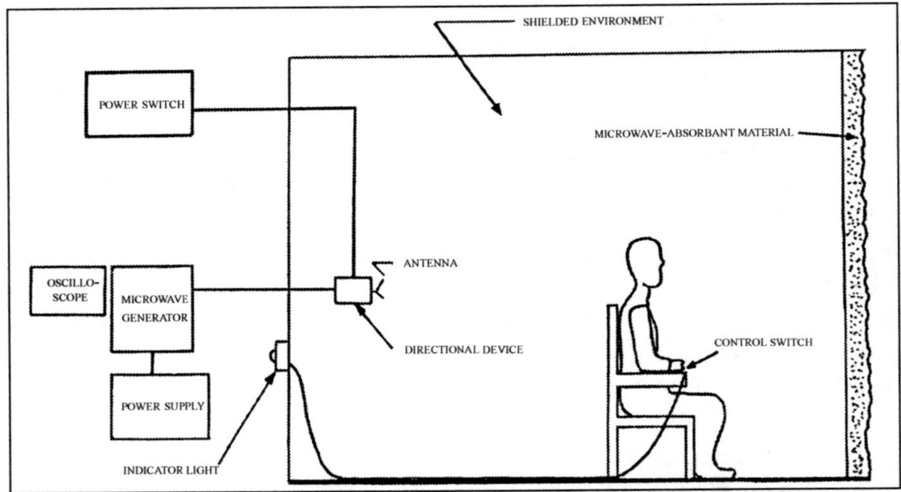

Fig. 17 – Experimental laboratory for research into the effects of the Auditory Microwave Phenomenon on human beings.

underscored that they were "clearly hearing" that noise when the "Lady" was speaking with Lúcia "without moving her lips."

This detail comfortably sustains the notion, maintained by the accounts, that the "buzzing" or "humming" phenomenon would be audible within a determined area around the three children and would come from a *source external* to the onlookers. In our working hypothesis, the means of communication between the "luminous lady" and the principal "message" receptor was the previously described beam of focused light.

Table 3: Phenomena Testified to by Eyewitnesses (except at "The Miracle of the Sun")

Phenomemon	June	July	August	August 19th	September	October
Lightning			❍			
Buzzing	❍	❍				
Thunder	❍	❍	❍	❍		
Clouds in sky			❍		❍	❍
Clouds of smoke	❍	❍	❍		❍	❍
Colors in air		❍	❍	❍	❍	❍
Decreased light	❍	❍	❍	❍	❍	❍
Cooling	❍	❍	❍	❍	❍	
Breezes	❍	❍	❍		❍	
Flying objects			❍		❍	❍
"Foo-fighters"					❍	❍
"Angel hair"					❍	
Ramps of light					❍	❍
Odors				❍		❍
Bending foliage	❍					

Naturally, new cross-trials will be necessary and desirable, given their potential to provide controllable and statistically representative data, with a view to the study of psycho-physiological reactions and human (as well as animal) behaviors at those levels of radiation in the electromagnetic spectrum. We cannot even speak to the immense field of analysis which is openly anticipated, having as its target the structure of the discourse of the religiousand para-religious "messages" and their semantic content within the phenomenology of the "unidentified" processes involved.[4]

Lastly, let us address the hypothesis set forth by Claude Rifat, when he confronted the apparent distortions and anachronisms of content, i.e., the obvious unreality and irrationality of the UFO-type experiences and the "Marian Apparitions." In the magazine *UFO Phenomena*, Rifat emphasized the function carried out in these situations by the *Locus Coeruleus*, an important region in the mammalian brain. And it is there, according to Rifat, that the phenomenon of dreams is induced. Maybe, then, the source of Radiation "X" (flying saucer, "luminous being," what have you) might interfere in the normal functioning of the brain via the emission of microwave radiation. The distortion or alteration of the "message" (beyond the eventually suggested "images," i.e., those of "Hell"[5]) could be one resulting from the interference of that radiation at the level of *Locus Coeruleus*, while our unconscious would act as a rectifying "filter," actualizing and adapting the information according to the surrounding cultural context and time.[6]

Notes

1. LIGHTNING

[1] *O Mensageiro*, November 8, 1917.

[2] First written report from Lúcia. REIS, Sebastião Martins dos, *Uma Vida ao Serviço de Fátima*, Evora, 1973, p. 315.

[3] *Memórias e Cartas da Irmã Lúcia*, op. cit., p. 335.

[4] Ibid.

[5] *Parish Inquiry.*

[6] Letter published, anonymously, in the newspaper *A Guarda* [*The Guardian*], August 30, 1919, extracted from the original that we found in the *Arquivos Formigão* [*Formigão Archives*], cit. por d'ARMADA, Fina, op. cit., p. 321.

[7] *O Mensageiro*, August 22, 1917.

[8] MARCHI, João de, op. cit., p. 138.

[9] CASALDALICA, Pedro e ALVES, João, *Senhora do Século XX* [*Lady of the 20th Century*], Lisbon, "Reinado do Coracao de Maria [The Reign of the Heart of Mary]," 1965, p. 179.

[10] VALLÉE, Jacques, *Le Collège Invisible* [*The Invisible College*], Paris, Albin Michel, 1975, p. 37. This witness is also known as "Dr. X."

[11] CERPA, António Moya, *Stendek*, a publication of CEI, Barcelona, no. 30, December 1977, pp. 18-21.

[12] *Memórias e Cartas da Irmã Lúcia*, op. cit., pp. 330-331.

[13] McCAMPBELL, James, *Ufology*, Belmonte, USA, Jaymac Company, 1973, p. 29 *et seq.*

2. "THE BUZZING OF BEES"

[1] *A Voz de Fátima*, no. 3, December 13, 1922.

[2] *Stella*, no. 77, special edition about Fátima, May 1943.

[3] 8th ed., Fátima, 1966, pp. 97-98.

[4] *Parish Inquiry.*

[5] *Era uma Senhora Mais Brilhante que o Sol*, op. cit., p. 114.

[6] *Eu Vi Nascer Fátima*, Porto, ed. Salesianas, 1966, p. 31.

[7] In the original, we found the word "guitar." In light of the context, we think that could be an error, since it should mention the sound of an insect. This is part of the *Arquivos Formigão.*

[8] *Arquivos Formigão.*

[9] When he went to Fátima, Canon Formigão was received by relatives of this witness, who live in Montelo. MONTELO, Viscount of, *As Grandes Maravilhas de Fátima*, Lisbon, 1927, pp. 80-85.

[10] The newspaper *Diário de Lisboa* [*The Lisbon Daily*], February 26, 1968.

[11] BOUGARD, Michel, *Des soucoupes volantes aux Ovni* [*From flying saucers to UFOs*], SOBEPS, 1976, pp. 166-167.

[12] VALLÉE, Jacques, *Chroniques des apparitions extraterrestres* [*Chronicles of extraterrestrial apparitions*], Paris, Denoel, 1972, p. 311. Published in America as VALLÉE, Jacques, *Passport to Magonia: On UFOs, Folklore, and Parallel Worlds*, Chicago, Henry Regnery, 1969. Republished in America as VALLÉE, Jacques, *Passport to Magonia: On UFOs, Folklore, and Parallel Worlds*, Chicago, Contemporary Books, Inc., 1993.

[13] *Memórias e Cartas da Irmã Lúcia*, Porto, 1973, p. 225.

[14] McCAMPBELL, James, *Ufology*, Belmont, USA, Jaymac Company, 1973, p. 44.

[15] REHN, K. Gösta, *Dossier Ovnis* [*UFO Dossier*], Portugal, Litexa, 1979, p. 110.

[16] PETIT, Jean-Pierre, "Une propulsion magnetohydrodynamique pour les Ovni [A magneto-hydrodynamic form of propulsion for the UFOs]," *Inforespace*, no. 30, November 1976, p. 26 *et seq.*

3. THUNDER

[1] *A Voz de Fátima*, May 13, 1923.

[2] *Arquivos Formigão.* Statement of November 13, 1917. All documents which make up part of these files, quoted here only in excerpts, are taken from d'ARMADA, Fina, *supra.*

[3] November 18, 1917 ed.

[4] *Cartas de Fátima* [*Letters to Fátima*], back cover, Editora Pax. Statement of December 8, 1966.
[5] The newspaper *O Seculo* [*The Century*], October 13, 1917.
[6] *Era uma Senhora Mais Brilhante que o Sol*, Fátima, 1966, p. 100.
[7] *A Voz de Fátima*, December 13, 1922.
[8] *Era uma Senhora Mais Brilhante que o Sol*, op. cit., p. 117.
[9] *Eu Vi Nascer Fátima*, Porto, ed. Salesianas, 1967, p. 31.
[10] *Era uma Senhora Mais Brilhante que o Sol*, op. cit., p. 156.
[11] Ibid., p. 138.
[12] Brasil, Melhoramentos de S. Paulo, 1977, p. 10.
[13] VALLÉE, Jacques, *Chroniques des apparitions extraterrestres*, op. cit., p. 271.
[14] FERNANDES, Joaquim, *Ovnis em Portugal* [*UFOs in Portugal*], Porto, Nova Critica, 1978, p. 19.
[15] The magazine *Insólito* [*Unusual*], Porto, no. 26, July 1977, p. 21.
[16] VALLÉE, Jacques, *Le Collège Invisible*, op. cit., pp. 37-40.
[17] McCAMPBELL, James, *Ufology*, Belmont, USA, Jaymac Company, 1973, p. 42.
[18] VALLÉE, Jacques, *Chroniques des apparitions extraterrestres*, op. cit., p. 382.

4. BIZARRE CLOUDS

[1] *Era uma Senhora Mais Brilhante que o Sol*, op. cit., p. 100.
[2] *Stella*, no. 77, May 1943, p. 11.
[3] MARCHI, João de, op. cit., p. 113.
[4] *A Voz de Fátima*, no. 8, May 13, 1923.
[5] *Encontro de Testemunhas* [*Encounter of the Witnesses*], Fátima, Sede Internacional do Exército Azul [International See of the Blue Army], 1961, p. 79.
[6] MARCHI, João de, op. cit., p. 138.
[7] Letter written to the Viscount of Montelo. *Arquivos Formigão.*
[8] Although we had to verify the original, this can be found in BROCHADO, Costa, *As Aparições de Fátima*, Lisbon, 1952, p. 118 *et seq.*
[9] *A Voz de Fátima*, March 13, 1924.
[10] The newspaper *Novidade* [*Latest News*], August 1937, cit. *Stella*, October of that year. Interview with the Viscount of Montelo.
[11] Transcript published in *A Voz de Fátima*, Lisbon, May 16, 1957.
[12] *Stella*, February 1959, pp. 15-16.
[13] *A Voz de Fátima*, December 13, 1922.
[14] *Arquivos Formigão*. Statement of November 13, 1917.
[15] *Gazeta de Lisboa Ocidental* [*The Gazette of Western Lisbon*], November 16, 1730.
[16] DURRANT, Henry, *O Livro Negro dos Discos Voadores* [*The Black Book of Flying Saucers*], Lisbon, Ulisseia, p. 50.
[17] DURRANT, Henry, *Os Estranhos Casos dos Ovni* [*The Strange UFO Cases*], Amadora, Bertrand, 1977, p. 37.
[18] VALLÉE, Jacques, *Chroniques des apparitions extraterrestres*, op. cit., p. 364.
[19] DURRANT, Henry, op. cit., p. 143.
[20] *Parish Inquiry.*

[21] McCAMPBELL, James, op. cit., p. 33.

[22] EDWARDS, Frank, *Flying Saucers: Serious Business*, photograph section, Bantam, 1966.

[23] DURRANT, Henry, *Le dossier des Ovni* [*The UFO Dossier*], Paris, Robert Laffont, 1973, p. 93.

[24] McCAMPBELL, James, op. cit., p. 38.

5. EFFECTS ON THE ENVIRONMENT

[1] *Fátima - Como Eu a Vi e como a Sinto*, 1967, p. 25.

[2] *Stella*, no. 65, special edition about Fátima, May 1942.

[3] *Arquivos Formigão.*

[4] *O Mensageiro*, August 22, 1917.

[5] MONTELO, Viscount of, *As Grandes Maravilhas de Fátima*, Lisbon, 1927, pp. 80-83.

[6] *Arquivos Formigão.*

[7] MARCHI, João de, op. cit., p. 139.

[8] Idem., p. 155.

[9] MONTELO, Viscount of, op. cit., pp. 59-60.

[10] Idem., p. 61.

[11] M.C.S.P., de Alcobaça, *O Mensageiro*, December 27, 1917.

[12] SANTOS, Gilberto dos, *Os Grandes Fenómenos da Cova da Iria...*, 1956, p. 174

[13] Inquiry carried out by the authors in 1979. The witness is a relative of Mr. José Lúcio, former official of the *Jornal de Notícias*, Porto, and to whom we are grateful for the contact.

[14] OLMOS, Vicente-Juan Ballester, *Ovnis: el fenomeno aterrizaje* [*UFOs: The landing phenomenon*], Barcelona, Plaza & Janes, 1977, p. 291.

[15] BENITEZ, J. Juan, *Documentos Oficiales del Gobierno Español* [*Official Documents of the Government of Spain*], Barcelona, Plaza & Janes, 1977, p. 249.

[16] We have relied mostly on the statement of the Viscount of Montelo, note 10.

[17] GUINDILIS, L.M., MENKOV, D.A. and PETROVSKAIA, I.G., *Phénomènes atmosphériques anormaux* [Abnormal atmospheric phenomena], translated into French by GEPAN, Toulouse. Condensed and annotated by SIDER, Jean, *Lumières dans la nuit* [*Lights in the night*], nos. 198-199, October and November 1980.

[18] According to an opportune epistolary correspondence which permitted us an exchange of suggestions and ideas about the fundamental scientific problems inherent in the phenomenology of Fátima.

6. ODORS

[1] FONSECA, Luis Gonzaga, S.J., *Nossa Senhora de Fátima* [*Our Lady of Fátima*], 3rd ed., Porto, Livraria do Apostolado da Imprensa, 1957, p. 53.

[2] There is a mistake in this testimony. It was not Lúcia, but Jacinta, who brought the little oak branch from where the Being came down.

[3] PASQUALE, Humberto, op. cit., p. 46.

[4] *Stella*, no. 70, October 1942, interview oriented around Maria de Freitas.
[5] VALLÉE, Jacques, *Un siècle d'atterrissages* [*A century of landings*], cit. por DURRANT, Henry in *Os Estranhos Casos dos Ovni*, op. cit., p. 82.
[6] *Boletim especial da SBEDV* [*Special bulletin from SBEDV*], Rio de Janeiro, Brazil, 1975, p. 18.
[7] McCAMPBELL, James, *Ufology*, Belmont, USA, Jaymac Company, 1973, p. 34.

7. LUMINOUS OBJECTS

[1] *Stella*, no. 77, May 1943, p. 21.
[2] *Arquivos Formigão*. Testimony given on November 13, 1917.
[3] *Arquivos Formigão* and the newspaper *A Guarda* of September 13, 1919.
[4] *Fátima – Como Eu a Vi e como a Sinto*, 1967, pp. 15-16.
[5] Gonzaga da Fonseca introduces the term "airplane," which seems to us to be an error in the translation. This statement was published for the first time in German in *Bote von Fátima*, 1933, p. 14, and then translated into Portuguese by that author in *Nossa Senhora de Fátima.*
[6] MARCHI, Joáo de, *Era uma Senhora Mais Brilhante que o Sol*, 8th ed., Fátima, Missões Consolata, 1966, pp. 167-168.
[7] BARTHAS, Canon C., *Fátima*, Lisbon, Aster, 1967, p. 132.
[8] OLIVEIRA, Canon Galamba de, *Fátima, Altar do Mundo* [*Fátima, Altar of the World*], 2nd vol., Porto, Editora Ocidental, 1954, pp. 90-91.
[9] Canonical Process of Fátima.
[10] *Arquivos Formigão.*
[11] REIS, Sebastião Martins, *Na Órbita de Fátima* [*The Orbit of Fátima*], Évora, D. Manuel Mendes da Conceição Santos Center for Studies, 1958, p. 80.
[12] The newspaper *Notícias* [*News*], Lourenço Marques, December 17, 1954, cited by BUENO, B. Sánchez, *Os Ovnis e a Vida no Universo* [*The UFOs and Life in the Universe*], Lisbon, António Ramos, 1978, p. 67.
[13] *O Grande Livro do Maravilhoso e do Fantástico,* Lisbon, *Selections from Reader's Digest*, 1977, p. 571.
[14] *Insólito*, Porto, no. 37, January-March 1979, p. 14.
[15] CLEREBAUT, Lucien, *Historique des Ovni* [*A History of the UFOs*], Brussels, SOBEPS, 1975, p.26.
[16] KEYHOE, Donald E., *Les ètrangers de l'espace* [*Strangers from Space*], Paris, France-Empire, 1975, p. 280.
[17] FERNANDES, Joaquim, *Ovnis em Portugal* [*UFOs in Portugal*], Porto, Nova Crítica, 1978, p. 105.
[18] BOUGARD, Michel, *La Chronique des Ovnis* [*The Chronicle of the UFOs*], Paris, J.P. Delarge, 1977, p. 198.
[19] STEIGER, Brad, *Proyecto Libro Azul* [*Project Blue Book*], Madrid, EDAF, p. 147.
[20] The magazine *Phénomènes Spatiaux* [*Spatial Phenomena*], no. 14, December 1967, pp. 26-27.
[21] HOBANNA, Ion and WEVERBERGH, Julien, *Les Ovni en URSS et dans le pays de l'Est* [*UFOs in the USSR and in the Eastern Bloc Countries*], Paris, Robert Laffont,

1976, p. 204.

[22] FERNANDES, Joaquim, op. cit., p. 23.

[23] MARCHI, João de, op. cit., resp. pp. 100 and 84.

[24] HEERING, Jan, *UFO Physics* – part 2(a), FSR, vol. 24, no. 5, p. 21.

8. RAMPS OF LIGHT

[1] *Memórias e Cartas da Irmã Lúcia*, Porto, 1973, resp. pp. 335 and 331.

[2] *Ibid.*

[3] SANTOS, Gilberto F., *Os Grandes Fenómenos da Cova da Iria e a História da Primeira Imagem de N. Sra de Fátima*, 1956, pp. 29 and 32.

[4] *Memórias e Cartas da Irmã Lúcia*, op. cit. , p. 333.

[5] CLEREBAUT, Lucien, *Historique des Ovni*, 1975, pp. 99-100.

[6] *O Incidente de la Dulce* [*The Incident at La Dulce*], personal communication of Alejandro E. Chionetti, investigator for SIU-UFO PRESS, San Isidro, Buenos Aires.

[7] "Les aspects physiques des manifestations des Ovnis" ["The physical aspects of UFO Manifestations"], the magazine *Inforespace*, nos. 39 and 41, May and September 1978, resp. pp. 24 and 35.

[8] *Si: están – aproximación científica a los Ovnis – los Ovnis en España* [*Yes: they're here – scientific approximations about the UFOs – UFOs in Spain*], Stendek Selection, Barcelona, ed. 7 ½, 1978, p. 7.

[9] PETIT, Jean-Pierre, "Une propulsion magnetohydrodynamique pour les Ovni [A magneto-hydrodynamic form of propulsion for the UFOs]," *Inforespace*, no. 30, November 1976, pp. 26 and 27.

[10] "Commentaire concernant les aspects physiques du phénomène Ovni et les faisceaux lumineux tronqués" [Commentary concerning aspects of the physics of UFO phenomena and the lights with a conical-tubular shape], *Inforespace*, no. 40, July 1978, pp. 2 *et seq.*

[11] PANNETIER, V., *Controle des rayonnements ionisants* [*Control of ionizing rays*], Paris, 1966; WILLIAMSON and others, *Table of range and stopping*, Commission de Energie Atomique, Saclay, 1966, cited by MEESSEN, Auguste, *Inforespace*, no. 40.

[12] "Réponse de Jan Heering au prof. Meessen" ["Jan Heering's response to Professor Meessen"], *Inforespace*, no. 42, November 1978, pp. 18-19.

[13] GOUPIL, Jean, "Les manifestations physiques des Ovni – tentative d'explication" ["Physical manifestations of UFOs – a tentative explanation"], in *La Nouvelle Vague des Soucoupes Volantes* [*The New Fad of Flying Saucers*], Paris, France-Empire, 1974, p. 201.

9. BREEZES

[1] *A Voz de Fátima*, December 13, 1922.

[2] MARCHI, João de, *Era Uma Senhora Mais Brilhante que o Sol*, p. 113.

[3] *Raio de Luz*, September 1, 1917.

[4] VALLÉE, Jacques, *Chroniques des Apparitions extraterrestres* [*Chronicles of extraterrestrial Apparitions*], Paris, Denoel, 1972, case no. 72, p. 268.

[5] *Si: están*, op. cit., p. 99 *et seq.*
[6] BOUGARD, Michel, *Des Soucoupes Volantes aux Ovni* [*From Flying Saucers to UFOs*], SOBEPS, 1976, p. 208.

10. ANGEL HAIR ["THE RAIN OF FLOWERS"]

[1] OLIVEIRA, Canon Galamba de, *Fátima, Altar do Mundo*, 1954, p. 91.
[2] SANTOS, Gilberto F. dos, *Os Grandes Fenómenos da Cova da Iria e a História da Primeira Imagem de n. Sra. De Fátima*, p. 174.
[3] *Encontro de Testemunhas*, op. cit., p. 93.
[4] BARTHAS, Canon C., *Fátima*, Lisbon, Aster, 1967, p. 134.
[5] CRUZ, Marques da, *A Virgem de Fátima* [*The Virgin of Fátima*], Brasil, Melhoramentos de São Paulo, 1937, p. 29.
[6] BARTHAS, C., op. cit., pp. 133-134.
[7] This must be a typographical error. In the original, it should have been "flakes."
[8] *Arquivos Formigão*, cited by d'ARMADA, Fina, *Fátima – What happened in 1917*, Amadora, Bertrand, 1980, p. 371.
[9] *Memórias de Um Médico*, 1967, pp. 121-124.
[10] FARIA, P.O., *Perguntas sobre Fátima e "Fátima Desmascarada,"* Porto, 1975, p. 249.
[11] SANTOS, Gilberto F. dos, op. cit., p. 81.
[12] *Stella*, October 1961.
[13] GENS, José Pereira, op. cit., p. 124.
[14] REIS, Sebastião Martins dos, *Na Órbita de Fátima*, 1958, p. 98.
[15] The newspaper *Diário Ilustrado* [*Illustrated Diary*], July 18, 1960.
[16] PERRIN, R. Jack, *Le mystère des Ovni* [*The mystery of the UFO*], Pygmalion, 1976, p. 329.
[17] Op. cit., Lisbon, António Ramos, 1977, pp. 26-28.
[18] BERENGUEL, Raul, *Ovni: Portas para o Ano Zero* [*UFO: Portals to the Year Zero*], Porto, Nova Crítica, 1978, p. 164.
[19] FORT, Charles, *Le Livre des Damnés* [*The Book of the Damned*], Paris, Eric Losfeld, 1967, pp. 62-64.
[20] SACHS, Margareth and JAHN, Ernest, *Celestial Passengers, UFOs, and Space Travel*, New York, Penguin Books, 1977, pp. 136-138.
[21] WILSON, Clifford, *UFOs and their mission impossible*, New York, Signet Books, 1974, p. 196.
[22] McCAMPBELL, James, *Ufology*, Belmont, USA, Jaymac Company, 1973, p. 77.
[23] See note 17.
[24] SENELIER, Jean, "*Le neige d'Octobre*" ["*The Snow of October*"], the magazine *Phénomènes Spatiaux* [*Space Phenomena*], no. 16, June 1968, p. 8.
[25] Vol. XIII, no. 105, p. 24.
[26] DURRANT, Henry, *Les dossiers des Ovni*, Paris, Robert Laffont, 1973, pp. 148-156.
[27] Cited by DURRANT, Henry, op. cit., Portuguese ed., p. 178.
[28] LOEB, L.B., *A tentative explanation of the electrical field effect on the freezing of super cooled water drops*, J. Geophys Res., vol. 68, no. 15, 1963, pp. 4475-4476.
[29] BOUGARD, Michel, From Flying Saucers to UFOs, SOBEPS, 1976, cited in

Maurice de San, *Inforespace*, no. 11.

[30] BOZZONTTI, Yvan, "La propulsion des soucoupes volantes – engime résolue?" [The propulsion of flying saucers – enigma resolved?"], *OURANOS*, 4th trimester of 1975, p. 111.

[31] GARDES, François, *Chasseurs d'Ovni* [*The UFO Hunters*], Paris, Albin Michel, 1977, p. 214.

[32] SILVA, General Conceição e, *Comentário ao Relatório sobre o "Organismo Desconhecido"* [*Comments to the "Unknown Organism" Report*], forwarded to CEAFI (renamed CNIFO), Porto, Portugal, on December 12, 1978.

[33] AMARAL, A.J. Guedes do, *Um estranho ser caído do espaço – Relatório dos extraordinários factos observados no dia 2 de Novembro de 1959, na cidade de Évora* [*A strange being fallen from space – Report of the extraordinary facts observed on November 2, 1959, in the city of Évora*], dated January 10, 1960, p. 11.

[34] AMARAL, A.J. Guedes do, op. cit., p. 14.

[35] SOTTOMAYOR, José, SOUSA, José Manuel, and RIBEIRO, Fernando, *Inquérito em Évora* [*Inquiry in Évora*], CEAFI Record (Lisbon Center), June 1-13, 1979.

[36] *Boletim mensal da Sociedade de Astronomia Popular de Toulouse* [*Monthly Bulletin of the Society of Popular Astronomy of Toulouse*], no. 497, June 1967, cited by Henry Durrant.

[37] "A recent analysis of angel hair," *Inforespace*, no. 36, Nov. 1977, p. 14.

[38] FERNANDES, Joaquim, "A fibralvina dos Ovnis" [The angel hair of the UFOs], *Insólito* magazine, no. 38, May 1979, p. 4.

[39] By "tinsel" is meant the shiny, silver threads that are used to adorn Christmas trees.

[40] Author's inquiry, June 1979.

11. EFFECTS ON ANIMALS

[1] "A New FSR Catalogue, the Effects of UFOs upon Animals, Birds, and Smaller Creatures," *Flying Saucer Review*, vol. 16, January-February 1970 *et seq.*

[2] OLMOS, Vicente-Juan Ballester, *Ovnis: el fenomeno aterrizaje*, Barcelona, Plaza & James, 1978, p. 329.

[3] McCAMPBELL, James, *Ufology*, Belmont, USA, Jaymac Company, 1973, p. 76.

[4] Ibid., p. 75.

12. THE TESTIMONY OF THE "FOURTH SEER" – THE SMALL, "TELEPATHIC" HUMANOID

[1] General Management of LUCF, 1941, p. 5.

[2] REIS, Sebastião Martins dos, *A vidente de Fátima dialoga e responde pelas Aparições*, Braga, Franciscana, 1970, p. 61.

[3] Folha 18 v. in the original, cited by d'ARMADA, Fina, *Fátima – O Que se Passou em 1917*, Amadora, Bertrand, 1980, p. 358.

[4] We think that the witness meant to use the Portuguese verb "emolir," which means "to soften" or "to soothe."

[5] PEREIRA, Jader U., *Les extraterrestres* [*The extraterrestrials*], 2nd special number of the magazine *Phénomènes Spatiaux*, Paris, GEPA, 1974, p. 37.

[6] PEREIRA, Jader U., op. cit., pp. 45 and 51.

[7] OLMOS, Vicente-Juan Ballester, *Ovnis: el fenomeno aterrizaje*, Barcelona, Plaza & James, 1978, p. 291.

[8] PEREIRA, Jader U., op. cit., p. 37.

[9] VALLÉE, Jacques, *Chroniques des apparitions extraterrestres*, Paris, J'ai lu, 1969.

[10] BASTIDE, Jean, *La mémoire des Ovni* [*The memory of UFOs*], Mercure de France, 1978, p. 205.

[11] KEEL, John, *Strangest Creatures from Time and Space*, Sphere Books, Ltd., 1976, pp. 154-169.

[12] FERNANDES, Joaquim, *Microstrutura do Fenómeno Ovni – um caso Português* [*Microstructure of the UFO Phenomenon – a Portuguese case*], communiqué to the First Iberian Congress of Ufology, Porto, October 7-8, 1978.

[13] OLMOS, Vicente-Juan Ballester, "Dados biométricos extraídos de dezanove casos de passageiros de Ovnis" ["Biometric data extracted from 19 cases of UFO passengers], in DURRANT, Henry, *Primeiras Investigações sobre os Humanóides Extraterrestres* [*First Investigations regarding the Extraterrestrial Humanoids*], Lisbon, António Ramos, 1978, p. 181 *et seq.*

[14] McCAMPBELL, James, *Ufology*, Belmont, USA, Jaymac Company, 1973, p. 102 *et seq.*

[15] BOWEN, Charles, *En quête des humanoïdes* [*The quest for humanoids*], Paris, J'ai lu, 1974, p. 101 *et seq.*

[16] OLMOS, Vicente-Juan Ballester, *Ovnis: el fenomeno aterrizaje*, op. cit., p. 254.

[17] In her *Memórias*, written 20 years after the fact, the seer Lúcia included the observation of "angels" in 1916. These accounts do not appear in this book; they must be part of another work. Here, we merely leave a summary of "physical" characteristics of that "angel."

[18] Naturally, in 1916, the heights of the youngsters which served for comparison to the "angel" did not approximate those of contemporary youngsters of the same age. In recent decades, better nutrition in early infancy and other marginal factors have resulted in the hyper-development of heights in adolescents, a fact well known by all.

[19] The interrogation of D. José Pedro da Silva, cited by REIS, Sebastião Martins dos, op. cit., p. 56.

13. EXPERIMENTAL OBSERVATIONS OF THE EFFECTS OF MICROWAVES

[1] McCAMPBELL, James, *Ufology*, Belmont, Jaymac Company, 1973.

[2] Proceedings of the IEEE, vol. 68, no. 1, January 1980.

[3] PETIT, Jean Pierre, personal communications, 1983.

[4] RIFAT, Claude, "The induced dream hypothesis," *UFO Phenomena*, Bologna, vol. 2, 1977.

[5] The images of "Hell" were presented in July 1917 to the seers of Fátima. They comprise part of the "secret," which was already divulged by Lúcia in her *Memórias*, but not developed in this work.

[6] Ibid. "A theoretical framework for the problem of non-contact between an advanced extraterrestrial civilization and mankind; symbolic sequential communication versus symbolic non-sequential communication, *UFO Phenomenon*, Bologna, vol. 3, 1978-79.

PART THREE

THE DAY THE SUN DANCED IN THE SKY

Phenomena Associated with "The Miracle of the Sun"

"Suddenly, a luminous disk the size of a great host... appeared, as if it stood out from the Sun (or placed itself before it.)."
– Eyewitness

October 13, 1917 dawned ashen. The clouds threatened a tempest. At a given height, it began to rain, drenching the walkers. "The rain was such," we were told in July 1978 by eyewitness Júlia Franco, "that I remember us taking off my sister's jacket and wringing it out. It released as much water as wet laundry does."

At the site, all muddied in red mud, the people waited impatiently. They waited for they knew not what – they waited for anything. "There wasn't anywhere to sit," Franco recalled. "And it was cold in that arid place, without shelter, without a house nearby."

All at once, "I saw a dark cloud coming from the East," a farmer would later remember. And it was in this manner that the "anything" for which they were waiting arrived.

1. METEOROLOGICAL CONDITIONS ON THE DAY OF OCTOBER 13, 1917

Before seeing how that meeting took place, let us pause to consider the meteorological conditions of that day. We obtained this important data by consulting the *Observações Meteorológicas, Magnéticas e Sísmicas* [*Meteorological, Magnetic, and Seismic Observations*], a work edited in 1918 by the Meteorological Observatory of Coimbra (which was the facility of that nature closest to the site of the Apparitions).

The figures that follow, which we found in volume LVI of that compilation, refer to the period of time on October 13th nearest to the hour of the "Miracle."

– Atmospheric pressure (at 1:00 PM): 749.7 millimeters (mm)
– Temperature:
  – at 1:00 PM – 13.2°
  – at 3:00 PM – 14.7°
  – at noon – 13.39°
– Atmospheric vapor tension (at noon): 9.97 mm

- Relative humidity (at noon): 87.04%
- Wind and rain direction (from noon to 2:00 PM):
  - predominant bearing: west by northwest
  - rain in millimeters: 9.5

- Wind velocity:
  - at 1:00 PM: 7 kilometers (Km)/h (hour)
  - at 2:00 PM: 24 Km/h

- Cloud configuration (at noon): Nimbus, cumulous; cumulous nimbus
- Visibility of the Sun (from 1:00 PM to 2:00 PM): 0 h and 6 m
- Total duration of Sun's brilliance on that day: 3 h and 45 m
- Angular height of the Sun at solar midday: 42° 44'
- Astronomic refraction at solar midday: 1' 05"

With a view to how these factors may have interacted on that day, let us see then what happened after the arrival of the "mysterious cloud."

2. THE ANTECEDENTS OF THE "MIRACLE"

When the "dark cloud" arrived, who was there waiting for it?

At Cova da Iria, there were not merely to be found believers and the superstitious, children and the sick, visionaries and liars. At the site itself, there was a far richer multitude, well chosen, were one to look beyond normal social patterns. It was, at once, heterogeneous, spontaneous, and mixed – perfectly representing the population of our planet. It included journalists and university professors, farmers and housewives, city folk and country folk. And they were not alone. They wore vestments rich and poor, male and female, hats and adornments, beautiful shoes and boots, in a broad sampling of human clothing. Very close by, one could find all manner of vehicles – from donkey-drawn carts to the best automobiles of the age, "in an area that extended to almost one kilometer" – according to the correspondent for *Raio de Luz.*[1] For his part, the reporter from *O Século* wrote: "Someone counted more than 100 automobiles and more than 100 bicycles and it would be impossible to count the diverse cars which blocked the road, one of them an autobus from Torres Novas, within which were united people from every social condition.”[2]

Carlos Silva, who published his impressions eight days later, thought “the snaking of so many creatures over the hill” lovely.[3] “I inquired where they were from... and upon hearing named all their places of origin, I marveled how those souls had come from so far to bear witness to what two children affirmed.”

Avelino de Almeida described how the entire multitude consisted of “thousands of creatures… many leagues around… who were joined by the faithful… from various provinces – Alentejanos and Algarvios, Minhotos and Beiroes – [all] congregated around the small oak....”

That was the epicenter of the encounter – a tree that was no longer a tree. According to Carlos Silva, the tree had been so thoroughly stripped for souvenirs that it survived only as “a fragment that protruded 10 centimeters out of the ground.” Maria Carreira recounted: “Now it was nothing more than a stump, which I, the night before, had decorated with floggers and ribbons of silk.”[4] Nonetheless, it was the judgment of Avelino de Almeida that the tiny tree was visible to the throng, because it stood on a small height around which a crude portico could be seen upon which two lanterns swayed.

And with what did the multitude occupy its time while it waited?

Maria Augusta Saraiva Vieira de Campos, who in October published the first pamphlet on the subject, would record how “among the crowd we took up places, and began to pray or say the Rosary in chorus, and sang the *Ave de Lourdes* (which the crowd and the women accompanied), and the *Queremos Deus,* and recited the Prayer to San Bernardo, and so on.”[5]

If the Lady had made an appointment to meet a military commander rather than three illiterate children, perhaps the troops would have waited for her on that 13th day. As it was, however, the 50,000 people brought with them provisions, umbrellas, rosary beads, and coats, but left their rifles at home.

Oddly, in the apparitions at Lourdes, the Being seemed to fear the presence of the French gendarmes at the scene. Thus, on February 22, 1858, when these followed the Seer, the Lady did not keep her appointment. Bernadette justified the fact by saying that the Lady was afraid of the guards. And that could not have been too far from the truth, because Angla, who, like other children, *received messages in her mind without knowing from whence they came*, told Father Cros, historian of these apparitions, that she had heard: “While the Commander of the Guard is there, I shall not see her.”[6]

The “cloud,” which came from the West, must have arrived punctually at solar midday – around 1:37 PM. The longitude of Lisbon is + 0 hours: 36 minutes: 34 seconds past Greenwich Mean Time. However, in 1917, at Fátima, the multitude was beset with great confusion as to the actual time. A new time scheme – Daylight Savings Time – was in effect, that had begun on February 28th and that would end on October 14th. As a result, the witnesses later offered discrepant times – times which span a period of some three hours!

This ambiguity can be resolved by resort to the time identified by Pinto Coelho. He was a prominent legal advisor and pillar of the community. His opinion as to the arrival time of the Apparitions can be relied upon with some certainty as to its accuracy. "1:37:30 – solar midday – was the announced time of the vision, which was expected to coincide with the phenomenon of the sky," Coelho was quoted as having said in the October 16th issue of *A Ordem* [*The Order*]. "At that time, it continued to rain. Minutes later, the rain diminished, and when it was 1:15 PM ceased completely. The Sun, until then covered, showed itself...."

In light of the fact that the dialogue with the Seers lasted some 10 minutes, it is probably true that the "cloud" could have arrived at the site exactly at solar midday. Ten minutes later – at approximately 1:46 PM – the "Miracle" that had been announced three months previously then began.

"I saw a dark cloud coming from the East," stated Joaquim da Silva Jorge, a farmer.[7] To a farmer, one accustomed to capably distinguishing clouds in the atmosphere, even regulating his work by them, this cloud must have looked different from the ones that he usually saw.

Yet, there were other "clouds" before "The Miracle of the Sun." Quite possibly, from the "dark cloud" emerged... a smaller one.

"I saw a little cloud that moved away," we are told by Maria dos Anjos, Lúcia's sister.[8]

Her other sister, Glória, also testified: "A type of little cloud of smoke moved directly, parallel to the ground, in the direction of the Seminário da Consolata, east of the site of the Apparitions. Lúcia said: 'Remove your hats, Our Lady is coming'."[9]

The Being always proceeded from the East. Ferreira Borges, who arrived late – at the time the dialogue between Lúcia and the Lady was taking place – related: "I heard people saying that they had seen a white cloud come from the East and pause over the bush and that they were still seeing it."[10] This would be seen during a UFO incident in Brazil in December 1973, when João Rodrigues Terra saw "a white cloud [that] descended from the sky, that was much whiter than the other clouds."[11]

There were those for whom the hovering object suggested more a star than a cloud. The correspondent from *Raio de* Luz, for instance, left this written account: "Many (including persons of credibility) saw a pretty star moving in the direction of the oak tree of the Apparitions with a flash."

As the primitive "cloud" continued in space, Lúcia proceeded to converse with the Lady, while the onlookers observed the characteristic "cloud of smoke" over the tree. At the same time, "in the sky, where the *cloud* diverted itself, it grew clear, and to our amazement a silvery globe appeared that made a small gyration...."

The dialogue completed, the Lady "turned the palms of her hands upward,"[12]

Fig. 18 – The crowd coming to the site of the Apparitions. Moments later, a "dark cloud," different from the others, came from the East. The "Miracle" was about to begin.

"pointed with her finger to the band where the Sun is,"[13] and, as if she had made a signal to the silver globe, a "street of colored lights," detected by Gilberto dos Santos, began to retreat "little-by-little." The Being turned around because "she was leaving with her back turned towards us."[14] She disappeared "head first, then her body, [and] the last thing that I saw were her feet."[15]

Afterwards, according to eyewitness Angélica Pitta de Morais, "the rain stopped and *a very white and brilliant little cloud raced across the sky*, and all the people who [had] surrounded the oak trees fell to their knees without concern for the mud. I heard a voice say what I was at the same time thinking: *'It is a cloud passing before the front of the Sun, something which often happens.'* At this, the brilliant Sun appeared...."[16]

And then the "Miracle" began.

3. THE FUNCTION OF THE CLOUDS

The thunder reverberated close by.... The air grew thicker with a sound that called to mind the buzzing of bees. Suddenly, the clouds began to move in the sky... and from those clouds a light emerged – like lightning from behind them.... The clouds appeared to be descending, and bringing in

> their bulges peculiar flashes of colored light that appeared to ricochet from one cloud to another.... From the other side of the landscape, there emerged a massive, darker cloud formation.... Within the clouds, there was something like a fireworks show....

A witness of the events at Fátima did not bequeath this long description, in extracts, to us. Thunder and lightning, the buzzing of bees, disconcerting clouds moving through the sky with colors that called to mind fireworks, "massive cloud formations" – all of these were witnessed in 1917. The description above, however, was not merely observed by 50 thousand people at Fátima. Six decades later, it was also seen by millions of moviegoers who watched Steven Spielberg's film about alien contact, *Close Encounters of the Third Kind.*[1] But why include this particular account in our work?

Let us return to October 13, 1917 to review the statements of several of the witnesses present at Cova da Iria, as illuminated by both previous and subsequent events in UFO history.

Higino Faria, while residing in California in 1960, provided this testimony to Haffert:

> [T]he clouds became a *very dense and dark mass*, giving the impression of an eclipse. At that moment, I looked to the multitude and had the impression that it was the Final Judgment. Faces seemed thinner, longer, yellowed. Then the *black cloud opened*, divided itself, and *through the opening* we saw the Sun shine, spinning like a ball of fire.[2]

It is interesting to note that Faria made reference to a "black *cloud*," in the singular, which so closely resembles what farmer Joaquim da Silva Jorge described as the "dark cloud" that he saw approaching the Fátima site from the East.

Maria Romana wrote in *A Ordem* on October 25th: "The cloud began tearing itself in pieces and opened itself – allow me the comparison – as if it were the curtain of a theater to allow the Sun to be seen shining...."

Another witness who was present, Miss N., told Martindale: "[T]he dense clouds did not disappear *but opened a hole*, and then we saw the Sun."[3]

Manuel da Costa Pereira also stated that when "the stars suddenly opened, one could clearly see the Sun, which did not hurt [one's] eyes...."[4]

Eight days after "The Miracle of the Sun," a lady from Lisbon, who was named "da Guarda," shared her impressions in a letter to a friend, who was named "Mimi," and these missives were later published in the January 12, 1918 edition of *A Guarda*:

> There were torrential rains and everybody, standing on their feet,

> maintained themselves until two o'clock, the time at which *the clouds moved aside to allow the Sun to be uncovered,* and immediately, rolls of light, yellow clouds like gold, purple, and the color of carnations began to pass, in front of the Sun.... I saw within the vacuum a marvelous crown of such clouds in various colors.

Other witnesses noted the chromatic aspect of the clouds as they opened to either side. The lawyer Luís António Vieira Magalhães e Vasconcelos, who was the Baron de Alvaiázere, wrote a statement on December 30th that today is part of the official document entitled *Processo Canónico de Fátima* [*Canonical Process of Fátima*].[5] He confirmed the accounts of others when he wrote: "The Sun could not be seen, covered by the clouds, and none there would have ventured to say that it would reappear on that rainy and brusque day. At 1:00 PM on the dot... I saw the clouds, running lightly, leave the Sun exposed." He then added additional coloration to the historical record by stating, "Diaphanous, vaporous clouds, some purple, some orange, went by."

In his own account, a prominent journalist, Eduardo Teixeira, wrote:

> [T]o the black [clouds], [came] tempestuous clouds [that] succeeded one another, lighter and filled with whiteness. The Sun, in [its] turn, began to unveil itself and soon afterwards, all the people noted that some *small clouds, a lovely pink in color, distinguished themselves from the others,* [then] came to pass beneath the Sun, and disappear. This happened repeatedly....[6]

But the "thickness" of the multitude was more surprised itself by the break up of the clouds, without there being any wind, than by its colors.

The Canon Formigão affirmed: "As if by enchantment, *the clouds suddenly ripped apart* and the Sun, at its zenith, appeared in all its splendor...."[7]

Ferreira Borges wrote to Canon Barthas: "At this moment, I got out of the car, and when I was extending my hand to my wife to help her out, it was then that the *accumulated clouds* disappeared, without even the slightest breeze blowing, and the Sun gleamed in a pure sky!"

Avelino de Almeida, at the behest of an ex-seminary, who was then president of the Chamber of Santarém, wrote in another statement on October 29th, this to the magazine *Ilustração Portuguesa* [*Portugal Illustrated*]: "...What did I see on the moor [at] Fátima that was truly strange? The rain, at the pre-announced time, stopped falling, a *dense mass of clouds broke apart*, and the Sun – [a] disk of dull silver – at its complete zenith, appeared...."

The correspondent of the *Diário de Notícias* told us on the 15th: "There had been people, according to what we heard some say, who thought they saw the Sun abandon its fictitious orbit, *break the clouds*, and descend to the horizon."

Gregório Tavares, in the *Concelho de Mação* for November 18th, stated: "*The clouds, running swiftly, opened clearly,* and the Sun appeared, shining with rays of gold...."

And Jacinto de Almeida Lopes testified to the *Parochial Inquiry*: "As the approximate [time] approached, it was then, as if by enchantment, [that] the rain ceased, and the Sun broke the *dense and black clouds*, [and] showed itself shining with its luminous rays...."

An even more vivid picture was painted by our well-known Mrs. J, who found even more precise language to describe what the eyewitnesses saw, as reported in the *Correio da Beira* [*The Beira Post*] newspaper of November 10th: "In the sky, in the place *where the cloud was diverting itself,* it cleared... and we saw the silver globe...." He went on to elaborate: "[T]hat globe or sphere... *broke*... in all its splendor, *a cloud or brilliant red flame* that covered it."

Transporting ourselves forward in time to Svoarzed, Hungary in 1958, we find the following observation: "George Barroinski saw a greenish, phosphorescent cloud, coming from the northwest. The center became constantly more brilliant, rapidly changing color, becoming dark green. *An oval object appeared and left the area, followed by some type of flame....* "[8]

It appears that the "Sun" at Fátima did not limit itself to "breaking the clouds." The testimony of Mrs. J. confirms the fact that, as depicted in Spielberg's film, the "cloud" opened up, accompanied by flames, flashes of light, and lightning.

Let us examine additional testimony that emphasized this detail.

Joaquim da Silva Jorge (the farmer who saw the cloud arrive from the East) added: "[The cloud] opened in a *girândola* of sunlight." Beyond having been merely poetic, this witness provided valuable information. A *girândola* is a type of firework that, instead of producing half a dozen shots and resulting lights, is comprised of dozens of flashes of light that appear and disappear very rapidly.

Other witnesses referred to the incandescent flashes seen in the skies above Fátima.

Maria Cândida da Silva, then a child, told us: "Then, suddenly, the rain stopped, and a great flash appeared...."[9]

Maria Guerra affirmed: "The lightning opened the clouds and the Sun began trembling."[10]

It seems, however, that a strange cloud, seen in Fátima, presented other Ufological peculiarities. For example, it appeared and disappeared, showing itself to possess mutable chromatic effects. Mrs. L. de S., in *Raio de Luz,* told us of this detail: "A lovely cloud, now colored like fire, now purple, now rose-colored, now gold, successively showed itself and disappeared, reflecting the colors not on all the onlookers as much as upon the whole area."

A similar description can be found in a work by Robert Roussel, which refers to an observation made in Vendée, France, on October 10, 1975:

> Mr. M. P. André saw, in a southwesterly direction in the sky, an ash-colored machine, likened to a *sort of* Sun, covered by a cloud of many colors overlaid: red, green, yellow, and orange. That phenomenon called to mind a *round Moon of dull color* that did not merge with its cloud of scintillating color.[11]

There are witnesses who point to the fact that just as these emanations were liberated from the surface of the "globe or sphere," likewise, they were gathered to it.

Augusta Saraiva Vieira de Campos, in her previously cited pamphlet, wrote: "Screams could be heard from everywhere when from the Sun a white form stood out... coming toward us, returning again to the Sun, and finally, *hiding itself the third time among the clouds.*"

Mrs. "J", blessed with a visual acuity that was "out of the ordinary," perceived that after the maneuvers of the globe, "a golden yellow cloud moved across the scene; and it was, thus, that this reality, which to us mortals, appeared to be a dream, proceeded to disappear!" This anticipated by many years attempts to interpret the phenomenon in light of its circumstances, some that were to come in a very culturally superior manner, but all of which have led to the lament: "Where it came from, and how it left, we know not how to explain." And she was Catholic, having even stayed on the previous night, as if a daughter, in the residence of the parish priest.

Let us compare this last function of the "cloud" of Fátima with descriptions gleaned from the compendia of Ufology.

Koninsberg, Prussia, March 17, 1716

> "Around nine o'clock, toward the northwest, a *very black cloud* could be seen, that cast from itself rays of fire and, having continued in this manner for about half an hour, *various lucid bodies of varied colors were seen to exit from it, which they later returned for and gathered up.*"[12]

England, July 2, 1963

> Three youths saw a machine that "moved vertically and *entered a cloud.*" One of them declared to a reporter that "the machine was silvery and shone intensely. The cloud into which it vanished was uncommon in color," but he could not describe exactly its tone.[13]

Lastly, in Cova da Iria, we have the statement provided by Maria Romana that after the globe was picked up, "the clouds began disappearing a little at a time from the firmament, which became clean, serene, and blue as there has been none to equal in this, our beautiful Portuguese land."

But, before this, what was presented to the multitude that would cause them to abandon their homes, fields, and cattle, and the exercise of other professions, to attend the announced Miracle?

4. A DESCRIPTION OF THE PHENOMENON

The so-called "Miracle of the Sun" was truly a superior event, without parallel in recorded human history. Maybe the lady from Lisbon was right when she wrote in a letter to her friend "Mimi": "It was the greatest miracle of the last centuries, a miracle that was seen by believers and non-believers." In truth, it was on a level with the greatest accomplishments of the 20th century, when the magic of the Unknown would cross paths with the superstition of Normalcy. Today, we detect several important elements already known to us. At each step, accompanying the experiences of every witness to which we turn, are clues to the reconstitution of the event.

Let us begin with the description of the "solar" object that the Beings used as a translator of their "techno-magic" that we could understand. The multiplicity of the statements is a factor that enriches the experience, enabling us to test varying sensibilities and, moreover, providing investigators with other indications no less precise about the intrinsic relationship between the phenomenon and its witness. Therefore, let us continue to observe the "Miracle" through the eyes of the Portuguese of that time.

The lawyer José Proença de Almeida Garrett related:

> Moments before, the Sun had broken overhead through a dense layer of clouds that would have [otherwise] hidden it, [allowing it] to shine clearly and intensely. I turned toward that magnet that attracted every gaze, and I could see that it was similar to a *disk with a distinct and lively border, luminous and lucent*, but harmless.

The comparison to a dull silver disk, which in Fátima I had heard still made,

> did not seem entirely accurate to me. The color was more clear, active, and rich, multi-faceted, having the opalescence of a pearl. In no way was it similar to the Moon on a crystal clear night, because it could be seen and felt to be a living star.
>
> *It was not spherical, like the Moon, it did not have the same tonality or the chiarra-obscuro. It seemed like a polished wedge, cut from the nacre of a conch shell.* This is not some banal comparison of cheap poetry. My eyes saw it this way. It was also not to be confused with the Sun as seen through the fog (which, as a matter of fact, there wasn't at that time), because it was opaque, diffuse, and veiled. In Fátima, it had light and heat and drew itself distinctly and with a banked, recessed edge, like a game board....
>
> The marvelous thing is that, during a long while, one could gaze at the star, flame of light, and hot coal of heat, without any pain in one's eyes and without any dazzle in the retina, which blinded.[1]

The lady from Lisbon, still under the thrall of the event, told her friend "Mimi": "Suddenly, it was the Moon that appeared, but it was only for a moment, because immediately it was transformed into the Sacred Eucharist wherein the Cross can be seen as if sunken in that *opaque material the color of wheat flour, very white.*"

After having received diverse letters describing the phenomenon, the newspaper *Beira Baixa* communicated to its readers: "The Sun uncovered itself, and had a strange light, [and]... able to be gazed at, like a full Moon, passed through diverse *gradations*, appearing sometimes like the solar globe... enclosed by an aureole of flames, [and] other times a *metallic disk as if of silver.*"[2]

Aside from appearing to be a "metallic disk" – one having a strange similarity to a star – there were those who called it a "magnetic disk." The engineer Mário Godinho looked upon the "Sun" through the eyes of a technician and left us this account published in *Stella*:

> In a radiant sky, the Sun could be looked at straight-on and with eyes wide open, without blinking, as if we were looking at a *disk of polished glass*, illuminated from behind, with a rainbow of iridescence on its periphery, seeming to have a rotating movement.... And the Sun did not have the brilliance that hurt our eyes on normal days, as it was a majestic disk, *magnetic*, which attracted us and sort of revolved in the immense sky....[3]

This same witness told Haffert: "It was like a disk of steamed-up crystal that had been illuminated from behind, a disk of opaque glass."[4]

Ermelinda Vilhena Barbosa, however, did not find the disk to be opaque. In her view, "it turned turquoise blue, and appeared to be *transparent*, and one could see the sky behind it."[5]

"Disk – metallic; disk – silvery; disk – magnetic and made of dull, opaque glass; disk – transparent"– and still they called it the Sun.

Yet there exist three statements that give it other designations. Two of them were chosen by the parish priest to accompany his report. The Leiria newspaper *O Mensageiro* reported on November 29th: "The parish priest of Fátima, my friend Father Manuel Marques Ferreira, remained always withdrawn from everything, conducting himself so as to even avoid going to Cova da Iria on the days of the Apparitions. Only as the result of many pleas did he go there on the last day."

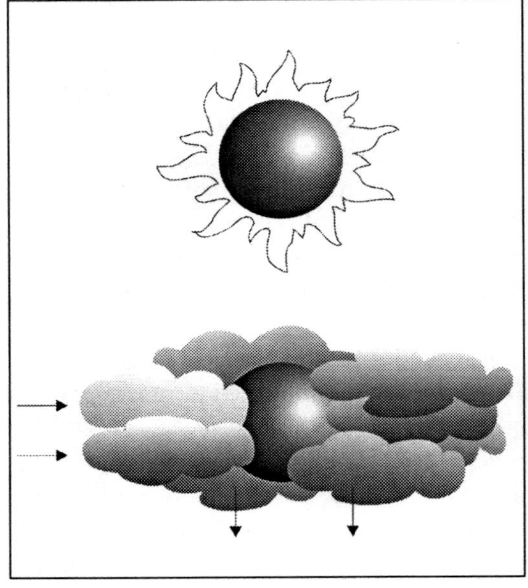

Fig. 19 – The advent of the "special cloud" carrying the mimetic "Sun" that disguised the actual Sun.

If he went, then he observed the "Miracle."And he must have been convinced that it was not the Sun, because, among many statements that he must have known regarding this strange phenomenon, he chose two that did not presume that our Sun had set itself to dancing. In addition, he disregarded statements published in the Catholic newspaper *A Ordem* and those made by Avelino de Almeida. Here are the two statements that he selected instead:

Maria Augusta Saraiva Vieira de Campos:

> We saw a silver veil, *rounded in shape,* as if it were a full Moon.... Screams could be heard from every quarter *when what appeared to be a form that was white as snow, brilliant*, and that did not hurt the retina, appeared to *emanate from the Sun,* and come toward us....

Mrs. "J":

> Suddenly, everything was bathed by the splendor, very different than usual, a red and very brilliant cloud or flame, which covered it, and, several moments later, *that globe or sphere* [that same one which before had made a small

> gyration] agitated itself nervously, as if impelled by electricity....

Beyond these two accounts, there exists yet another that has been kept forgotten. It is that of the correspondent of the religious periodical *Raio de Luz*. Either no Fatimist author came upon it, or it was disregarded because of its anti-Sun evidence. Let us hear it. It reads:

> Suddenly, a *luminous disk* the size of a great host, but one which could be gazed upon as one gazes at the Moon, *appeared, as if it stood out from the Sun (or placed itself before it)*, descending visibly.... The horizon was limited in a perfect circle by *luminous flashes equal in size and distance from one another*, giving a little bit of an impression of campfires, more by the yellow tone that one sometimes notices at sunset. All this effect was lasting, and the flashes to which I allude were appearing one after another. Simply marvelous and amazing!

And we might add: "Simply Ufological!" "Simply explainable in light of the observations of our day!" Thus, in the belief of this witness, it was not the Sun, but a luminous disk that superimposed itself over the Sun, offering a series of maneuvers to the thousands of spectators watching it from below. And the reality of that fact was not only divulged as early as November 1, 1917, but, in a second contemporary account, by a very religious woman.

Other statements, of course, exist, although less detailed, less rich, and less exact about the description of the object. They provide us, in the meanwhile, some indications, as to the structure and characteristics of the disk or globe.

Gilberto dos Santos: "I saw the Sun, seeming a dull, silver disk, but more luminous than the Moon."[6]

Pereira Gens, physician: "At its zenith, the Sun defined itself like a colossal host."[7]

Inácio Lourenço, priest: "It was like a ball of snow...."[8]

Madalena Patrício, author: "The ashen luster of mother-of-pearl transformed itself like on a *plate of gleaming silver.... The silver Sun, wrapped up* in the same light ashen gauze...."

Manuel Pereira da Silva, priest: "Immediately the Sun appeared with a *well-defined circumference....*"[9]

Carlos de Azevedo Mendes, lawyer: "I saw the Sun, as if it were a *ball of fire,* begin to move in the clouds...."[10]

Maria Romana: "The Sun gave the appearance of a *globe of dull silver* surrounded by a very dark purplish disk...."

Ana Maria da Câmara: "I saw a *very clear, silvery blue disk*, without rays...."[11]

This established, let us now place side-by-side these descriptions of the witnesses to the Fátima phenomenon with accounts made by people who have observed phenomena associated with modern day UFOs.

FÁTIMA	**OTHER LOCATIONS**
"We saw a silver veil with a rounded shape" *Maria Augusta Saraiva*	"They saw a shape that was round and silver in color" *Portugal, 1950* [12]
The Sun appeared to be "transparent and... the sky could be seen behind it" *Ermelinda Barbosa*	"A large sphere which turned transparent.... [T]hrough the object, the stars could be seen" *The Canary Islands, 1976* [13]
"The Sun was like the Moon, only much larger"*Júlia Franco*	"A Moon-shaped object began to draw near.... While descending, it was double the size of the Moon" *Portugal, 1966* [14]
The Sun "had light and heat and drew itself distinctly and with a banked, recessed edge" *Almeida Garrett, Junior*	"The object, spreading a white-yellow light, had distinct contours, [a] circular edge" *France, 1971* [15]
"I saw the Sun appearing to be a disk of dull silver" *Gilberto dos Santos*	"I saw an object... the color of silver or aluminum in the shape of a disk" *Romania, 1967* [16]
"I saw a very clear silvery blue disk... that, resuming its natural color, began rolling" *Ana Maria da Câmara*	The object "presented brilliant clear blue light, surrounded by a ring of white light, and seemed to spin" *Brazil, 1969* [17]
"The silver Sun was seen to roll and spin around" *Madalena Patrício*	"Observed a silver disk.... [T]he object spun upon itself" *França, 1954* [18]
"Suddenly, a luminous disk... that all could gaze upon" *L. de S., in "Raio de Luz"*	"A strange body unexpectedly arose. It was in the shape of a luminous disk"*Portugal, 1957* [19]
"I saw the Sun as if it were a ball of fire" *Carlos de A. Mendes*	"A ball of fire resembling the Moon" *Fátima Station, 1974* [20]
"The solar globe appeared to be a metallic disk, as if [made] of silver." *"Beira Baixa"*	"All of it seemed to be made of metal, similar to brilliant silver."*Portugal, 1974* [21]

It is not only in our day that we find descriptions like those of Fátima. Throughout human history, startled Earthlings have written accounts that, given the relative state of human knowledge, have interpreted alien craft in metaphor. Let us examine several of these "metaphorical" accounts.

The first is not an observation from our time. It was written 2,600 years ago, in Babylon: "I looked and saw... a thick cloud accompanied by flashes and a mass of resplendent fire around it; in the middle of it, something could be seen which had the aspect of resplendent metal." And within that "mass of fire," the witness did not make out an odd humanoid form, but God in human form. The description is none other than the now famous, formerly strictly metaphorical, account by the prophet Ezekiel found in the Bible.

This translation is a bit liberal.[22] In the original text, Ezekiel did not write "similar in aspect to a resplendent metal," but "like a sort of electro." But what was this "electro" of which he wrote? According to the Roman historian Plinius, "it [was] a very fine metal composed of four parts gold and a fifth of silver."[23]

Moving forward in time, to shortly before the time of Jesus, we find a second interesting account, this one written by the Roman orator Cicero in 50 BC:

> How many times did our Senate not ask the Decenviros [a class of judges in the Roman republic] to consult the Oracles... when two Suns were seen, or when three Moons and tongues of fire were pointed to in the sky, or on the other occasion, when the Sun rose at night, when noises were heard in the sky, and the very same Moon seemed to shine, noting strange orbs in the sky?[24]

By the 6th century, we find this description, in France: "We saw, during two consecutive nights, in the middle of the sky, a type of very luminous cloud that had the shape of a helmet."[25]

And in the 13th century, in England, on August 3rd, in the year 1290, something was observed which also reminds us of Fátima. The Abbott Henry, prior of Byland Abbey, Yorkshire, and his monks, were terrorized when they saw "an enormous silver disk pass slowly over them."[26]

At times, such apparitions were attributed to a divine source, as they were at Cova da Iria.

In the 16th century, on December 5, 1577, at 7:00 AM, in Tubingen, Germany, a beautiful ballet of disks with cupolas could be seen exiting clouds that, in turn, were flowing from the Sun. Note the marvelous description this "miracle" was given 460 years before Fátima:

> Numerous black clouds appeared around the Sun, like those we see when storms are announced; a little later, other clouds of fire and blood, and then other yellow clouds (like saffron) emerged from the Sun. From those clouds

> were emitted light effects, in the shape of large hats, tall and wide, and the ground itself turned yellow and reddish, and was covered with tall and wide hats that turned different colors, such as red, blue, green, and black. Each of us can easily comprehend this miracle and know that mankind should do penance and repent.[27]

The strange clouds and the strange disks, you see, have continually visited us in diverse eras and places. In the 17th century, Japan was chosen. There, in Kyoto, in May 1606, it was recorded that:

> [S]everal times, balls of fire flew over the area. On one occasion, countless samurai noticed a ball, similar to a wheel of fire, that spun and leveled over the Castle Nijo. On another afternoon in September 1702, during various consecutive days, the Sun became the color of blood, and it is said that strands of cotton fell, which apparently came from them. Chaos reigned in all Japan when, on January 2, 1749, three round objects, similar to the Moon, appeared, and remained there four days.[28]

And was it not again described as a "miracle" the Moon remembered to "do," in Bucharest, Romania, on December 27, 1793, at 7:30 PM? On that evening, a man who was present would later write: "[T]he ground trembled three times. I was dining in Floresti [Bucharest] with the venerable Constantin Poenaru. The next night, at the same time as the night before, the Moon performed a miracle: she *transited through the sky for half an hour.*"[29]

There are endless analogies such as these that could be drawn.

So it was in 1917, at Fátima, that a "luminous disk," likened to the Sun and the Moon as in other locations centuries before, was seen to sketch strange maneuvers in the sky. Indeed, in our travels throughout the centuries and in our investigations of contemporary cases, the same reality confronts us, and the same questions present themselves. Who, or what, maneuvers these machines? And, what do they want from us?

Perhaps Mrs. "J" had understood, by intuition, the intentions of the occupants of these satellites, which are similar to our neighboring asteroids. "It seemed to swell and to wish to hurl itself or *speak to the Earth*, to announce a matter of joy and terror!"[30] Might not fear and happiness be, in truth, the sentiments that manifest themselves, when two universes collide?

5. CHROMATIC EFFECTS

The annals of Fátima establish that the chromatic effects were verified:

1. In the "Sun"
2. In the atmosphere

COLORATION OF THE "SUN"

In respect to the iridescent aspects of the object, the following characteristics are known:

a) Iridescent aspects on the whole surface
b) Iridescent aspects on the periphery of the "Sun"
c) Constant succession of colors
d) Posterior luminosity

a) Iridescent aspects on the whole surface

The human eye does not register colors uniformly. What for some is green, for others is blue. It is not surprising that because of this, we might find many different colors in the eyewitness testimony.

A Lucta, October 18th: "...[S]traight away it gained a paleness like the Moon, which right away was stained in a fluid *blue*, a *bruised yellow*, and other faint tones."

Antónia da Câmara: "The Sun showed a *dark green* color."[1]

Nascimento e Sousa, attorney: "I only saw a much pronounced *yellow*, and it seemed to me that I saw a *black* color under the solar disk, but this one I cannot guarantee."[2]

The lady from Lisbon: "Suddenly, it was the Moon that appeared, but it was only for a moment, because immediately it was transformed into the Sacred Eucharist... opaque... the color of wheat flower, *very white.*"

One of the witnesses present, who has been much-pigeonholed, was the Dean of Mathematics at the University of Coimbra, Gonçalo de Almeida Garrett. In a letter to the Viscount of Montelo, he wrote: "[T]he Sun took on a violet color, and afterwards *orange.*"[3]

Ana Maria da Câmara:

> Seconds later, this exclamation flew from my mouth: 'It is the Moon!' I saw a very clear, *silvery blue* disk, without rays, which, taking back its normal color, right away, began to roll frenetically. Later, the disk took on different colors, and hurled from itself rolls of smoke, the center of which was colored, but it always retained its perfectly round shape, without rays and able to be gazed at perfectly. On a certain occasion, I saw it color itself a *bright, vivid, rose color....*

Others perceived different colors.

Ermelinda Vilhena Barbosa wrote: "The Sun turned itself *light* green, which changed to *sky* blue, as if it was apparently transparent and one was seeing the sky behind it. And later it changed to *emerald green*, the color it remained for several minutes, and always trembling."

In turn, Maria Carreira told us: "It made different colors, *yellow, blue, white....*"[4]

But let us now look to see what the official documents say:

Vicarial Process

This document was concluded on October 25th of the year of the Apparitions. Sixteen witnesses were deposed – 15 men and one woman. The Vicar from Porto de Mós, Reverend Joaquim Vieira da Rosa, wrote the report and submitted it to the Archdiocese of Lisbon dated November 11, 1917. The author of this document explained: "I consulted many people about the matter, and all of them confirmed what was said in the witnesses' statements... and for that reason I abstained from requesting that their testimony be written."

Even though the Vicar had handled their statements quite summarily, what do those witnesses chosen by him tell us about the chromatic effects of the "Sun?"[5]

Maria da Silva Rosa, the sixth witness: "...before the Sun [had seen] diverse colors."

Manuel Carvalho, eleventh witness: "[I] saw the Sun... redress itself in various colors."

Parochial Inquiry

In this document, we find the account by Jacinto de Almeida Lopes, who declared to the parish priest that the Sun "shows itself to be shining with its luminous rays, that very slowly take on the colors *yellow, scarlet, and green.*"

Canonical Process of Fátima

We can read here the statement of Luís de Andrade e Silva, Bachelor of Law and Theology: "The solar rays presented the colors *yellow, green, blue, and purple*, according to what they saw, but I saw only the color *yellow*."

The Official Interrogations of 1923

Manuel António Paula was quoted in this document as saying that he worked in Lisbon, but was spending his vacation in Fátima in the months of September and October. He declared:

> Suddenly, the priest [Father José António da Cruz Curado, who was from Penacova] looked to the Sun and said that the Sun during an eclipse is not like this. The deposer also looked and saw that the Sun did not give off light. A white fog ran across it, it was like a Moon that didn't glow. The Sun remained to the left, the remainder of the sky was covered....

In short, perhaps Jacinta's father was right when he told João de Marchi: "We were looking directly at the Sun and it did not bother us. It seemed to turn off and it illuminated once in one direction and then in another. It emitted beams of light to one side and then to the other."[6]

Some later statements indicated the colors of the rainbow.

Canon Formigão: "...successively recapitulating all the colors of the rainbow and projecting light beams of a surprising effect."[7]

José Frazão: "...shooting all the colors of the rainbow."[8]

Maria do Carmo Meneses: "...It descended like a ball of fire, taking on all the colors of the rainbow...."[9]

PARALLELS IN UFOLOGY

Canada, April 4, 1952

A UFO witness stated: "Its color shot out *orange*." Afterwards, "the color turned *reddish*. When the object reached the southern zone, it directed itself towards the horizon and the color turned to *orange*, then to *green*, and finally to a *silvery white*."[10]

Guarda, Portugal, September 10, 1977

A student observed "a flying object which was initially *yellowish* in color. The object changed afterward to a still more intense *blue*, changed again suddenly to *yellow* and, finally, to a *vibrant red*.[11]

b) Iridescent aspects on the periphery of the "Sun"

Many witnesses, however, stated that only the edges of the "Sun" appeared iridescent. And the majority were witnesses of that time.

One stated: "The light underwent different gradations, the solar globe appearing some times surrounded by an aureole of flames, at other times by a metallic disk like silver."[12]

Father José Curado, in his rather detailed account about the colors of the "Sun," wrote:

> It appeared to be wrapped in flames and appeared to us a plate of dull silver... [I]t lit itself on fire shortly afterwards... finding itself then again *wrapped* in *rose-colored* flames and also without projecting rays over the ground. Perhaps a minute having passed, it again lost its light and flames, and found itself once again, now, a *white* plate.... Yet a third time, the Sun... *wrapped itself* in *bluish flames*, which followed the loss of light.[13]

These two statements point to the alternation of coloration (on the periphery) and to the metallic appearance of the disk.

Another statement of the time is that of a jurist that was published on October 16th, in *A Ordem, who observed that the "Sun" was "at times surrounded by scarlet flames, at other times by an aureole of yellow or subdued purple...."*

Maria Romana, on October 25th, was quoted in the same periodical: "The Sun presented then the aspect of a globe of dull silver, [and] *encircling it* [was] *a very dark purplish disk* as seen when eclipses are not total."

In the November 18th edition of the *Concelho de Mação*, Joaquim Gregório Tavares wrote:

> The Sun appeared shining rays of gold in the natural sense, but changed to the color of dull silver, finding itself *surrounded* immediately following by scarlet flames, and at a given moment, became animated by a rapid rotating movement, [and] appeared to slip from the sky and fall to the Earth, and changed to a subdued purple. Immediately it turned green and, finally, a vivid yellow that was prolonged over time.... We were paralyzed with fright. And so that the slightest doubt would not remain in our spirits, we looked, after such a stupendous phenomenon, to the Sun, not noting in it the slightest alteration after the cessation of the yellow color."

As for the engineer Mario Godinho, he always declared quite clearly that "the disk of polished glass" that he saw was "*iridescent on its periphery.*"

The professor from Coimbra, Gonçalo Almeida Garrett, in his letter to the

Viscount of Montelo written on December 3, 1917, added that the "Sun" flashed "*sparks of light on its borders*, similar to those that are given off by the well-known fireworks [with] wheels.

Other witnesses confirmed: "Then the Sun, breaking from the clouds, lit itself up in a more vivid brilliance, *itself ringed in a dark circle...*" (as cited in *A Lucta*, October 18th edition).

In his turn, an acquaintance of journalist Eduardo Teixeira declared: "A fire-colored ribbon began spinning alternately in one and another direction, around the Sun. And *going around it*, equally along all its circumference, *an enormous splendor equally fire-colored ....*"[14]

It remains to us to make sense of these accounts in light of what the official documents tell us.

In the Vicarial Process

• António Ramos Mira, the first witness: "...observing at the same time that *around it* there was a reddish yellow color"

• Romano dos Santos, the fifth witness: "... looking to the Sun, saw that it *was surrounded by* different colors"

• Adriano de Matos, the eighth witness: "... saw different colors *encircling said star*"

In the Canonical Process

• The Baron of Alvaiázere wrote on December 30th: "Suddenly, I saw an intense, rose-colored edge *surrounding the "Sun"* that looked like a disk of dull silver"

This chromatic detail is also not an exclusivity of the "Sun" of Fátima. In modern times, we undeniably have had similar accounts.

PARALLELS IN UFOLOGY

Hamburg, Germany, August 1960

"Something like a disk appeared... with a pulsating, yellow *halo.*"[15]

Lynn, Massachusetts, USA, August 25, 1964

On this day, Richard Pratt observed "a silver, oval object, surrounded by a light white halo."[16]

It seems that nothing new exists on the face of the Earth.

c) Constant succession of colors

The evidence indicates that varied colors appeared on the surface or the periphery of this "similar-to-the-Sun" object. Did they appear in an amalgam, at random, without defined characteristics? According to some witnesses, the colors followed a pattern, whereby they returned to their origin and located themselves at specific points on the periphery of the "solar" object.

Maria Augusta Saraiva addressed that characteristic with particularity: "We saw a silver veil, round in shape, as if it were the full Moon. Shortly, it turned vivid purple, then to red, then to emerald green, and *finally back to its original color.*" That seems to suggest that, according to this witness, the object evinced a chromatic sequence of sorts.

Curiously, Avelino de Almeida was prescient in identifying early the ordered nature of this color scheme. "There are those who would say that he saw it change color *successively.*"In the October 29th edition of *Ilustração Portuguesa*, he expressed his own opinion, saying: "...such beautiful and glittering colors were taken on successively by the solar surface," hence referring once more to the term "successively."

Angélica Pitta de Morais explained this even better: "The Sun successively took on various colors, like lilac, blue, rose, orange, the color of fire, *repeating these several times*."

How might this chromatic succession be provoked? Perhaps Mrs. L de S., from *Raio de Luz,* who wrote her statement that same month (and we can guarantee that, until then, she had never read a modern Ufological description), wrote something disquieting, but which might also explain this detail of the appearance of sequential colors:

> The horizon [this might refer to the exterior circumference of the luminous disk that descended before] was delimited in a perfect circle by *luminous flashes*, equal in size and distance one from the other, giving the impression of "campfires," but in the yellowish tones that are from time to time noted at sunset. This entire effect was lasting and *the flashes to which I allude appeared one after another.*

The explanation can be found here, not only for the chromatic sequence but also for the descriptions that suggest coloration merely on the peripheral part of the "Sun."

d) Posterior luminosity

There exist two other statements which establish that a light emanated from the posterior area of the object and not from its entire surface. Godinho, who wrote that the "Sun" was iridescent on its periphery, added: *"it was illuminated from behind.*"Now let us look at his statement to *Stella* in January 1962: "In a radiant sky, the Sun could be faced straight-on and with open eyes, without blinking, as if we were looking at a disk of polished glass, having a rotating movement."

The lady from Lisbon also stated in her letter to her friend Mimi, "The Sun, *with its light from behind,* seemed to strain the clarity as though through colored glass...."

This image of "strained clarity" was also supported by Madalena Patrício: "The light turned blue in an odd [way], *as though it came through two stained glass windows* of an immense cathedral.... The blue extinguished itself slowly, so that the light appeared to be strained through yellow stained-glass windows."

But it was not merely the globe or disk taken by the Sun that presented strange chromatic and light effects. The entire area became rainbow-colored, encompassing both the multitude and the mountain.

COLORATION OF THE ATMOSPHERE

Ana Maria da Câmara affirmed:

> On certain occasions, I saw it color itself a vivid rose color. From behind every head, a gauze-like veil of the same color rose up. Field and multitude, everything reflected it. It was grandiosely lovely, and in the meantime, a sentiment of inexplicable fear grew in the soul, even if one did not have a conviction about the supernatural. No one said aloud what they saw, but from the redoubling of the ardor of the invocations to Our Lady... one could perceive that everyone, more or less, saw and felt the same thing.

"It threw off sparks of light to one side and toward the other it painted everything in different colors – the trees and the people, the ground and the air," Manuel Marto, the father of the seers, poetically expressed.

Júlia Franco told us: "It was a different yellow, as I had never seen before. It wasn't just on the faces, but it was everywhere, all over Cova da Iria."

Many accounts expressed sheer amazement. The one provided by the lady from Lisbon to her friend Mimi embodied these: "The people were the same color as the clouds (gold, purple, metallic). This happened all around the valley selected for so many marvels, like simple ornamentation, some [spots] stained with the three predominate colors."

Various spectators utilized the term "stains." Besides the lawyer, Almeida Garrett, there was Madalena Patrício, who said: "Yellow stains [after the blue] were now falling upon the white kerchiefs, on the dark, poor skirts of rough surge. They were stains that indefinitely repeated over the low-lying oak trees, over the rocks, over the mountain." But the Baron of Alvaiázere observed: "At various points on the line of the horizon, contrasting with the lead-colored hue of the sky, I also saw reddish stains. On the landscape and the people, I could also make out rose-colored and yellow stains."

In her time, Emília Alves, a housekeeper, told us: "Everyone could look directly at it. It was merely the Sun; its rays had disappeared. What it made were colors.... We looked at one another to see those colors – blues, scarlets, yellows and the color of the sky – very vivid!"[17]

Maria do Carmo Meneses wrote in a letter to her brother, the poet: "All of us took on those same colors [of the Sun]; our faces, our clothing, the very ground [we stood on]; screams could be heard and many tears could be seen... I said, quite impressed: 'My God! How great is Thy power!' "

Naturally, in Ufology we find similar accounts. In Dai-el-Aonagri, Morocco, on July 29, 1952, a man named Pitejan saw a luminous object, some 20 meters in diameter, "launching bluish bolts."[18] Our renowned farmer Joaquim da Silva Jorge remained surprised when "his" cloud "opened in a girândola of Sun, that came to descend to the Earth, and suddenly, the ground turned blue."

"I looked around," stated Maria Romana, and "the aspect and the colors of the landscape were the same that can be observed during the duration of an eclipse – the same *bluish light, sui generis* of that ultra-special, electric blue."

But there was not merely the color blue on all things. Angélica Pitta de Morais stated that the Sun "successively took on various colors, like lilac, blue, rose, orange, the color of fire, repeating these several times, and all the ground, the cars, the people were inundated by those colors."

Father João Gomes Menitra "looked around surprised to see that the crowd was turning various colors: yellow, white, blue...."[19]

The *Concelho de Mação* of November 18th reported that "right away it turned a green color and finally to [a] vivid yellow, that prolonged itself longer and with such intensity that the color of the Sun was seen to pass to the Earth, appearing to us to be the atmosphere and the closer objects adorned in that color."

Returning to Ufology, let us see what a Brazilian observed in 1973: "All of a sudden, there appeared a luminous object that was orange in color... the field, at a distance of some 300 meters, was totally illuminated by the 'ball' as if it were daytime."[20]

And what do the official documents tell us of the coloration of the landscape?

In the Parochial Inquiry

Jacinto de Almeida Lopes affirmed that the solar rays "took on the colors *yellow, scarlet, and* green, turning the objects that were under their influence those same colors."

Manuel Gonçalves, Jr., in his turn, told the parish priest, who wrote:

> With eyes always fixed upon the oak trees, in order to see some extraordinary thing, without purposely gazing at the Sun, he noted that, on the same occasion in which the crowd was screaming loudly and exclaiming, because of what it saw in the Sun, the people as well as the trees and everything on which his gaze rested in the direction of the oak trees, took on different colors.

In the Vicarial Process

Auzebino Francisco Mira "also saw different colors on the crowd and on the horizon and all at the same time as the facts that took place on the 13th of each of the five months transacted."

Above the statement of Manuel Ribeiro de Carvalho, it noted that "at the same time he observed the colors blue and scarlet on the horizon."

António Maria Menitra "saw different colors on the Sun and on the crowd."

As for António Ramos Mira, he affirmed that around the Sun "there was a *reddish yellow* color that was reflected upon the crowd and on the horizon." This recalled the case of Tubingen, Germany, that took place in 1577, where "clouds of fire and blood had emerged from the Sun and others were yellow... and the ground itself turned *yellow and reddish.*"

In The Official Interrogations of 1923

Manuel António Paula, "pulling his gaze away from the Sun, saw the crowd was a very vivid scarlet, and exclaimed: 'Oh, gentlemen, look at the crowd how it is! All scarlet!' To which the priest [Father José Curado] replied: 'Could they be scarlet handkerchiefs?' To which I responded: 'How could that be?' Then everyone had agreed to wear scarlet handkerchiefs on their backs! Afterwards, the crowd appeared the color of gold."

And the statements continued to manifest the fear of those who had looked upon the colored spectacle. The October 18th edition of *O Mensageiro* cited Carlos Silva as having said: "I heard several... pleas to the Virgin and Holiest Mother and I saw faces of the tremendous attendees laden in a rose color, then it transformed to indigo and, quite suddenly, to a cadaverous, yellow hue."

Gilberto dos Santos conveyed the general sentiment with this gloomy description:

> [M]y gaze swept over that great multitude, and that is when I saw diminish, almost suddenly, the clarity of the day, and I saw the entire multitude inside of a thick darkness, like castaways in a black sea, with only their heads exposed! The bodies [were] almost invisible due to the darkness and the heads [were] visible as if [seen] during the day.[21]

Lawyer Almeida Garrett described in this eyewitness account in another vocabulary what had so frightened dos Santos:

> [D]uring the solar incident... there were impressive colors in the atmosphere. I looked at what was close and extended my sight to the extreme horizon and everything was an amethyst color. Objects, and the sky, and the atmospheric layer, were the same color. The oak tree-turned-violet, that rose up before me, cast a dark shadow upon the Earth.
>
> In Fátima, an atmosphere, although purple, remained transparent up to the confines of the horizon that could clearly be distinguished, and I did not have the sensation of a cessation of the universal energy.
>
> Continuing to look at the Sun, I noticed that the atmosphere had cleared. Soon after, I heard a rustic who was near me say in frightened amazement: "The Lady is yellow!"
>
> In fact, everything now changed, near and far, taking on the color of old, yellow damask apricots. The people appeared sickly and jaundiced. I smiled to myself at finding them, frankly, ugly and inelegant. Laughter could be heard. *My hand had that same yellow hue.* Days later, I conducted the experiment of staring at the Sun [for] brief instants. Withdrawing my gaze, I saw, after several moments, yellow blotches, which were irregularly shaped.
>
> It did not look to be of one uniform color, as if, in the air, a topaz had been rendered volatile, rather, like specks that move about because of the movement of the air. My hand had that same yellow tone.

The same thing happened in 1956 to a student of fine arts in France, in the region of Loiret (close to Serdon). There, on a night in September, a married couple, of which this student was part, was traveling by automobile when they saw "an enormous, unmoving, silent mass above them." A strange light flowed from that mass descending to the ground as if it were a rope ladder unwinding. All around, everything became illuminated in various colors, producing an effect similar to the light of iodine. The witnesses noticed a great variation of colors. *The woods, which were green, turned a dark blue.* It is not surprising that this student of Fine Arts might have been marveled, writing: “At a given moment, *my hand was caught* by the luminous ray. *It turned yellow-orange.*” That color and the blue of the forest impressed her to the point that she proffered that she would never forget. And she added, “It was an inhuman sensation.”[22]

Her words evoked those spoken at Fátima by the engineer Mario Godinho, who concluded with this poetic expression: “Everything around it became unreal, as if the Earth had been made divine!”

*

Based on the myriad cases of luminous UFOs endowed with different colors, it is possible to theorize about their chromatic composition. McCampbell studied the luminous component of the phenomenon, fundamental to its observation at night, in the light of day, when the colors being studied are less prominent and the object tends to reveal its metallic aspect.

This scientist found that the colors observed are, often, pure, in other words, a complement of precise waves being selectively excited. In this way, McCampbell traced the emitted colors to traces of the emission of molecules in the air. Rare gases (helium, neon, argon, krypton, and xenon) seem to him to be the best candidates, because of either their low ionization potential or the high number of traces they generate in the visible spectrum. The necessary energy would be transmitted to the ambient air via some form of radio frequency electro-magnetic wave, or one slightly lower.

The descriptions of the witnesses, as we saw, point to the metallic aspect, but also the spectral colors, the brilliant white and the pale white. When more than one color was implicated, the witnesses indicated that they were surging in a repeated series. In relation to the metallic nature, of the 56 witnesses that made up McCampbell’s study, 13 used the terms “silver,” “silvery,” or some other polished surface of white metal. (At Fátima, 15 percent indicated the color “silver,” excluding other polished surfaces, such as the conch nacre or mother of pearl). On another note, almost all the colors of the visible range of the EM spectrum were described, from blue-violet, passing through green, yellow, orange, and red (see color table below).[23]

McCampbell suggests that the source of the luminosity associated with UFOs is not, therefore, the object itself, but the surrounding air excited by the UFO’s energy or propulsion system. In light of this theory, it becomes necessary to know which specific atoms are responsible for the light that is produced at a given height in the atmosphere. In the case of Fátima, as with so many others that occur in rural areas, where the air is relatively pure, hydrocarbons are insignificant as a source of light. It is evident that it becomes difficult to associate each gas specifically emitted in the atmosphere to a given color surrounding the UFO. Nevertheless, it is known that some gases are more responsive to an electrical field. The scientific measure of this threshold for each element is known as its *ionization potential* – the same quantity of energy required to elevate an electron from its fundamental state to the state immediately above it.

The most easily stimulated gas appears to be *xenon*, which has an ionization potential of merely 12 to 13 volts. Following McCampbell's rationale, let us suppose that, by unknown means, the UFO liberates a growing potential of energy over its surrounding gases. At a given point, the atmosphere, absorbing the energy, becomes luminous, which, in its primary state, corresponds to the excitation of xenon. A later augmentation of energetic "transfer" activates the other gases in inverse order of its limits, and, in this manner, its light would join that emitted by the first gas.

Table 4: Colors Observed in UFOs

Spectral Colors	Pure	Combined
Violet	Blue-Violet **Purple**	
Blue	Blue Brilliant Blue Luminous Blue Incandescent Blue	
Green	Incandescent Green Greenish Brilliant Green	Bluish Green
Yellow	Yellow Pale Yellow Copper-Burnished	Yellow-Red
Orange	Incandescent Orange Brilliant Orange Orange-Red	
Red	Fire Red Brilliant Red Intense Red **Purple** Luminous Red	Yellow-Red

The light of xenon is seen as intense blue and pure ("brilliant blue" or "luminous blue," say witnesses). If the UFO increases the transference of energy to the surrounding atmosphere, other colors would appear. Red-orange is quite probable, McCampbell thinks, because of the neon. The purple would result from the xenon, and the red, from the argon. The resulting colors would be derived from the excitation of the remaining gases already referred to, and their respective mixtures.

Another important aspect, one demonstrated in an exemplary manner at Fátima, is the sequence of the colors presented by the pseudo-Sun, which underscores with eloquence the different movements and corresponding accelerations of the object over Cova da Iria. How is it possible that the random assemblage of witnesses at Fátima could have anticipated such an internal consistency, one discovered, by the scientist that we have been citing, some 60 years later?

The energy originated by the UFO itself would, in this way, be responsible for the atmospheric luminosity seen around its periphery, where different levels of energy would create different colors. McCampbell expanded the search for the relationships between the colors and the UFO's movements and accelerations. In Table 5, we present his findings linking the states of energy of a UFO and the underlying physical basis for the change of color that appears at different states.[24]

Table 5: Energy States, Color, and Physical Principles (UFOs)

State	Color	Physical Principle
Zero	Metallic Appearance	Inadequate energy to excite perceptible light
One	Incandescent Blue	Merely the excitation of xenon
Two	Orange-Red	Selective excitation of neon
Three	Incandescent White	Weakening of the altered nitrogen
Four	Brilliant White	Limited ionization of all gases increased by the mechanism of the "ball of light"

When referring, in particular, to some cases of the observation of UFOs and the consequent chromatic alterations that could justify the proposed model, the scientist refers to his agreement with Michel when, in anticipation, he foresaw that "the mentioned colors appear associated, in some way, with velocity, or most probably to the rate of acceleration. The ashen silver, with an aureole of dark red, is seen when the object is still or when it is moving slowly. Afterwards, comes the vivid red. At great velocities… the colors… white, green, blue, and violet appear."[25]

It will be useful to add that this chromatic production, according to the various energetic regimes, was itself confirmed in the laboratory in the experimental works of Petit and the astronomer Maurice Viton. They established that "one can expect to see every possible color, in agreement with the regimes, electronic values, and ionization temperature. They move from dark red to yellow, passing through blue and violet, and up through dazzling white."[26]

As to the green-blue color, McCampbell believes he can associate it with the element hydrogen. Having a low threshold, hydrogen is easily excitable, even if the percentage of free hydrogen in the atmosphere is less than one part per million. But, as the cited investigator points out, each molecule of water vapor in the atmosphere contains an atom of hydrogen, permitting it, therefore, to ensure an adequate supply. The concentration of hydrogen would be greater on rainy days, when the relative humidity of the air is 100 percent and the air is full of water droplets.

This deduction deserves investigation, because we know that the atmosphere in Fátima was nearly saturated at the time of "The Miracle of the Sun." If it could be proven that on humid days the color green-blue is predominant in UFOs, the source could well be hydrogen, as McCampbell presumes. Note that at the onset of the "Miracle," the UFO above Cova da Iria had to break through saturated clouds, and there is no lack, as we know, of descriptions of the colors green and blue surrounding the "Sun."

There is still one other chromatic aspect emphasized by the witnesses at Fátima: the alteration of the environmental light. Relative to this, we note, once again, the words of Meessen:

> [T]he light produced directly or indirectly by the UFO, in some cases, might be more or less monochromatic, and thus all objects do not necessarily reflect that light. This could cause the *transformations of the color of the objects*, like those observed many times under the influence of sodium lamps placed along highways."[27]

6. MOVEMENTS OF THE "SUN"

At the time of the Fátima incident, what most surprised the witnesses were the movements of what they judged to be the "Sun." Naturally, the anticlerical republicans of the day mocked the "Miracle," considering it an anecdotal event, the invention of the credulous. On October 15th, the newspaper *Portugal* reported:

> It has been many years now since the Sun was considered, relative to our

> planetary system, as a fixed star; and the affirmation of this truth cost some sorrows to its discoverer. Now three small delinquents come along, who hit on the scientific truth to be overturned, causing, by the influences of those who dispose of the court in the sky, to dance the Sun over the chosen place of Fátima.

In our day, skeptics no longer have a basis to joke about UFO phenomena or to assert that they are the fanciful inventions of simple-minded rustics. It is evident that the Fátima witnesses spoke the truth. Thus, it is our task to investigate more deeply how the "solar" movement actually took place, so that at an earlier time, it could astound the people of Portugal.

Basing our analysis on the witness statements, we can divide the movement of the "luminous disk" into six categories:

1. Gyrating movement – spinning upon itself
2. Gyrating movement – merely on the periphery
3. Other movement
4. Position of the "Sun" in the sky
5. Movement on its descent
6. The ascent and a return to normalcy

GYRATING MOVEMENT – SPINNING UPON ITSELF

Many witnesses saw this type of movement. Let us examine the accounts of several of them:

• For the lady from Lisbon, and friend of Mimi, "It... began a *rotary* movement with an incalculable speed."

• The newspaper *Beira Baixa* reported: "The disk could be seen to rapidly *spin upon itself.*"

• Father José Curado commented: "It appeared to us to be a plate of dull silver, having a rapid and quite visible *rotating* movement."

• The newspaper *Diário de Notícias* described how "[T]he Sun appeared with the color of dull silver, in a circular *agitation*, as if it were affected by electricity."

• In the view of Inácio António Marques, "The Sun *spun about itself....*"

• *A Guarda* newspaper noted the presence of "a disk of dull silver, in a circular *agitation....*"

• The *Concelho de Mação* newspaper stated: "...At a certain moment, it was seen to be animated by a rapid *turning* movement."

• Ana Maria da Câmara did not equivocate. She said: "I saw a very clear disk, silvery blue, without rays, which quickly resumed its natural color, [then] began rolling in a dizzying manner."

• The engineer Mário Godinho described the object as "...having a movement that was like a *rotation.*"

• To Angélica Pitta de Morais: "...Immediately it became as if it were a disk of dull silver... *it turned upon itself.*"

In the official documents, there is also discussion of how the object moved so that it gyrated upon itself.

In the Vicarial Process
Manuel Ribeiro de Carvalho: "[I] saw that the Sun *spun upon itself...*"

In the Canonical Process
Luís de Andrade e Silva: "The globe of the Sun, similar to a disk of dull silver, was *spinning around upon an imaginary axis.*"

In the Parochial Inquiry
Jacinto de Almeida Lopes: "It made some *rotating*, vertiginous movements...."

And we uncovered still other witnesses:

• João Carreira: "I saw the Sun *toss and turn...* it was like the wheel of a bicycle."[1]

• António dos Reis Novo: "The Sun seemed to transform itself into a window frame, spinning very quickly...."[2]

• Júlia Franco: "Afterwards, the Sun began to *spin very* quickly, with an extraordinary speed, moved by I know not what."

• Maria dos Anjos, Lúcia's sister: "Suddenly, it stopped raining, and the Sun appeared spinning and spinning *as if it were a disk.*"

• José Maria Almeida Garrett, the lawyer: "That nacre disk had the dizziness of movement. It was not the scintillation of a star in full life. *It spun upon itself* with a breakneck speed."

• Pinto Coelho, in *A Ordem:* "...[At] other times, it seemed animated by an extremely fast *rotating* movement...."

• Father Inácio Lourenço, who viewed "The Miracle of the Sun" from 13 kilometers away: "It was like a ball of snow *rolling upon itself.*"

GYRATING MOVEMENT – MERELY ON THE PERIPHERY

Gonçalo Almeida Garrett, the mathematics dean, stated clearly that *merely the edges of the "Sun" executed the rotating movement.* He is the witness, it seems to us, whose testimony cannot easily be rebutted, especially because he described the phenomenology of what he was viewing with such rigor, even enumerating its phases. Thus, in phases three and four:

> The Sun, three times, manifested a *rotary movement on its periphery*, flickering sparks of light on its borders, similar to those that are seen [around] the wheels of the very well-known fireworks.
>
> That rotating movement on the borders of the Sun, three times manifested, three interrupted, was rapid, and lasted between eight and 10 minutes, more or less.[3]

Fig. 20 – A reproduction of a drawing published by the Capuchin Missionaries in 1955, showing the movement on the periphery of the "Sun."

It was not merely this professor who provided details with this level of particularity. A relative of reporter Eduardo Teixeira from *Jornal de Notícias* pointed out:

> The solar disk lost its brilliance and turned black; a *ribbon* the color of fire *began spinning alternately* in one and another direction, *around* the Sun. And *going around this*, equally along its entire circumference, a tremendous splendor, also the color of fire, full of majesty and of *giant dimensions*, appeared to the eyes of the many thousands of spectators.[4]

But perhaps this movement could be better explained by a design executed by Capuchin missionaries.[5] Observe Figure 20: the rotating movement on the periphery of the "disk" can clearly be seen in that design (the one the university professor observed). It has been ascertained that 14 percent of the witnesses referred to coloration being present only on the borders of the "Sun." But Father José Curado affirmed that only when it transformed into a plate of dull silver did it spin *upon itself.*

Professor Gonçalo Almeida Garrett provided a comparison that can help us. It was: "Three times, the Sun manifested a *rotating movement upon its* periphery, flashing sparks of light on its borders, like those that are given off by the firework wheels that everybody is familiar with." The priest José Curado [6] offered the same comparison: "Maybe four minutes could have passed when the Sun, *similar to a piece of stationary fireworks,* that after being lit makes a luminous circle in the middle of the dark night, made the clouds, which had been overcast, quickly disperse, [thereby] also making a circle." Beyond that, it was only when the object took on the aspect of a plate that it spun upon itself.

Canon Formigão: "The Sun at its zenith… spun dizzyingly upon itself *like the most beautiful wheel of fireworks* that one could imagine."[7]

Maria do Carmo Marques da Cruz Meneses: "...It went away like a wheel of fire."[8]

Maria Romana: "A marvelous thing was then seen! The Sun spun rapidly *as if it were a wheel of fireworks.*"

Of the 16 witnesses who testified in the *Vicarial Process*, 12 referred to the Sun spinning like "a wheel of fireworks." They were: Auzebino Francisco Mira, Romano dos Santos, Maria Vieira da Rosa, Manuel João, Sr., António Vieira Amado, João Vieira Gomes, Manuel Carvalho, Domingos Pedro, and another four who confirmed what the others had described. These witnesses signed their statements on October 25, 1917.

Maria Celeste da Câmara e Vasconcelos, the sister of the Baron de Alvaiázere, declared: "The Sun began to spin *in circles* of every color, like a wheel of fireworks."[9]

Higino Faria: "...Through the aperture [of the parted cloud], we saw the Sun shining, spinning like a *wheel of fire.*"

Maria Teresa, de Chainça: "Afterwards, it began spinning like a *wheel of* fire during popular celebrations."[10]

Mariana Pinto Coelho: "I saw it rolling with speed, like the *little wheels of stationary fireworks.*"[11]

António Marques, de Chainça: "It began to *roll* in a circle of maybe more than one meter."[12]

Another statement exists containing this same measure – that of Maria Teresa de Chainça, who, after stating that "it began spinning like a *wheel of fire during* popular celebrations," added, "It stopped for some time and began spinning, in a circumference of, perhaps, more than a meter in diameter."

When it was his turn, José Joaquim from Assunção did not speak of a circle, but of an agrarian measure with the format of a cube: "*The Sun began to draw back* within what could be a half alqueire [in Portugal, 4.84 hectares]."[13]

Beyond the gyrations, other movements are cited, including the famous dancing. Foreign authors who cover the topic habitually designate the Fátima phenomena "The Dance of the Sun." But the "dance" was only one of the various movements that the surprised multitude observed.

OTHER MOVEMENTS

In this category we include the *dance,* the *tremor,* the *sudden* and *shaky movements.* Let us let the spectators tell us what they saw:

Avelino de Almeida even entitled his report "How the Sun Danced at Midday in Fátima." He wrote in one place: "To the impressionable eyes of the crowd… the Sun *trembled*, the Sun had never seen *sudden movements*, outside of all the cosmic laws – the Sun "danced," according to the typical expression of the country folk." And he added: "A great number confess that they saw the trembling, the dancing of the Sun; others, however… swear that the Sun spun upon itself like a wheel of fireworks…"

In his article, published in *Ilustração Portuguesa,* de Almeida described what he himself saw: "What did I still see? The Sun – a disk of dull silver – in full zenith appeared and began *dancing in a violent and convulsive dance* that a great number of people imagined to be a serpentine dance...."

Manuel Pedro Marto: "At a certain height, the Sun stopped and then *began to dance.…*"[14]

The October 18th edition of *A Lucta* also spoke of the diverse movements: "It was shaken, at last, by irregular, arrhythmic movements – it trembled – trembled and was silent."

Manuel da Silva, who was 18 years old at the time: "The Sun appeared clearly and moved itself."[15]

Carlos de Azevedo Mendes: "We all saw the Sun dancing and taking on aspects that I had never seen before."[16]

Mrs. J: "…That globe or sphere agitated itself nervously as if impelled by electricity.…"

Maria Celeste, sister of the Baron de Alvaiázere, also confirmed: "I saw the Sun… *dance*."[17]

This "dancing" to which certain witnesses referred perhaps was an oscillatory movement.

Now let us see what we are told by Ana Maria da Câmara:

The clamor was immense at the moment in which the Sun descended, a movement that I observed distinctly, as well as the *movement to the right and left or vice-versa, but already at the regular altitude of the Sun.* These last two movements were much less clear than the descending movement and I cannot attest to the fact that they immediately followed this one.

Dr. Vieira Guimarães, an intransigent atheist, observed the phenomenon and, so as not to give his arm for twisting, declared that he had already seen the same thing "many times," which was, evidently, not true. That kind of response was commonplace. "The Sun appeared, being seen as if to *dance* through the diaphanous clouds...."[18]

Ferreira Borges attested also: "I saw the Sun move as though it were dancing."[19]

But there are those who pointed to different movements.

António Marques was one of them: "The clouds broke apart and the Sun appeared to tremble. It seemed to be descending, rose up in an impulse, and began to *roll in a circle* of maybe more than one meter [in size]. It stopped, and then spun, and spun again, as if it were a wheel of fire."

Maria Teresa de Chainça was another: "...the Clouds parted and the Sun appeared to *tremble.*"

In the Vicarial Process

António Ramos Mira declared: "The Sun had unusual signs... spinning upon itself, *trembling....*"

Still, it was Father José Curado who bequeathed to us the most detailed statement of the movement of the "Sun" seen above Fátima. His description included its colors, which apparently cannot be disassociated from it. Here is his account:

> Maybe four minutes had passed, when the Sun, similar to the stationary fireworks, that after being lit make a luminous circle in the middle of the dark night, made the clouds, which had been overcast, almost quickly disperse, also making a circle, and making it possible to observe a phenomenon that appeared to everyone to be extraordinary. The Sun, now without clouds, did not project its rays over the Earth, but it seemed to be wrapped in flames of a faded color. Suddenly, it lost all that light or flames and appeared to us to be a dull plate, as *O Seculo* accurately stated, having a rapid and very visible rotating movement, appearing to draw even closer to

the Earth. It could be gazed upon indefinitely without bothering the eyes.

It caught fire soon afterward, and let me say it this way, found itself then once again wrapped in rose-colored flames and still without projection of rays upon the Earth.

One minute, perhaps, having passed, it again lost its light and flames, and was seen, once again, to be a plate, now very white, with the same very rapid rotation.

Yet a third time, the Sun, which appeared to have *sudden, shaky movements*, became wrapped in bluish flames, to which followed the loss of light and the rotating movement of the plate. Then the phenomenon was over.

If we are to give credence to the account of Father Curado, the "Sun" had movements that were:

– sudden (trembling),
– shaky (oscillatory),
– circular with a wheel of fire (gyrating around its periphery),
– gyrating, losing its colors and looking akin to a dull silver plate (rotating upon itself.)

THE POSITION OF THE "SUN" IN THE SKY

Is it possible that this "plate" was in the Sun's place, in other words, in the actual spatial position of the star at the center of our solar system, the Sun?

For the majority of those present, what they had seen was the Sun; therefore, they were only impressed when it descended to the Earth.

One witness, however, claimed to see the "Sun" in numerous positions in the sky: Ferreira Borges stated: "I saw it assume *four different positions* in space, marking the three angles of a triangle."

In the Canonical Process

The Baron de Alvaiázere: "...[A]t the same time, it gave me the impression that it was *moving from its primitive position.*"

Father Manuel Pereira da Silva: "Immediately, the Sun appeared with a well-defined circumference. It approached as if *at the height of the clouds* and began spinning...."

Almeida Garrett, the lawyer, left us this interesting detail:

> The clouds, which were running lightly from west to east, did not obscure the light of the Sun, giving the easily comprehensible and explainable impression of *passing behind* [it], but, at times, the white sparks that it gave off seemed to take on, as they slid in front of the Sun, a rose or diaphanous blue tone.

Mrs. L. de S. also told us: "Suddenly, a luminous disk the size of a great host, but which we could look to as one looks to the Moon, appeared, as if it *stood out from the Sun, descending visibly* in a rotation that followed, and which after it stopped, repeated again."

MOVEMENT ON ITS DESCENT

What precise movements did it truly execute when it descended upon the crowd?

There are five designations:

- spinning
- zigzagging
- in a spiral
- dancing
- like "autumn leaves"

We can synthesize these five designations into only two:

- circular movements (spinning and spiraling)
- falling like dead leaves (zigzagging, dancing, and "autumn leaves")

Which of these two movements does the evidence support? This is not easy to determine.

a) Circular movement

Almeida Garrett, lawyer: "The Sun, conserving the celerity of its rotation, stood out in the firmament and, sanguine, advanced over the Earth, threatening to smash it with its igneous nature and the weight of its huge size. They were seconds of terrifying impression."

Ferreira Borges: "...appearing to approach the Earth in *spiral movements*."

Maria dos Anjos, Lúcia's sister: "When it descended, it appeared to us that it came *in a spin,* in a spin, in the same way as I have already seen a record playing. It appeared to be coming loose from the sky and to be suspended at the end of a wire, spinning."

But the most convincing witness in this category was the Baron de Alvaiázere. The Fatimist author Sebastião dos Reis asked him once:

> "Could Your Excellency describe for me exactly the solar phenomenon?" "Why not? Look – it was like this...." And with his index finger he drew the Sun *spinning* rapidly *upon itself*.[20]

As can be seen, the drawing exemplifies a "spinning" descent.

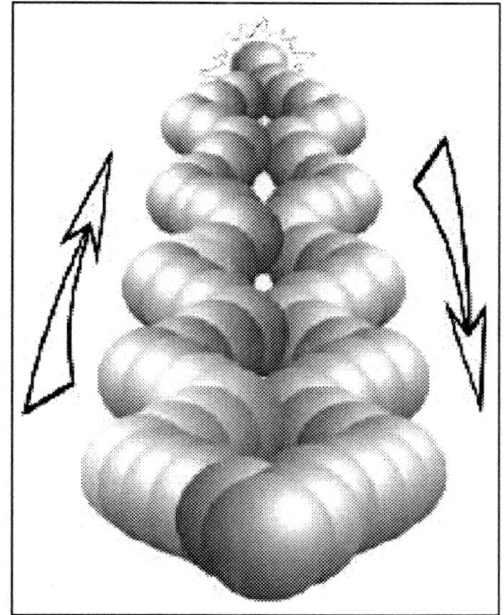

Fig. 21 – Movements indicated in the sketch made by the Baron of Alvaiazere.

b) Falling like dead leaves

There were others who spoke of another type of movement. Maybe this rotary movement was carried out merely on the ascent. As the majority were frightened upon seeing the "Sun" descending, in truth, we do not have many descriptions of that aspect of the Fátima incident.

Maria Celeste da Câmara Vasconcelos (Alvaiázere): "I saw the Sun *descend to Earth, dance, and turn and rise in a spiral,*" she told a reporter from *Stella*.

If we are to believe this witness, the Sun descended and danced (possibly oscillating "right and left, or vice-versa," as Maria da Câmara said) and ascended in a spiral.

There exists, in the meantime, a description that discussed this in a very clear way. We offer it with some reservation, because it was the statement of an indirect witness, and in this work, we have pledged to include only the direct statements of eyewitnesses. Nonetheless, it seems improbable to us that a member of the clergy, Father Alves Vieira, in a work published in 1952 [21], could have invented the following description without having taken it from observers of the "Miracle":

> Here, without delay, another even more moving prodigy was produced.... Suddenly, the Sun appeared to separate from the sky. And the crowd saw it, not precipitate itself in a dizzying fall, but *oscillate*, descending in *slow zigzags*, [in] the rhythm of a *dry leaf that falls from trees in Autumn*.... [S]creams of "Miracle! Miracle!" could be heard imploring mercy and forgiveness.

He was describing the "falling leaf" pattern familiar to all Ufologists. Was this a coincidence, or was it drawn from a description given by a heretofore-unidentified witness?

It turns out that 13 kilometers away, in Alburitel, another Catholic priest, Father Inácio Lourenço, also identified the same characteristic movement: "Afterward, suddenly, it appeared that it was *descending in a zigzag*, threatening to fall upon the Earth."

In addition to what has already been revealed, there remain two problems related to the descent:

– How many times did the "Sun" descend?
– How far did it descend?

c) How many times did the "Sun" descend?

Basing our findings strictly on the documents (and we can do nothing else), it is very difficult to conclude whether the "Sun" descended one, two, or three times. Curiously, when, in 1978, we spoke with two of the witnesses, Júlia Franco insisted that the "Sun" descended *three times*, whereas Maria dos Anjos, Lucia's sister, left us without a doubt that, in fact, it had descended only *once*. The problem has no easy solution. Fourteen percent of witnesses maintained that it fell only once, five percent said three times, and another 11 percent said that it drew closer as it spun. Only two people said it spun twice. They were Mrs. L. de S. and Manuel da Costa Pereira, in a letter addressed to the Viscount of Montelo: "I saw pass, over the upper part of the Sun, two clouds, which were illuminated by the Sun, and which ran *a second time* to the Earth."[22]

The disparity must originate from the fact that, while evincing a gyrating movement, the "Sun" seemed to descend. Dr. Pereira Gens said: "Suddenly, it began to spin around, with dizzying speed, and, at a certain altitude, it was as if it drew nearer and threatened to come down over us." Further in his account, he claimed that, in "its strange dance, rolling upon itself," it gave all "the sensation that now it drew near, now it moved away." Father José Curado, for his part, stated that, as to the rotating movement of the plate, it appeared "even as if it were moving closer to the Earth."

It seems to us, therefore, that, in its triple gyrating movement, it gave the sensation to some witnesses of descending from its initial position, and from that must have sprung the accounts that speak of the "spinning" descent. In its final movement, however, as the more qualified accounts establish, the "disk" descended quite a bit, maybe in the rhythm of a leaf falling to the ground, thereby justifying the accounts that maintain it descended only once.

> I cannot explain what then happened. The Sun began to dance and, at a given altitude, it seemed to break free of the firmament and, in wheels of fire, hurl itself upon us.
>
> My wife – we had been married just recently – fainted, and I did not have the courage to assist her. It was my brother-in-law, João Vassalo, who supported her in his arms. I fell to my knees, forgetful of everything. When I stood up, I don't know what I said; I think I began to scream like the others.[23]

This witness, who intentionally came from Lisbon, was not a country person but an intellectual. There are myriad accounts of crying, wild praying, people fainting, and all manner of madness. "There was even a lady who in a loud voice gave a general confession – 'I did this, that, and the other thing'," joked our own Maria Carreira.[24]

It is perhaps a telling fact that none of these manifestations of fear was ever described three times. From this we can surmise that the "luminous disk" must have descended only once, but in a very noticeable manner. That, incidentally, is the official opinion of the Catholic Church.

d) To where did it descend?

Father João Gomes Menitra: "I saw the Sun roll at great speed and *very close to me.*"

Manuel Francisco, a farmer, 27 years old: "The Sun began to come down to the point where it appeared as if *we were almost at the foot of it.*"[25]

Maria dos Anjos: "[I]t descended so much, so much, so much, that it acted as if it was going to fall on the Earth. It seemed to us that it only stopped descending when *it got to the trees*. Still today it seems to me that it was as if *poised over that fig tree.*"

Glória, Lúcia's sister: I saw it "descend upon the Earth, until [it was] *at the height of mid-afternoon or more.*" From this witness' statement, it is not certain whether she saw it arrive at this height while it spun or at the time during which it was closest to the multitude.[26]

A nun in the Rectory of the Colégio Português in Rome in 1953 described how: "The Sun descended downward through the sky until arriving *at the height of a pine tree.*"[27]

Since the Pines in the Leiria zone are tall (some 30 to 40 meters in height), and given the secondary effects that the "Sun" demonstrated during its descent, this statement, which correlates the fall of the "Sun" to the height of the surrounding pine trees, seems to us the most plausible.

THE ASCENT AND A RETURN TO NORMALCY

Returning to the testimony of Maria Celeste Alvaiázere: "I saw the Sun descend to the Earth, dance, and ascend again in a spiral." It seems there can be no doubt as to the movement that the "disk" executed on its ascent.

Father Alves Vieira, in his indirect report, added the detail of a falling leaf or ascendant movement, saying: "Slowly, and always with a snail's pace... it goes ascending; and recovers its usual splendor in the sky."

Descriptions such as "snail-like," "spiral," and "spinning" indicate to us a constant as to the movement executed during the ascent to its initial position.

There is a question as to how much time elapsed during all of its maneuvers, from its beginning to its return to normalcy.

Here, too, the accounts vary, although the majority of those that address this point tell us that it was 10 minutes. In the view of its witnesses, the "solar" phenomenon lasted from five to 20 minutes:

Jacinto de Almeida Lopes: "...some five minutes."

Angélica Pitta de Morais: "...some five minutes maybe, or more."

Father Manuel Pereira da Silva: "...more than eight minutes."

Almeida Garrett, dean of mathematics: "...from eight to 10 minutes."

Canon Formigão: "...close to 10 minutes." This duration was also that indicated by lawyer Almeida Garrett, engineer Mário Godinho, Joaquim Vicente, António Marques, and Maria José Monteiro.

Maria do Carmo Meneses: "...a quarter of an hour, more or less."

Carlos Silva: "...some 20 minutes."

The most probable time to us seems to be the one estimated by the professor from Coimbra, who said: "The phenomenon lasted from eight to 10 minutes."

PARALLELS IN UFOLOGY

• "[They] saw the Sun spinning like a wheel of fire...." *Vicarial Process, 2nd witness*

• "They saw a ball, similar to a wheel of fire that was spinning...." *Japan 1606*[28]

• "The Sun had never before seen movements...." *Avelino de Almeida*

• "The object was animated by restless movements..." *Portugal, 1958*[29]

• "The Sun seemed to have sudden, shaky movements, which were followed by… rotating movement." *Father José Curado*

• "It moved in an odd way, with small, transverse movements and rolling upon itself."*Lisbon, 1977*[30]

• The Sun "had unusual signs spinning upon itself, trembling…." *Vicarial Process, 1st witness*

• "A youngster saw an object… spinning upon itself and vibrating…."*Spain, 1974* [31]

• "I observed distinctly the movement to the right and left, or vice-versa." *Ana Maria da Câmara*

• The object had "light movements to the left and to the right, every so often."*Azores, 1976*[32]

• "It then began a rotating movement with an incalculable speed." *The lady from Lisbon*

• "A large disk… spinning upon itself at great speed was seen by a boy." *France, 1954*[33]

• "We all saw the Sun dancing and taking on aspects that were never seen before."*Carlos de Azevedo Mendes*

• "The object… which was at the height of the trees, oscillated like a pendulum." *Spain, 1968*[34]

Descending

• "I saw it spin around…and appear to draw closer to the Earth in spiral movements." *Ferreira Borges*

• "...Took notice of a phenomenon that descended from the sky in a spiral…." *France, 1976*[35]

• "Suddenly, it seemed to descend in a zigzag, threatening to fall upon the Earth."*Inácio Lourenço*

• "Suddenly, one of them fell toward the ground in the movement of a falling leaf." *France, 1954*[36]

• "The multitude saw it descend… in the rhythm of a dry leaf that in Autumn falls from the tree." *Father Alves Vieira*

• "Observed an object… that oscillated slowly with a movement like a falling leaf…" *Spain, 1968*[37]

• "I saw the Sun descend toward the Earth, dancing…." *Maria Celeste Alvaiázere*

"... Observed an artifact… that tottered near the ground." *Spain, 1966*[38]

Ascending

• "... And once again ascend in a spiral." *Maria Celeste Alvaiázere*

• The object, "when it rose, made a spiral movement." *Moscow, 1958*[39]

"Slowly, and always curling, it goes ascending." … And thus, the "Sun" seen above Fátima returned to its place, in other words, disappeared from the location of the actual Sun, which we hope will maintain its good state for millennia to come.

Flight characteristics of UFOs constitute an obvious challenge to the

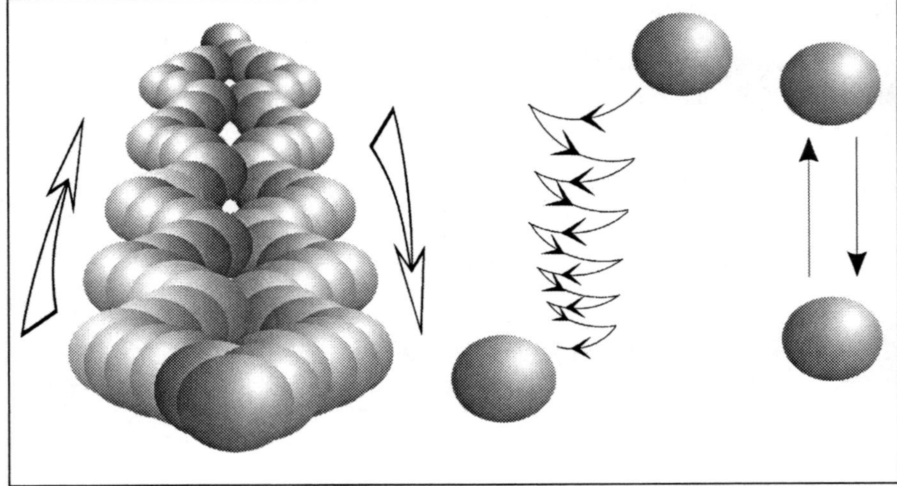

Fig. 22 – Typical movements of the "disk" that Fátima witnesses reported.

laws of physics as they pertain to inertia, gravity, and so on. By now there is no need to debate these aspects. Rather, we shall abide by the current interpretation of the facts that, in one way or another, UFOs nullify the effect of gravity upon their mass and must also annul somehow their behavior when inert. As superior beings (which we believe they are), the Ufonauts must know how to evade – and, indeed, surpass – the laws that constrain us.

We do not intend to imagine what compels these "anti-gravitational processes." Rather, the answer may lie in the plausible data of current studies into the magneto-hydrodynamic concept. Meessén thinks that UFO propulsion might be executed by reaction, which would be achieved by a dislocation of ambient air. This would be possible, without mechanical means, by electromagnetic action over the conjunction of particulates that are charged by the ionized air that envelops the craft.[40] The MDH model, let us remember, was studied by Petit and Viton and could be applied to flight in the lower atmosphere. Another scientist, cited by Meessén, the American physicist Stanton Friedman, likewise admits that plasma energy could be the basis for the propulsion system of what he has called "terrestrial excursion models"– smaller alien craft used in Earth's atmosphere.[41]

The Belgian physicist Meessén, on the other hand, conscious of the difficulties of conceiving of an anti-gravity field produced by the UFO and by which it would propel itself, suggests, as an alternative, that the craft might exert a force of repulsion over the Earth. This would act upon the craft by reaction, producing something tantamount to the effect of an "antigravity" force.

Returning to the prototype by Petit and Viton, which they designated an *aerodyne MHD*, we are confronted by its discoid form, although we see other classical forms observed ("cigars," "spheres," and so on). "Our" UFO would share – say the investigators – "a certain parentage with the helicopter and – why not? – it would have the same unstable descent (an *oscillating descent*, like falling leaves). Its *aerodynamic stability* or *immobilization* might be achieved via a velocity very weakly induced. The larger the rotor of a helicopter, the smaller the rate of speed it needs to keep the craft elevated."[42]

We can now confront what actually happened at Fátima. The weight of the evidence – from the diverse types of movement, the hovering of the object, the descent followed by the ascent, the falling leaf pattern – readily support a finding that the Fátima incident was a UFO close encounter and not a Marian apparition. This was a conclusion that the frightened people of Portugal of that time could not even consider, much less invent.

In his analysis, relative to the typical movements of UFOs, McCampbell refers initially to *suspension* or *immobilization*: the UFO does not totally defy gravity. To the contrary, it would not remain suspended forever. The investigator thinks that it could, however, have a reduction in weight and effective mass on the order of 99.3%.

As to the *descent* and the *ascent*, such a process would imply the utilization of small, lateral movements with gradual loss of altitude. The "falling leaf" or "pendulum" pattern is observed in many fly-overs at low altitude (as was the case at Fátima).

The *accelerations* are another prominent flight characteristic of these crafts. UFOs have been seen to change direction and velocity much more rapidly than known spacecraft; rather than exhibiting long curves through space, they have exhibited spins in close circles. Such erratic flight, with rapid changes in speed and altitude, was one of the consistent pieces of evidence of October 13, 1917.

Lastly, the *oscillation* (or *tremor)* and the *rotation* are movements that can be verified in the whole object or in parts, such as what is sometimes seen on the periphery (Fátima confirmed this). McCampbell notes that every type of UFO contains these characteristics. The rotation of the entire vehicle or one of its components is apparently used to maintain its stability in the air, and this would be to maintain the axis of rotation in a constant direction because of its angular acceleration.[43]

In summary, we can conclude that the movements of the pseudo-Sun of Fátima were the classic ones that have been deduced from worldwide UFO sightings and attributed, in major part, to disk-shaped objects. We can identify in them various, distinct phases:

Phase One: spinning upon itself, wherein the stabilized object shows a dull silver color (metallic);

Phase Two: *rotation on its periphery, wherein the object shows iridescent borders* (dark red, purple, or even black);

Phase Three: oscillation (sudden movements or tremors) tied to its rotation, wherein the object descends toward the ground and rises again, producing a color sequence;

Phase Four: return to the stabilization achieved during phase 1.

7. THERMAL EFFECTS

The silver globe, as well as the Sun, emitted heat when it descended to the ground. While perusing the documents of Fátima, however, one finds different statements pertaining to this detail.

Maria Teresa, de Chainça, who was 30 meters from the site of the Apparitions, told Haffert: "The sky was covered with clouds and it was raining heavily. We could not see the Sun. Then, suddenly, at noon, the clouds parted and the Sun emerged, as if trembling, appearing to descend, and *giving off great heat.*"[1]

The jurist Pinto Coelho, quoted in the October 16th edition of *A Ordem*, also confirmed that "separating itself from the Sun, [the object] approached the Earth, and *radiated strong heat....*"

In the Canonical Process

Luís de Andrade e Silva testified on December 30, 1917:

> Someone at my side called my attention to the Sun, and I noted something in its behavior that until this day I had never seen. The orb of the Sun, similar to a disk of dull silver, spun around on an imaginary axis, and at that moment appeared to descend in the atmosphere, towards Earth, accompanied at times by an *extraordinary brilliance and a very intense heat.*

As it turns out, identical accounts of a "very intense heat" being associated with UFOs are found in the annals of Ufology.

We can cite two cases, demonstrating, once again, that the "Sun" seen above Fátima has manifested itself in other parts of the world with identical characteristics and without the aura of the divine and the miraculous.

PARALLELS IN UFOLOGY

France (between Bessaillin and Cologne), December 17, 1954

A butcher saw a light over the street, which, later on, took on the shape of an object, at 80 meters. The light became more brilliant, and the witness *felt a wave of heat* and thought he was going to die.[2]

During the "Miracle," not all of the witnesses made reference to this "very intense heat," possibly because of the nature of the location. But there were those who indicated that they were affected by such heat.

Mariana Pinto Coelho, in a letter addressed to her aunt, the Marquesa da Ribeira Grande, wrote in October 1917, "I saw the Sun descend to the Earth in an extraordinary manner, and *the heat managed to be bothersome*."[3]

New York State, U.S.A., July 1956

A Starfire F-94 jet aircraft approached a brilliant, disk-shaped UFO tracked by radar at Griffis AFB. Suddenly, a *suffocating heat* enveloped the aircraft. The pilot parachuted to safety, while the plane crashed over Walesville.[4]

In the *Vicarial Process*, two testimonies also referred to the aspect of heat. António Ramos Mira, from the parish of Reguengo de Fetal:

> ...saw, a quarter hour after the rain stopped, the multitude in great clamor and almost all kneeling, turning toward the Sun, which showed signs of the unusual. [The Sun was] spinning upon itself, trembling, and he observed at the same time that around it was a reddish-yellow color that was reflected upon the entire multitude and on the horizon, having at the same time a slackening of light and *an increase of temperature.*

Manuel Ribeiro de Carvalho, also a Reguengo de Fetal native, "saw that the Sun spun upon itself, drew near to the people, and *threw off much heat...*"

These two statements, in addition to mentioning heat, refer to the matter of the "Sun" executing a rotating movement.

Let us now examine other analogous UFO cases, which, while producing heat, were seen to spin or emit different colored rays, and were similar, as in Fátima, to our Moon.

Dympep, India, October 27, 1967

"An object, [that was] spinning and emitting red and green lights, descended in the direction of the river, creating a sudden agitation of the water, [and then] rose above the forest, followed by a *gust of heat*."[5]

The heat produced by the "Sun" was not lost on the witnesses at Fátima. Among the hundreds of statements that we have chosen as the foundation of our work, 11 percent included a reference to heat in their description of the "Miracle."

Maria Augusta Saraiva de Campos made one of those:

> The rain stopped as if by enchantment. Hats were removed. *A heat that seemed as if we were entering a heated stove* was felt and the solar disk grew visible, so that it could be perceived clearly in the grayish brown layer that covered the whole sky.
>
> *The heat increased.* And the Sun seemed to descend, descend evermore, presenting new and multi-faceted changes.

Potomac, Maryland, U.S.A., October 5, 1966

On this date, a young boy saw a disk-shaped object at ground level. It elevated itself at great speed, provoking a *great wave of heat, and lost itself in the clouds*.[6]

In Fátima, there was even one who insisted that heat was only felt when the "disk" descended. Júlia Franco passed on to us this fact: "As it was spinning, it was drawing closer to us. *And when it drew closer, it grew hot.*"

At times, the increase in temperature produced by the UFOs gives rise to a rapid drying of the atmosphere. Hence, in various parts of the world, accounts like the following one have emerged:

Insigny Forêt, France, October 20, 1954

Roger Réveille saw an oval object, six meters long, at the level of the treetops, *and felt an intense heat*. The object rose vertically, and a cloud of dense smoke formed in the rain. Fifteen minutes later, the witness approached the site and found *the trees, the grass, and the ground perfectly dry*.[7]

We verified that in the Réveille case, it was rainy, there was the observation of an object, and a rapid, unnatural drying ensued. Likewise, it was also raining at Cova da Iria, when a "silver orb" was seen that produced rapid drying. But in 1917, such drying could not be understood. So it was regarded as a form of incontestable proof of the miraculous nature of the Apparitions by those who believed in them and ridiculed by those who did not. Without minimizing that fact, nor considering the drying as divine in origin, let us return to the witnesses of that day.

Emília Alves, the housekeeper, told Sebastião Martins dos Reis:

> The Miracle of the Sun I saw perfectly well.... It had been raining very much. Suddenly, when it was the hour of Our Lady's arrival, the Sun emerged hot, as is natural for it to do. Suddenly – because it was truly of a sudden – *the people were feeling soaked and also dry*. Everyone began to discuss the matter, crowing: "But how can this be? How can everyone have dried off so quickly?"

> And we looked at each other, remarking that we were dry. And we said: "This is a miracle! This is a miracle![8]

Inácio António Marques, the popular postman, claimed: "The Sun spun around upon itself, and *all who found themselves wet appeared dry, as I was one of them.*"[9]

Physician Gens also testified: "If it was true that [the] solar luminosity... weakened, the heat maintained itself, because my suit, still drenched a short while before, I felt now to be almost dry." And in another part of his book, he wrote: "The first thing we noticed, my uncle and I, was that our suits, which just a short time before [had been] completely drenched, were now perfectly dry."[10]

When asked "Did anything else extraordinary occur?"João, the son of Maria Carreira, told Haffert: "The heat rapidly dried my entire suit."[11]

Even our guileless farmer, who saw the "cloud" arrive, affirmed: "I was all wet because it had rained, and I became dry soon afterwards." We should regard this as direct evidence.

Maria Cândida da Silva, from Leiria, who at the height of the events was 31 years old, exchanged the following dialogue with Haffert: (Haffert) "You did not observe anything when you recovered your senses?" (Maria)"*My clothes were wet,* because it had rained a lot, *but they quickly* dried."[12]

Haffert interrogated many witnesses in 1960, preserving the testimony of the illiterate. He was very preoccupied with the detail of the drying of the clothing of those present, and many of those whom he interviewed responded in the affirmative.

Another helpful witness, the engineer Mario Godinho, stated:

> One fact that transpired, however, and to which I forgot to allude to, was that on that day, October 13th, [I was] completely soaked by the rain, which totally drenched my suit, as I had to change a tire in the rain. [But] without knowing how, *I found myself, immediately afterwards, with my clothing perfectly dry.*[13]

Carlos Silva, in *O Mensageiro,* stated on October 18th: "What really amazed me is that being all wet moments before, *I noticed that I was now dry*. Was this a miracle? I don't believe so. What I believe is that the same thing happened to many people."

It is odd that the majority of the statements do not confirm such drying. There even exist accounts from witnesses who clearly affirmed that they remained drenched.

Leonor Salema Manuel Atalaia, in a letter to a friend, wrote: "Oh, how we were soaked! I had a big furry coat, which I was taking for the cold, but not... my rain hat. Well, that coat stuck to me like a sponge, my suit beneath and my skin, from head to toe."

Maria Emília de S. José Lobo Moura de Vilhena Barbosa Cardoso also said, "*At 10:00 PM,* when I went to bed, *I still had my completely wet clothes on.*[14]

The group that accompanied Júlia Franco also did not have the privilege of returning home dry. One of her sisters arrived so wet that she stripped off her clothes and climbed into bed. "We, our brothers, Clementina, and Mr. Acácio's Maria...[and] Mr. Prior, *all remained wet,"* she clarified for us in 1978, "and of course dried off, because afterwards the Sun illuminated as though it were any other day." It is possible that Avelino de Almeida and other important witnesses also did not dry off, for they did not refer to this fact.

*

For Meessen, the *sensation of heat, the rapid drying after it rains*, and, in other cases, the burns that have been found on trees, on the ground, and on witnesses, can be attributed to low-frequency electromagnetic radiation, which provokes vibrations and rotations of matter on a molecular level. This principle is involved in the process known as heat-induction."[15]

McCampbell has given equal attention to these effects. He has concluded, "Heat is a common sensation in proximity to UFOs." He has cited cases where, on a rainy day, total evaporation was verified; when trees, shrubs, and the ground itself were found to be completely dry soon after a UFO had stationed itself over a location.[16] The scientist notes that the heating and evaporation of water are typical of microwave radiation, since water molecules absorb that form of energy quite efficiently.[17] Another result of this effect is the calcification of the roots of plants without visible damage to the stem and the leaves. The investigator of a case that occurred in West Palm Beach, Florida, suggested that the only known way to produce such calcification would be via heat induction through a "powerful" alternating magnetic field.[18]

The heating and drying which took place on October 13, 1917 were not metaphysical wonders. Rather, they were among the very physical causes that can be produced by the trajectory of a UFO.

Yet, were these thermal effects the only unusual or supernatural events that occurred at Cova da Iria?

Let us probe further.

8. MECHANICAL BREAKDOWNS AND SUCTION EFFECTS

"The motor of the automobile driven by Mister Fillomenau, a stonemason by trade, stopped before the approach of a great ball of fire. The car battery hesitated and the headlights went out."[1]

Accounts such as this are commonplace in Ufology. As a rule, automobiles stop, or merely lose power, for no detectable reason. The driver exits the vehicle to find out what is happening... and comes face-to-face with yet another UFO sighting.

The approach of a UFO sometimes even prompts fire.

Provençal, Louisiana, U.S.A., November 1957

Haskell Raper, Jr. was returning home by car one rainy night when he became aware of a huge object hovering over the roadway. Truck lights illuminated it. Suddenly, a ray of light was emitted from the object onto the road. This beam seemed to exert a strong power over the automobiles traveling on it, causing them to reduce speed and stop within a distance of five meters. A wave of heat enveloped the highway. The witness rushed from his car in a panic, just as his vehicle was catching fire.[2]

Still other Ufological accounts have referred to the interesting effect of suction caused by an unknown craft. The French periodical *Phénomènes Spatiaux,* for example, has described UFO close encounter incidents where car windshields have been broken as if by suction.[3]

"Other witnesses speak of a suction-like effect that the UFOs exert over automobiles," the magazine stated.

"A French fireman driving a *2 CV* [a popular, low-cylinder sedan made by Renault] encountered a UFO that passed over him. The sun visor and a part of the *windshield flew* in the same direction taken by the object. They were found 1.5 kilometers from the site." This happened on November 2, 1965 in France.

A similar case occurred on October 29, 1970 in Norway:

> A man was traveling by car near Helleland when a light similar to the arc of a welder's torch blinded him. He stopped, and saw a stationary object hovering over the highway. Suddenly, the UFO rose in the air without making any noise and sped away at a terrific speed. The man fell backward and at the same time heard a tremendous racket. It was the *windshield of his car, which was shattering into splinters.*

Let us remember two facts about these last two cases – namely, that a sun visor flew away from a vehicle and a glass windshield disintegrated into a thousand pieces.

Now, let us open the copy of *Liberdade* published in Porto, Portugal, on October 20, 1917. Turning to the third page, we read a news column entitled: "Lisbon Diary – notes and impressions." The article concerned events of the previous day.

> Two friends, whom we shall designate by the initials E.L and Mr. S. – [the latter of whom] is well known for his financial vision and great erudition in banking matters – decided to travel to Fátima.
>
> Mr. S., is Portuguese, but of foreign birth. A very serious man, he is not one who, today, might be said to be accustomed to believing in miracles.
>
> The two friends went in the same automobile, and during the trip, were laughing in anticipation of the popular superstition. Along the way, they talked about the "Miracle," and commented upon it, laughing.
>
> At a given moment, the *gasoline* they were carrying *caught fire*. It caught fire, say the experienced motorists, for no explainable reason. At the time that it caught fire, it was raining heavily.
>
> There was nothing – neither crash nor spark – to explain the phenomenon....
>
> They obtained water finally and put out the fire.
>
> The trip continued....
>
> Several kilometers later, without any impact, such as from a rock, the windshield *broke apart into thousands of pieces* and the *hood of the car was ripped off*, as if a Herculean hand had pulled it off....
>
> They stopped the car and inspected the road where the disaster had occurred, in search of some wire or tree branch that might have explained what happened.
>
> No tree branch was found! Nor the shadow of any wire!
>
> Today, Mr. S. declares that he doesn't allow anybody to talk about the Apparition of Fátima in his presence, because he considers what happened to him or her *punishment* for having laughed at the "Miracle." They are persons of high social standing and quite well known in Lisbon.

And, as so often happens in UFO cases, they requested anonymity.

In short, that which in 1917 was seen as a *punishment* for mocking Fátima as an apparition by 1970 was understood to be the "*effect of suction*" caused by a UFO. Whether one wishes to attribute to it a divine or an extraterrestrial origin, a pattern of automotive breakdown afflicted the profane, such as the vandals who attacked the shrine in 1917, as we can see in this excerpt from the *Diário de Notícias* of October 25th, published under the headline "Miracle of Fátima":

> Last night, in the middle of the night, a group that had traveled to Fátima by automobile went to the site where the very famous phenomenon took place on October 13th, of which the press has been occupied, and using an axe, cut down the tree under which the three shepherds had presented themselves on that day.
>
> They took the tree, as well as the table that some believers had set up as a modest shrine, upon which had been placed: a religious image of Our Lady; the arch that covered her… two paper lanterns; [and] two crosses, one made of wood and the other of cane wrapped in silk paper.…
>
> While leaving the vicinity, their automobile broke down, causing the driver and his companions to flee in fright, for they were fearful of being found there. The event undoubtedly produced great vexation in the spirit of believers and among good Catholics of Fátima and its outskirts.

The facts surrounding mechanical failure involving a third automobile were revealed in *A Voz de Fátima* on July 13, 1932:

> The driver and owner of the vehicle is a well known mechanic in Santarém.
>
> It was in a tavern in Santarém, in the presence of several friends, that last night, with regard to several other foolish things said by colleagues in respect to the miracle, the following was told:
>
> "As we were leaving Fátima… *the car stopped on me suddenly, in spite of the fact that the motor continued working. The third attempt gave me the impression that the front part [of the car] was rising, and afterwards it began to move*. The following day I wanted to take the car from the garage, but I could not get it to work. I examined it and did not find anything wrong with it. I took it apart and examined its behavior for 15 days. Only after that did the car begin to work. What it was I don't know, but what I do know is that my friends and I consider it a *punishment*."

Lastly, we will relate an episode that may shed some light on the incidents involving mechanical breakdown.

In 1922, adversaries of the Apparitions placed five bombs at the site. Four bombs were placed in holes in the chapel walls that had been made for that purpose. According to the Viscount of Montelo, the fifth "was placed in the cove where one can find the root of the oak tree over which, two seers told us, rested the feet of the Apparition, but it did not explode. The walls of the chapel, although quite damaged, remained standing." He added that when the dynamite was thrown to a man from Santa Catarina da Serra, he held it in his hands and even unscrewed it, removing the contents of the bomb from its casing.

Why did the fifth bomb not explode? Was it simple luck?[4] This is a pertinent question, although it might be outside the realm of the miraculous!

The Viscount of Montelo, interviewed by *A Guarda* on May 13, 1922, described the explosive device in this way: "I had it in my hands for several moments. It must have weighed three kilos. It was cylindrical and measured 13 centimeters long by eight in diameter."

Miracles? Punishments? Mere chance? Or mysterious UFO field effects?

In a study by NICAP, the American UFO research group, we find a list of close encounters that caused temporary electromagnetic effects: stopped motors (47 cases), extinguished headlights (38 cases), disturbed radio reception (33 cases), among others.[5] Studying the possible effects of an oscillating, high frequency EM field, McCampbell says: "With respect to motors, there would be induced points of high voltage in the secondary stage of the coil, having as a consequence a gap in the sparking of the cylinders, disturbing the cycle function."[6]

One of the most current studies of the evidence for UFO interference upon automotive vehicles is the catalogue published by BUFORA, the prominent Ufology group in Britain, in which it is hypothesized with equal force that microwaves possibly disturb the proper functioning of motors, especially combustion engines.[7] We are convinced that had the automobiles of 1917 radios, or had the incident with the witnesses occurred at night, we would, at this moment, have, most likely, two other effects to compare.

EFFECTS OF SUCTION UPON THE OAK TREES

In June, before "The Miracle of the Sun," another interesting effect of suction had already been verified – not over the vehicles or trees of the street, but over the very oak tree chosen by the Being for her visitations. We refer to it here, and did not do so previously, because we think that the suction that ripped the sun visor and windshield from the car of the gentlemen from Lisbon was the same force that exerted itself over the "sacred" tree.

Our trustworthy eyewitness Maria Carreira, whose testimony about them was recorded in three sources, witnessed these effects.

In *The Official Interrogations of 1923*, she testified that in June 1917 "before the apparition, she saw that the sprouts of the oak tree were luxuriant and very upright. After the apparition, the sprouts were as though inclined *in a little wheel above, toward the East,* as if the dresses [of the Lady] had knocked them over in that direction."

To J. S. Tavares, of *Brotéria*, she expressly stated:

> I heard what Lúcia said to the Apparition, although I saw nothing and did not hear the responses. I noticed, nevertheless, something noteworthy. It was in June; the canopy of the oak tree was in full bloom. When, the apparition having ended, Lúcia signified that the Lady had gone to the East, all of the offspring of the oak tree were turned east, as if, upon her departure, the hem of Our Lady's dress had brushed over them.[8]

Maria Carreira should not have said that they were "all the offspring" of the oak tree. Nevertheless, *Stella* for May 1943 furnished a third verification of her account:

We then positioned ourselves to look toward the oak tree. It was in the full flower of its growth and now, on top of the oak tree, a little wheel could be seen about *the size of the brim of a man's hat*, with the branch all laid toward the eastern side. I began to pull some of its little leaves and everyone did the same. Lúcia said, "Do not pull leaves from the top, pull them from below."

We performed a search to learn what men's hats in the Fátima region were like in that era. We found these measurements:

– circular crown, a tall little wheel: 9 centimeters
– interior of the wheel: about 18 centimeters

Naturally, these values were only approximations.

It seems that when the "luminous ramp" retreated, taking the Being with it, the shoots of the oak tree leaned towards the beam. But in a surprising and previously unpublished detail, we find that the "crown" formed by the tips of the leaves inclined in the *opposite* direction of the "ramp"! This fact tends to verify an effect typical of suction or aspiration.

According to Meessen, "the effect produced is similar to that of a force that acts upon the bodies in relation to their mass, like the force of gravity but in a contrary sense, making it tempting to admit that this 'levitation' is really

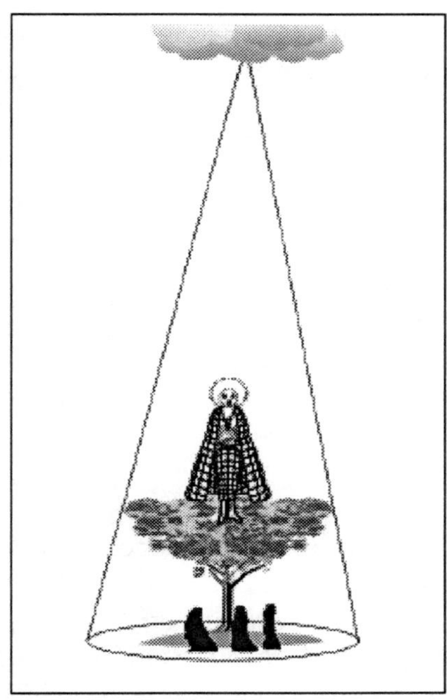

Fig. 23 – The "luminous ramp" that carried the Being toward the Seers, according to the description provided by Gilberto Fernandes dos Santos.

produced by a force of that kind." The fundamental hypothesis that he advances to justify the totality of effects– "anticipated" in the phenomenology of Fátima – is the existence of a force field, of a gravitational type, acting upon all the parts of the craft and its immediate ambient environment. This conforms to the "anti-gravity" hypothesis that has yet to be verified by contemporary physicists.

Meessen has proposed a model of how such a UFO might be shaped. He supposes a craft that pushes the air out of its way, ejecting it out of its tail, formed in a type of bell. In the posterior part of the craft, there would be a depression for the creation of a strong quasi-vacuum. The tendency to compensate for this depression would translate, according to his model, for *the effect of aspiration in a limited zone*, situated in the interior of the faring, where the air is dislocated toward the rear.[9]

Such an effect – the cases attest to it – is capable of lifting animals from the ground. It is even strong enough to affect the performance of a military helicopter in flight. This was confirmed on October 18, 1973, when a reserve U.S. Army captain found his machine "sucked" along by an unknown object.[10] Let no one be astonished by the fact that sun visors, windshields, and trees can also be aspirated, such as occurred at Fátima during the months of the "Miracle." We

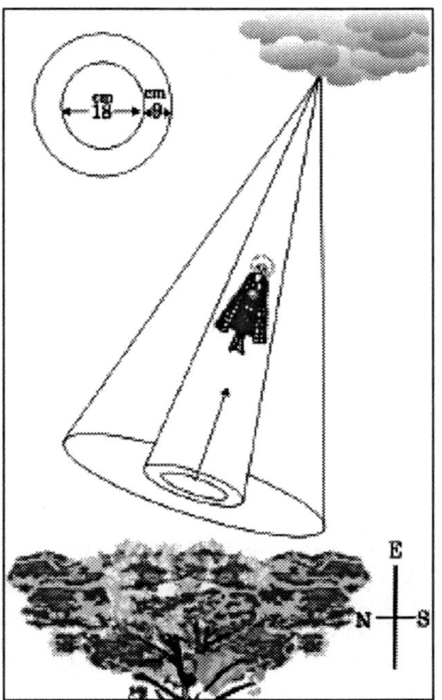

Fig. 24 – The "luminous ramp" carrying the Being, moving back to its point of origin at the oak tree, a movement that produced a "crown-like" suction effect, according to Maria Carreira, the fourth seer.

think, therefore, that the small oak tree at Cova da Iria may have been the first earthbound object – in known annals – to have experienced the effect of suction from a UFO. But it was in no way the last.

There were two later cases:

Sainte-Foy-les-Lyon, France, June 12, 1952

A UFO hovered over the Bramatan castle some 20 meters above the ground. The occupants of two roadways, who were driving along nearby, pulled over to observe the craft as it moved in various gyrating pulses. The branches of the trees and the witnesses' hair both seemed to be attracted to the object.[11]

Matosinhos, Portugal, January 21, 1980

Maria Helena Araújo Ferraz, a hospital employee, observed a luminous object in the shape, she said, of "Saturn" hovering stationary above a stone pine tree. At a certain moment, she saw that from the object arose a beam of transparent, white light that bathed the tree. The witness reported "the extremities of the tree-top were standing erect in the direction of the object, forming a concavity, giving the impression that the branches were going to be ripped out."[12]

It seems unnecessary for us to call attention to the fact that in this last case, the beam of light was associated with the flexing of the branches toward the object. It bears saying that here also the luminous beam is described as having defined limits, contrasting with the darkness of the horizon. Needless to say, the young witness was unaware of the description of 1917.

We believe that the presence of this factor involving the object will be determined in accordance with the hypotheses already exposed.

9. SIMULTANEOUS CURES

When the silver disk descended, nearing the multitude, other "miracles" took place. Some witnesses, without it having been asked for by them, and without prayers or penances performed on bended knees, found themselves suddenly cured. There were others who discovered when they arrived home that they were better. Still others noticed days later that they were free from chronic illnesses.

Might those cures, occurring in Fátima on October 13, 1917, have a supernatural explanation, a divine origin? Might they be the fruit of believers' fantasies? Or could they be a secondary effect similar to what has resulted, in other parts of the world, from direct contact with the UFO phenomenon?

Once again, let us compare what we have been told by citizens of different countries closer to our time with the statements of witnesses present at the famous "Miracle of the Sun."

PARALLELS IN UFOLOGY

Southeastern France, November 2, 1968, 4:00 AM

We have purposely referred, *supra*, to the "thunder," "lightning," and "whitened clouds" perceived by the French physician who woke to the screams of his infant son. The reader will recall that the doctor approached "the terrace and saw, at a short distance, two identical objects in disk form, that progressively drew closer to each other, until they fused together into a single object." After having heard an explosion, seen the object instantaneously disappear, and detected a "whitish" cloud, that lingered in the sky where the anomalous craft had been, he found himself the object of a "miraculous" healing:

> Three days earlier, the doctor accidentally wounded himself in the leg with a piece of wood, which caused a bruise. Shortly after the disappearance of the UFO, the doctor woke his wife, to alert her as to what had just transpired. He realized that at that moment, the wound in his leg was completely healed. Furthermore, other symptoms resulting from the war, such as partial paralysis on his right side, with difficulty standing, *were gone after the observation*, enabling the witness to perfectly balance over his right foot.[1]

As we can see, this account shares four commonalities with the phenomena observed at Fátima:

- *lightning* reported prior to a storm;
- the *sound of an explosion,* popularized as "thunder" heard at Fátima;
- a whitish cloud traveling close to the ground;
- the *healing* of recent wounds and long-standing infirmities.

But let us select from the annals of Ufology several other cases of spontaneous healing that occurred outside of the religious context.

United States of America, July 30, 1954

Buck Nelson boasted of receiving in his home humanoid beings that disembarked from a flying saucer. He stated: "The most extraordinary and frightening part of this visit occurred when I tried to signal the disk with my lantern. A very brilliant ray of light, *much hotter and more luminous than the Sun*, exited the craft and reached me with great force, causing me to fall down. Since I suffer from *lumbago and neuritis*, I was afraid to move or to get up, as I might receive another blow.... But when I wanted to rise, I was alarmed to find that I had no pains. *They never troubled me again.*"[2]

Damon, Texas, U.S.A., September 3rd and 4th, 1965

On September 3, 1965, an alligator bit policeman Robert Goode on the left hand. That night, his wound was still bleeding and suppurating while he patrolled State Road 36 with his fellow officer, Billy MacCoy. "Precisely after midnight, they saw a UFO in the sky that measured 60 meters in length by 15 in width. When they accelerated their patrol car to flee, a *luminous ray reached Goode's left arm,* which was resting on the door frame, *giving him a sensation of heat*." A short while later, he discovered that "the pain was passing, the blood was staunched, the suppuration had stopped, and the scar was beginning to fade at a rate that was really beyond normal."[3]

Peru, December 9, 1968

> "At 3:00 AM, a customs officer was on the terrace of his house, when he saw a UFO moving at close to three kilometers. Suddenly, the craft *emitted a ray of light* in his direction, with a color that varied from dark-red to violet, and that irradiated his body. The officer stated that *he no longer required eyeglasses for his myopia, since his vision had returned to normal, and that he no longer suffered from rheumatism.*"[4]

To be sure, on October 13, 1917, the pilgrims did not go to the site of the Apparitions on crutches. They did not gather there to ask God for medical cures. Rather, they were motivated to attend by the announcement that a "miracle" would be performed. And what did they see? A "Sun" that emitted *rays* and that, at the time in which it approached the Earth, *irradiated heat*. Now, if that "Sun" was effectively a UFO, it would not be natural to see people freed from chronic ills, or to find inexplicable cures in witnesses who had not come there to solicit such blessings from their Father in Heaven.

Nevertheless, it seems evident that spontaneous healings took place at Fátima *when the "luminous disk" descended to Earth.* Just as in France, America, and Peru, so too at Fátima, surprised Earthlings received "medical treatment" without previous consultation.

But let us allow those who benefited from these unusual cures to speak for themselves, for on that day, it was they who established proof of a superior science.

Maria Emília de S. José Lobo Moura de Vilhena Barbosa Cardoso. In a letter written January 13, 1918, which is part of the *Arquivos Formigão,* she wrote:

> I did not think at all of being able to be cured there, not as the result of not believing in the power of God, but more from not having formed an idea of what would happen, although I might have believed that there was something supernatural going on. Once the great miracle had taken place, I asked for nothing that would give me respite. My mother, being aware of that fact, told me, "Someone asked for themselves; it was me." I asked her, "What did [you] request?" My mother stated, "One of her requests was for her health." I then noticed that since two days ago, *I felt no pain in my arm that I have always had, as the result of malaria.* Usually, it was not strong; because of the Word of God, however, it disappeared.... One of the doctors who had examined me previously had spoken of operating on it, an option that, in turn, was disapproved of by the attending physician. He declared that it would not heal and that my illness was incurable, which he affirmed to me again on July 6, 1917, adding that I should just resign myself to living with it.... The doctor just saw me again on December 8th. He knew nothing of my trip to Fátima and, tremendously spooked, told me that he found nothing wrong with me....

It is interesting that this witness was motivated to insert her account of the request for a healing made by her mother, as a way to rationalize her own unexplained healing.

Branca de Sousa Lobo Vilhena de Barbosa. She related in a letter, dated December 30, 1917, one that is also found in the *Arquivos Formigão*, that after attending the "Miracle," she was ill with a fever and began to perspire *the following day, and that as a result, she noted that she had none of the symptoms of malaria that had annoyed her constantly.* She would fully recover and return to her former activities.

Other remissions experienced at Fátima were even more spectacular.

Mário Godinho. His mother...

> "...had suffered from a tumor in the lachrymal sacral font [the principal tear duct of the eye].... "Over many long years, she was treated by doctors. But, periodically, the ailment increased in volume, and on October 13th it was quite obvious. Upon her return, however, and *already home, she noted that the tumor had completely disappeared.* It did not appear again, nor did she feel the slightest discomfort during the 35 additional years that she lived."[5]

Maria do Carmo, de Maceira. Another much related case in the bibliography of Fátima is that of Maria do Carmo, a native of Arnal, Maceira Parrish, Leiria Diocese. She was 47 years of age and married.

Gonzaga da Fonseca wrote:

> For five years, she had suffered from a malady that presented all the symptoms of tuberculosis, aggravated since the beginning of 1916, with acute and persistent pain in her entire body, and other ailments. A tumor in her uterus was suspected. A ray of hope illuminated her soul, and she made a promise to go four times to Fátima, on foot and barefoot, to receive intercession from the Holy Virgin for her longed-for cure.
>
> On August 13th, she wanted to act on her vow, but her husband was adamantly opposed. He said, "We are poor and do not have the money to rent a car. On foot, it would be impossible. You could die on the road. Be patient. I will not let you go." She insisted, however, so much so that her husband had to yield. Supported by him, she took to the road at 1:00 AM.[6]

Gonzaga da Fonseca went on to write that in August, she felt some improvement, and in September, still more. But on October 13th, "she was caught in a torrential rain, under which she arrived at the site of the Apparitions with her clothes soaking wet." Moving now to a parallel account authored by the Viscount of Montelo, who reported on this case in the October 5th, 1918 edition of *A Guarda* [from which da Fonseca extracted a summary], we find that "the pains disappeared, never to return. *The intumescences of her uterus and her arms and legs disappeared, as if by magic.*"

Higino Faria. Some of the reported cases suggest that healings took place on October 13th. Higino Faria, who lived 13 kilometers away, told Haffert that he saw pass in front of his house "caravans of people, trudging along in every possible way, many barefoot, many from distant provinces, like Alentejo and Algarve."[7] He was sick, and constipated, with a hoarse throat, but he asked anyway, "Where are all of these people going?"

Apparently, he could not resist the enthusiasm of the passing parade, for Faria wound up going and getting wet like everyone else. "When I arrived, at 11 o'clock, I was surprised to see the great throng of people on the slope of the hill," he told Haffert. He could see that the crowd was "completely wet, dirty, and shaking from the cold," yet "awaited the moment of the miracle."

At the end, Faria remembered, "everything ended up clean and dry. I, who was sick, *returned completely well.*" He was greatly affected by what had transpired, and told Haffert years later, "In appreciation for such bountiful Grace, and because of my cure, I promised to recite the Rosary all the days of my life."

The Viscount of Montelo worried considerably over the healings that were taking place in the province of Aljustrel. In his work *Os Acontecimentos de Fátima* [*The Events of Fátima*], he related a case involving the healing of a man's chronic maladies, as is sometimes reported in modern UFO cases.[8]

Joaquim Vieira, of Assentiz. We already know this witness for having left us his observations in the previous months. On October 13th, he also sojourned to the Cova. At the time, he was 47 years old. The Viscount of Montelo wrote: "*He suffered from long-standing and serious infirmities*, and had become disillusioned with doctors. *He was healed on October 13, 1917.*"

Maria Carreira. Maria Carreira, her daughters confirmed in 1978, had also lost faith in her physicians, when the miraculous intervened. She stated while she was alive: "It had been seven years in which I was told by my doctors that I had an incurable condition and would only have a short time to live. [Afterward], from the time I set foot on that blessed site, I neither felt any pain anywhere nor my illness in any way."[9]

While it is not clear if Maria Carreira can be counted among those who were healed on that momentous day in 1917, or shortly thereafter, we note, *en passim*, and with great interest, that she lived until 1949. The fact that she lived for 39 years after her doctors told her that her condition was incurable, and 32 years after the Fatima incident, may have been due, at least in part, to the healing energy that the "Miracle" brought with it.

Alas, what can we conclude? Was it the Virgin Mary who cured the pains of rheumatism, the symptoms of ancient ills, the cysts and tumors of the afflicted who found their way to Fátima, not in search of cures, but curious to bear witness to the miraculous? Or might it have been the result of the fact that their journey brought them within close proximity to the "silver disk," when it "descended to the height of a pine tree?"

10. THE CREW MEMBERS OF THE "SUN"

Among the people from the area who watched the "solar" exhibition was Maria dos Prazeres. She was standing beside a married couple that was observing the phenomenon with binoculars. Years later, describing her experiences for Haffert, she stated, "I saw the Sun spin upon itself. It seemed that it was falling from the sky. Near me were a man and a woman looking at the Sun with binoculars. *They were saying that they were seeing a ladder close to the Sun....*"[1]

This statement speaks to us of two objects. One was detectable with the naked eye; the other took the form of a ladder – in other words, an object rectangular in shape, visible only through binoculars.

Maria dos Prazeres continued, "They were viewing a ladder near the Sun, and could see that Saint Joseph and the Baby Jesus were there."

It would seem, therefore, that in addition to the seers, other people could make out anthropomorphic figures in the "stars," whose identity, at the time, could only be understood in terms of religious figures taken from their governing belief system.

But could the multitude manage to see them only using binoculars? In fact, there were those who said that they saw something *within* the Sun. This aspect is little known. It establishes that the Sun not only spun and descended – facts that already provoked alarm – but did so while carrying passengers. Imagine what would have happened, in that time and place, had it been concluded that the "Sun" was a manned space capsule.

As for the observation of entities seen within the "Sun," we can divide the statements made about them into three categories:

1. Lúcia's testimony;
2. The testimony of the other seers;
3. The testimony of the crowd.

LÚCIA'S TESTIMONY

As early as August 25th, the seer told the parish priest that in October, "Saint Joseph would come with the Baby Jesus to give peace to the world. Our Lord will come to bless the people. Our Lady of the Rosary will appear with an angel on each side. We will see Our Lady of Sorrows beneath an arbor of flowers."

So here it seems that Lúcia, much earlier than October, was already certain that she would come to "see" the aforementioned figures, a conviction that would be reflected in that which, on the last day, she stated that she observed.

Let us examine the diverse declarations that Lúcia made to the following parties:

a) *To the Parochial Inquiry*

The *Parochial Inquiry* summarized Lúcia's account as follows:

> Once lost from sight, [Lúcia] looked toward the Sun – but not because [Our Lady] had commanded it – and saw *Saint Joseph from the waist up,* dressed in white. Saint Joseph was to the left of the Sun and *was blessing the crowd with his right hand.* It seemed to her that he made three or four crosses over the people. Our Lady could be seen beside the Sun.... *This vision disappeared,* she said, and everything turned yellow for a few moments and then she saw Our Lord, who appeared dressed in white, to the right of the Sun; and to the right of Our Lord she saw Our Lady, in full form, standing.... All these visions had a yellow resplendence, *except that of Saint Joseph.* At the time that she was seeing these *representations,* the crowd screamed, "Look... look! How beautiful!"

b) *To the Viscount of Montelo*

Lúcia told the Viscount of Montelo: "The Lady appeared dressed as the Lady of Sorrows, but without a sword on her breast, and the Lady was dressed I know not how, but it seems to be that she was our Lady of Carmel." Asking himself if a simultaneous vision of these three figures was possible, the Viscount of Montelo put this question to the seer on the same day as "The Miracle of the Sun."

Lúcia responded: "First, I saw our Lady of the Rosary, Saint Joseph, and the Baby Jesus. Afterward, I saw Our Lord. Then, Our Lady of Sorrows, and finally, the Lady who seemed to me to be Our Lady of Carmel." The figures, Lúcia said, appeared "at the foot of the Sun, after Our Lady disappeared from the foot of the oak trees." She saw Our Lord "*...only from the waist up.*" The masculine figures, she stated, wore "scarlet robes."

On October 19th, she told the Viscount of Montelo that she saw "*a figure, that appeared to be a man,* beside the Sun."

To confuse the matter even further, we find that in the same month, she told the editor-in-chief of *O Mensageiro:* "I could not distinguish well, but *it seems to me that I saw the face of a man and a child.*"

c) *Other declarations of the seer*

On October 13th, she told Mrs. L. de S., of *Raio de Luz,* that "Our Lady appeared to her with Saint Joseph and the Child standing at Her feet. The Baron de Alvaiázere, questioning her days later, came to learn that the seer "saw Saint Joseph in the Sun." She told Gilberto dos Santos that "beside the Sun were Our Lady, Our Lord, and Saint Joseph, blessing the people."[2]

d) *Previous declarations*

In her statement of 1922, Lúcia informed us: "We looked to the Sun and saw, on the right side of the Sun, *a man from the waist up*, with a child on his lap, making crosses with his right hand, and, on the other, he had a child dressed in white." She saw that "They were surrounded by a great splendor, that did not allow us to look as long as we wanted." Again, figures identified with the Holy Family *disappeared*, reappearing, "located this time, on the right side of the Sun, Our Lord visible from the waist up. On the other side, Our Lady of Suffering, always covered with a brilliance that seemed to blind us. With this, they *vanished.*"

In 1924, Lúcia again testified, her statements designated *The Official Interrogatory of Lúcia*. In this text, she reaffirmed, with one or two minor alterations, previous statements that she had made with respect to the appearance and disappearance of the celestial figures. Curiously, she affirmed that, in relation to the human form, seen from the waist up, beside the Sun, *the idea came to her that the man might be Saint Joseph.*

This tentative identification by her of what she observed as figures corresponding to her religious preconceptions is confirmed in this statement extracted from her *Memórias,* redacted in 1941: "I saw Our Lady, who *gave me the idea* of being Our Lady of Sorrows.... *It seemed to me* I could still see Our Lady in a form similar to Our Lady of Carmel."[3]

In response to a request for information, Lúcia wrote Father Gonzaga, O.C., on August 27, 1946, "...As *they had already told us* that in the last month Our Lady of Sorrows and Our Lady of Carmel would come, from that came the *intimate certainty* that Our Lady was showing herself to us in those different aspects."[4]

Lúcia, on another occasion, claimed to have not observed "The Miracle of the Sun" at all. She said that while the multitude watched the phenomenon, she was diverted by the images, by which changes were produced. As she explained in 1947 to D. José Pedro da Silva, these were seen "*in sudden changes of light*."[5] A priest was said to have seen the Holy Family *during the "solar" movements, by not fixing his eyes on the Sun.* The figures were made of light, such as an angel might be. "*From the moment that I saw them, my gaze was riveted and I no longer saw the Sun.*"

By today's reckoning, this suggests two possibilities: first, either Lúcia perceived images not contemplated by the others, or, second, that it was not the actual Sun in which she saw the figures, rather some form of interstellar craft that was executing the "solar" movements. In light of the apparent spatial reference of the figures seen, these may have been projected images, somehow impressed on the minds of those present, evoking the religious personages fixed in their belief systems. Technically speaking, such an effect is no longer even an earthly "miracle."

THE TESTIMONY OF THE OTHER SEERS

Jacinta provided the most interesting detail to the Viscount of Montelo. She told him that the "Child" was on the right side of Saint Joseph, did not reach his waist, and was the same age as a child that she knew named Deolinda, who was about two-years-old. It was Jacinta who observed that the dress of the Lady situated at the foot of the Sun was different from the dress of she hovering over the oak trees. As to the vestments of Saint Joseph and the Child, "they were scarlet."

Francisco agreed with the comparison made between the Child and little Deolinda. He denied, however, seeing the Lady of Sorrows and the Lady of Carmel, stating that he merely saw Our Lady, Saint Joseph, and the Child "near the Sun." Yet, he was able to confirm, "Our Lady seems to have been the one I saw below, or looked like the one that I saw below. She was dressed in the same way."

THE TESTIMONY OF THE CROWD

Among those present, did some detect the beings within the "Sun" or near it? Indeed, they did. And those accounts can be most closely dated to the 13th.

After October, no one risked supporting that notion, and in public opinion there was a conformity approaching unanimity that it was the Holy Family that had been observed close to the Sun. In fact, it seems that it was in the very interior of the "Sun" that such observations were made. What others saw were three beings, the same as those Jacinta and Francisco saw – a man, a woman, and a smaller being.

OBSERVATIONS OF THE VIRGIN

Avelino de Almeida: "And afterward, they asked one another if they saw what they saw. A great number confessed that they saw the trembling, the dancing of the Sun; others, however, declared having seen *the smiling face of the Virgin herself."*

República, October 17, 1917: "There were those who saw, *in the light of the solar orb*, the face of the Virgin take shape."

Dr. Vieira Guimarães, the intransigent atheist: "The Sun appeared, seen as if dancing through the diaphanous clouds, which caused to be released, from the mouths of more than 15,000 people, rapidly and in unison, the exclamation *Miracle!*, as they arrived at great faith by seeing *Our Lady brilliantly shining in the day like a star*."

The Lady from Lisbon, in her letter to her friend Mimi:

> *Our Lady became visible* to several people; I was not visited upon by such grace, [for] it was not necessary [for such a thing to happen to me in order] for me to believe. It was Rita and Betina who had that happiness, and many other people.
>
> Rita saw *the face of Our Lady before the Sun, only her face*, and it was becoming... I know not how to describe it.... She lost track of time and cannot describe what she saw. She doesn't know. Nothing can compare to the beauty and sweetness of that smile. Betina, was then, the one who contemplated it most of all. She was Our Lady of the Rosary come, lovely, to descend to us.... For her *it vanished just at the moment that it neared the Earth*. She was telling Regina, while crying and shaking, "Don't you see? It is Our Lady of the Rosary. But don't you see?" Many other people saw.

A Lucta, October 18, 1917: "An illustrious doctor from my country, who was already the fine flower of local Jacobinism, I was told, was screaming, like one possessed, hands crossed, eyes rolled back into his head, 'There goes the Virgin! There she goes!' And I would not be surprised if the man saw her."

The eighth witness of the *Vicarial Process*: "Adriano Matos, married, of Alqueidão da Serra... says that he looked straight at the Sun without any discomfort and it represented itself to him so that he saw *Our Lady with the Child Jesus* in her left arm and different colors surrounding the star."

SAINT JOSEPH

Júlia Franco: "There was one who said that he or she saw *Saint Joseph in the Sun*. We saw nothing. The gentleman Prior of the See of Leiria also saw nothing else. We spoke about each step on that day, here at home, and all of us had seen the same thing."

A cynic: "The people from my land were returning from Fátima, with their bags on their heads, skirts raised, legs on view; by their priests' rigmarole, over-pious and narrow-minded. It was known that Saint Joseph had blessed the perverse people and that our soldiers would return from the war any day now...."

Maria do Carmo Marques da Cruz Meneses: "And, at the same moment, *I saw Saint Joseph with the Child* on his lap *in the Sun,* which *had stopped descending*, taking on, instead, its own natural color, but looked at as one looks upon the Moon, *without making the slightest impression*. And it was not only me who saw [this]; many people saw [it]."

Many who were there would be surprised that anyone had seen, within the dull, silvery disk, humanoid figures. It is important to remember that Ermelinda Vilhena Barbosa stated that it seemed to her that, at a certain height, the Sun had turned "transparent." Maria do Carmo Meneses said that it was at the end, when it stopped descending, that she observed beings *in the Sun*, and not beside it.

Glória, the sister of Lúcia stated:

> At the moment that I looked to the Sun, I saw, myself, like the majority of those present, Saint Joseph and the Child, *who had his arm extended,* as one who gives a blessing. The people, terrified, screamed, imploring the mercy of God. I became like a fool; I knew not what was to be done. While that affliction lasted, we noticed that the Sun shone with tranquility, already in its place.[6]

Was a blessing or greeting directed towards the multitude? Maria dos Anjos told the authors in 1978, "There were people who said that they saw, beside the Sun, a hand giving a blessing."

THREE BEINGS

"[Lúcia] further tells us that 'there were many people who saw the Holy Family.'" And it was that observation that went down in history.

There exists a statement in the *Vicarial Process*, however, that synthesizes all of the other statements and may correspond more closely to the truth. It reads: "António Vieira Amado, married, from Alqueidão da Serra... said that he *saw the Sun very clearly, and represented within it were to be seen* three images...." Even though this witness was deposed in an official document, one elaborated by a member of the Church, this witness did not associate the figures he saw with the principal figures of the Catholic religion. In front of the expression were "three images," he emphasized, "and in front of the Sun diverse colors." He saw, it would seem, three figures within the interior of the "Sun" and diverse colors before it.

Scarlet is a color associated with the Church, especially the Papacy and the College of Cardinals. Oddly, in the immense font of contemporary UFO cases, beings in scarlet vestments also appear.

PARALLELS IN UFOLOGY

Las Rosas, Grand Canary Island, June 22, 1976

"The medical doctor, Dr. Francisco Padron, accompanied by more than a dozen witnesses, observed a great, *transparent* sphere, flying at low altitude, through which the sky could be seen, and within which were two beings of great height, although *one was taller than the other*. The beings were standing on a totally spherical platform and were wearing uniforms scarlet in color.[7]

These beings were standing. Others, smaller, have been seen sitting inside transparent UFOs.

Itaperuana, Brazil, December 20, 1971

On this day, a witness observed "a strange round or oval craft, entirely illuminated by a strong bluish light.... The transparency of the object permitted the observer to see more than *two people similar to the first* [*90 centimeters in height*], *seated, apparently looking in her direction.*"[8]

Even more interesting is the fact that in other parts of the world, crewmembers of unknown craft have also extended their arms to the Earthlings observing them.

Papuásia, Boianai, Papua New Guinea, June 26, 1959

"The Rev. William Gill and several dozen indigenous people observed various circular objects hovering over the length of the island. One of them approached, and the witnesses saw *four silhouettes on its upper part*. Those present became engrossed with the presence of the UFO, which even parked itself over them. *Reverend Gill then attempted to communicate with the beings* seen in the object. *Waving his arms, he saw that his gesture of communication was answered by the occupants of the UFO,* who *likewise waved to the witnesses on Earth.*"[9]

Granja de Torrehermosa, Badajoz, Spain, August 1956

Two dozen youth observed a flying object that stopped some 500 meters away. It had a transparent window, and in its interior could be seen *the head and shoulders of two beings*. The youth and other people ran to the craft *gesticulating to its occupants, who reciprocated those gestures.*[10]

Comparing the beings seen at Fátima with the amiable crew members of UFOs observed elsewhere, we find the following similarities:

a) Partial observation of beings. At Fátima, they were seen from the waist up, or merely faces were seen. In the Badajoz case, the heads and shoulders of the beings were seen;

b) Different-sized occupants. At Fátima, the smallest was given the name of the Baby Jesus. In the Grand Canary Islands, although quite tall, one being was taller than the other. And in Brazil, the beings measured nearly 90 centimeters;

c) Different positions of beings within the craft. In Fátima, they were seen standing, partial, or in half-body. In Brazil, they were seen seated; in the Grand Canary Islands, standing;

d) Transparency of the "solar" object (cf. the cases in Brazil and the Grand Canary Islands);

e) Beings that move their arms. In Fátima, these movements were interpreted to be acts of blessing. In other places, they were believed to communicate something, or were interpreted as friendly greetings (cf. the cases in Spain and Papua New Guinea).

11. OBSERVATIONS ON THE SAME DAY

There are those who may defend the notion that "The Miracle of the Sun" was a collective illusion, consisting of images induced by the celestial beings, a surreal scenario projected on the minds of the multitude. Yet, the announced "Miracle" was not merely observed in Fátima nor was it limited to the same timetable. Those observations made on October 13th can be divided into two groups:

1. Simultaneous observations
2. Non-simultaneous observations

SIMULTANEOUS OBSERVATIONS

There were different people in the area that did not go to Cova da Iria. While some expected to see something in their region, the others never considered the possibility of observing anything.

One of the more privileged vantage points was Alburitel, which lies in a straight line, some 13 kilometers away. There the population prepared itself, procuring elevated sites, and waited, as did the spectators at Fátima. Could they really have seen the "Miracle?"

ALBURITEL

Mother Maria do Carmo da Fonseca, later the secretary to Canon Formigão, was then four years old and the daughter of Delfina Pereira Lopes, an elementary school teacher from the area. In a letter she wrote to the University of Coimbra professor, Pacheco de Amorim, in 1958, she related:

> I remember perfectly the alarm of the population on that day, the fear that overcame many people, because the phenomenon was seen there in a manner almost as spectacular as in Cova da Iria. There is a proof that I consider formidable, to attest to the prophecy of the Seers of Fátima. It was known beforehand that the miracle promised by the apparition would be given "in the stars." ...For that reason, on the morning of October 13, 1917, there were those who, in my town of birth – Alburitel – occupied themselves turning

> dark panes of glass by candlelight to be able to observe the Sun without damage to their eyesight. And still the sky was burdened with dense clouds. This fact is absolutely verifiable. I witnessed it myself. I remember it as though it were today. A group of "locals" gathered and, despite the bad weather, went to a hill from where a very vast horizon can be seen, making it possible to see, quite far off, the smooth mountains of Fátima. That group waited there until "solar midday."

Immediately following, Maria do Carmo da Fonseca transmitted her memories to Father Joaquim Lourenço, who, at the time at which he wrote – June 10, 1958 – was the Rector of the Sanctuary:

> Her Reverence perfectly remembers the pathetic and dramatic things that occurred on that hillside at that hour. Suddenly, the Sun pulled apart the clouds and showed itself in a dizzy, rotating movement, only to later descend impetuously, giving the impression that it was going to come loose from the firmament [and] kill us all. The people present – some 20 – began clamoring in loud screams, asking God and Our Lady for help, judging that they would die without delay. And when *the Sun gave a jump over them*, the panic could not have been greater. They threw themselves to the ground and awaited the smashing – seconds which must have seemed like years! Even as recently as last year, Reverend Dr. Joaquim Lourenço told me that, thrown to the ground and seeing that death was delayed, [he] lifted his head a bit and saw that *the Sun had climbed and turned around there above,* emitting, without hurting one's sight, a multi-colored light, something never seen. *That solar jump was tripled,* and each time, the people would throw themselves to the ground, screaming, judging it to be the end of their life.[1]

The mother of this "religiosa," who in 1958 was still alive at 86 years of age, found herself at school with some of her students. One of them, a nine-year-old, was Joaquim Lourenço's brother. His name was Inácio, and in 1932, when he was a missionary in Goa, he wrote his testimony, which is now broadly disseminated:

> It was midday, more or less, when we were scared by the screams and shouts of some of the men and women who were passing in the street before our tiny school. The teacher, very good and pious, but easily impressionable and excessively shy, was the first to run to the street and was not able to avoid all of the children running after her.
>
> In the street, the crowd cried and screamed, pointing to the Sun, without responding to the questions that, very upset, our teacher asked them.

> It was the great miracle that could be seen distinctly from the height of the hill, where my land is situated; it was "The Miracle of the Sun," with all of its extraordinary phenomena.
>
> I feel incapable of describing how I saw it or felt about it then. I stared fixedly toward the Sun, and it seemed pale to me, in such a manner as to not blind the eyes; *it was like a snowball rolling over itself. Afterward, suddenly, it seemed to come down in a zigzag, threatening to fall upon the Earth.* Terrified, I ran into the middle of the crowd. Everyone was crying, waiting from one moment to the next for the End of the World.
>
> When the crowd persuaded itself that the danger had passed, there was an explosion of happiness.[2]

There were other people who observed the phenomenon away from Alburitel. At a radius of about 20 kilometers, someone who expected to see nothing saw part of the "Miracle."

MINDE

In a town near Minde, a shepherd was going about his occupation when he noticed that the "Sun" was falling. His name was Albano Barros and he lived about 18 kilometers from Fátima. He later immigrated to Somerville, New Jersey, where Haffert interviewed him, who found that he had become a prosperous developer. Here is what he declared:

"I was tending the sheep – my daily work – *and suddenly, in the direction of Fátima, I saw the Sun start falling from the sky.* I thought that it was the End of the World…."

We asked if he could remember whether it had rained and if his clothing was suddenly dry.

"I was so perturbed that I don't remember anything else except the Sun falling. I don't even remember if I took the sheep home, if I ran, or what it was that I did."[3]

ALJUSTREL

Naturally, closer to Cova da Iria, there were also those who could see the strange phenomenon. When we conversed, in 1978, with Amélia de Jesus da Silva, she related her observations to us:

> I saw it from my mother's house. I was playing with some little kids of my

own age in a threshing floor where wheat and chaff were thrashed. I remember that we stopped playing and that we spoke thus: "Look at the Sun! Look at the Sun! Look at the Sun!" The people back then had no idea what that meant. I did not remember at all that it was Our Lady. *We saw the Sun there below, there below, of all colors, like the rainbow. And it came just so, until it almost reached the ground. It appeared to be quasi-poised, to come very slowly, turning around, again and again....*

LEIRIA

Perhaps because of the height of the intervening mountains, or Leiria's distance from Cova da Iria (some 26 kilometers by road, some 18 kilometers in a straight line), the great "Miracle" in Fátima was limited to a "red light" in Leiria. Guilhermina Lopes da Silva, who in 1960 lived in Leiria, on the Road of Our Lady of the Incarnation, bequeathed that detail to Fátima history. She wanted to go with the others who were heading to the locality, but ended up watching the multitude pass by her door, because her husband was not a practicing Catholic.

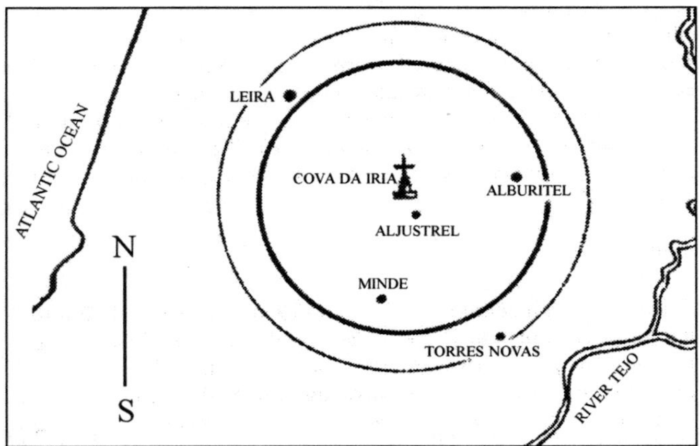

Fig. 25 – The area of the simultaneous sighting of the "solar" phenomenon on October 13, 1917 (Scale 1/834,000).

"Around midday," she told Haffert, "I was looking toward the mountains when I saw in the sky *a great flash of red light*. I called out to two men who were working for us. They also saw it and I will never forget it."[4]

TORRES NOVAS

It seems that "anything" was also seen in a nearby village – Torres Novas. We do not possess direct testimony, but in a letter that a witness, Adelaide Grego, wrote to a friend, at that time, on November 24th, we can read: "Here in Torres Novas, at the same time, something also manifested in the Sun, but from the description that they give me one cannot compare."[5]

NON-SIMULTANEOUS OBSERVATIONS

The Fatimist works also refer to simultaneous sightings in São Pedro de Muel (near Cascais) and Porto. Neither one of the accounts was based on direct observation. Could they really have been simultaneous? In light of the fact that in Leiria merely a flash of light was seen, it does not seem probable that in other localities farther away the "Sun" could be seen rolling and emitting different colors. It seems to us more logical to posit, therefore, that these other sightings would have occurred either before or after the events over Fátima. Moreover, we have an account – and one that is direct – that contends that, after entering the clouds, the "Sun" followed part of the multitude on their return home. It is possible then that it could have been detected near Porto and Cascais.

After observing the phenomenon, the multitude dispersed calmly. Leonor Salema Manuel Atalaia was one of the people who returned home by automobile. In a letter that she wrote from Cascais to a certain friend, Ana, on October 16th, she confessed that she had seen nothing in Cova da Iria, much like others present. Yet, she later stated:

> [Afterwards], we got on the road and *having covered some kilometers by automobile,* Mariana Ribeiro, who had seen everything, who had heard the child's message... told us: "Look to the Sun, which is still not back to normal." I then looked and saw – I can assure you, that I saw and would swear [to it] if it were necessary – *the Sun without brilliance, without* color, and I could look at it. A light cloud of white was passing. I said: "Let's see when the cloud has passed. It passed and I could still look at it. I saw it move through different colors that I cannot be sure about. *It turned itself green*, very green, surely, like green salsa, *with a golden halo around the wheel and spinning*, some long rays that seemed to touch the Earth, and *the Sun seemed to be separate from the sky*. Afterward, the sky took upon itself several rose-colored sparkles, turned yellowish in the wheel of the Sun and, farther away, [was] stained here and there. Several *long* moments having passed[6] – that I can't be precise about – everything returned to normal and I did not take a look at it.

São Pedro de Muel – In this locality, they say the poet Afonso Lopes Vieira observed the "Miracle." We do not possess his testimony, thus, we do not truly know what he saw. The poet Marques da Cruz later discussed the account of the sighting told by his friend.[7] According to da Cruz:

> [T]he illustrious poet Afonso Lopes Vieira told us, on the afternoon of October 20, 1935, on the veranda of his lovely home in São Pedro de Muel, which is located some 10 leagues from Fátima: "On October 13, 1917, I, who did not

> remember the prediction of the young shepherds, was enchanted by a dazzling spectacle in the sky, entirely unheard of by me, and which I attended from my veranda."

But he did not explain what the spectacle was. And despite various authors having written that they heard the tale from the mouth of the poet and his relatives who also had observed something strange, none of them left us a description. No information leads us, therefore, to reliably conclude that his sighting was simultaneous.

Granja – Granja is a locality near Porto. In a letter written by the wife of the Dean of Mathematics, Mrs. Joaquina Tavares Proença Garrett, written the day after "The Miracle of the Sun" and addressed to the Canon Formigão, we find the following passage: "His Excellency knows that here, in Granja, there were people who saw the movement of the rotation of the Sun and the same rose-colored cloud pass before the Sun?"[8]

Paço de Arcos – At this locality, an observation was also registered on the day of October 13th. The news was divulged for the first time in the March 13, 1938 edition of the journal *A Voz de Fátima,* in an article by Tomás de Gamboa. The correspondent wrote:

> On that autumn morning on which Lúcia summoned to Cova da Iria all those who wished to witness the sign that Our Lady would give of the truth of what she and her small companions assured, Paço de Arcos, the famous painter, the consummate artist of paper and pencil that is José Leite, was preparing to retouch a canvas in which his art was caressing a determined perspective touched by 1,000 enchantments. It was the hour in which the solar prodigy was announced at Fátima.

Concerning this observation, Mother Maria do Carmo da Fonseca decided to write to the daughter of the painter and ask her for further clarification. On August 17, 1959, Berta Leite responded:

> The miracle of Fátima that the little father saw was on October 13th. He liked to go by train to Santo Amaro de Oeiras and to be there to paint for several hours. It was on the Cascais Line. It was customary for me to go also, but on that day I did not go. We were in Parede. The little father went to paint the beach cliff and, suddenly, he had to stop. The Sun was spinning... spinning. He returned home enchanted [by this]... and would say: "It was lovely! It was lovely!"[9]

From the evidence, we do not consider this simultaneous observation to be correlated with the phenomenon of Fátima. At the time of the incident, timepieces were not accurate, and even if there had been a difference of two hours, everyone would have said that it was "at the same time." In the presence of a fact such as this, it would be logical that several witnesses, even those geographically dispersed, might feel solidarity in having contemplated what they considered a miracle. It would not be unexpected that emotion might supplant rigor as to what was the precise time.

But as to the colors seen, someone else detected strange colors in another part of Portugal – namely, in Leiria. João Cabral forwarded the statement to us from that city, because the witness, Maria do Carmo, did not know how to write. She found herself near the Caniços Bridge (the southern entrance to the city of Leiria). "She saw the water of the Lis River turn colors – it took various colors – and, looking toward the Sun, saw the same [thing], a colored Sun."

12. ANALYSIS OF THE STATISTICS OF THE WITNESSES

For a more refined analysis of the importance of the "solar" phenomenon at Fátima, we made a statistical compilation. Thus, we present here what observers saw under different conditions and the facts they furnished us, which served as the basis for our work. We gathered data without eyewitnesses, although we did not gather data without statements. In some cases, some were deposed verbally or in writing more than once, and those statements were subsequently collected and treated as a single statement and analyzed in their totality in reference to the same witness.

Hence, we proceed to the statistical analysis of the witnesses of "The Miracle of the Sun."

1. ***Locale*** - Cova da Iria (Fátima), an area of nearly 30 kilometers in diameter, in the province of Estremadura, Portugal
   Latitude - 39° 36'
   Longitude - 8° 36' W, Greenwich
   Altitude - 352 meters above sea level

2. ***Date*** - October 13, 1917

3. ***Time*** - 1:47 PM

4. ***Number of witnesses in their totality***

30,000 to 40,000 persons - Avelino de Almeida
40,000 to 50,000 persons - *Parochial Inquiry*
40,000 to 50,000 persons - *O Primeiro de Janeiro*
40,000 to 50,000 persons - Mrs. J
More than 50,000 persons - *A Guarda*
More than 50,000 persons - *Diário de Notícias*
Around 100,000 persons - *Concelho de Mação*

In summary, the statements of the time indicate approximately 50,000 witnesses.

5. ***Cultural sampling of the crowd***

In 1911, 75.1% of the population was illiterate; in 1920, it was 70.5%.

As the population present was composed of all socio-cultural levels, a simple progression supports our estimate that 72.1% of the witnesses were illiterate.

6. ***Origin of the statements***

6.1. Hand written 38 %

6.1.1. - *Among those written in their own hand*

16 - were transcribed in the press
4 - in books by the selfsame witnesses
9 - are part of the *Arquivos Formigão*
2 - part of the official document *Canonical Process of Fátima*
3 - private letters published by João de Marchi, Costa Brochado,

and Marques da Cruz
1 - published in *Fátima, Altar do Mundo*
1 - published in the work *Encontro de Testemunhas* by John Haffert
1 - published in *Fátima* by C. Barthas
1 - published in the *Episódios Maravilhosos de Fátima,* by the Viscount of Montelo

6.1.2. - *Of these 38% were rewritten*

- on the same day	2	5 %
- on the following day	4	11 %
- during the month of October	10	26 %
- in 1917	9	24 %
- after 1917	13	34 %

6.2. Gathered by others — 61 %

6.2.1. - *Among the statements gathered*

20 - deposed in the official documents:

Parochial Inquiry	2
Vicarial Process	16
The Official Interrogations of 1923	2

4 - by reporters of the age
25 - by John Haffert
3 - by João de Marchi
3 - by the authors of this work
2 - by Sebastião Martins dos Reis
1 - by Rádio Fátima
1 - by Martindale
1 - by *Stella*
1 - cited by P.O. Faria

6.2.2. - *Of the 62 % (considering the mix), were gathered*

- up until day 20	4	6.5 %
- in the month of October	16	26 %
- in 1918	2	3 %
- until 1950	6	10 %

- from 1950 to 1960	5	8 %
- in 1960	25	40 %
- after 1960	4	6.5 %

6.3. Mixed - direct testimony including gathering of the testimony of a future rector of the Sanctuary 1 %

7. *Observation site*

At Cova da Iria	94 %
Out of the area	6 %

8. *The identity of the witnesses*

8.1. - *As for the identification of the witnesses*

- have been completely identified	89 %
- have been partially identified	1 %

Of this 11%:

4 - undifferentiated witnesses who testified for the reporters of the day (one of these has been identified)
4 - we know the initials of their names
2 - we know the degrees of relationship to identified persons
1 - we know the locality where they lived and their friends

8.2. - *As to the physical picture*

- We know them personally or from photograph	38 %
- Are unknown to us	62 %

8.3. - *As to their gender*

- males	61 %
- females	35 %
- reporters who expressed the opinions of males and females	4 %

8.4. - *As to their ages in 1917*

- we do not know the exact ages of	59 %
- we know the ages of	41 %

Of this 41 %:

- children	6 cases
- 15 to 20 years	5 cases
- 21 to 25 years	9 cases
- 26 to 30 years	7 cases
- 31 to 35 years	6 cases
- 36 to 40 years	1 case
- 41 to 45 years	4 cases
- 46 to 50 years	2 cases
- over 50 years	1 case

8.4.1. - *Relative to the youthfulness of the witnesses whose ages are known to us*

80 % - were less than 35 years of age
20 % - were more than that age

8.5. - *As to their marital status*

Single	19 %
Married	31 %
Priests	4 %
Children (up to 15 years)	6 %
Unknown	40 %

8.6. - *As to the locality*

We know the locality of birth or residence of	93 %
Locality unknown	7 %

8.7. - *Professional categories of the witnesses*

Farmers	22 %
Housewives	22 %

Journalists (including reporters)	6 %
Lawyers	6 %
Priests	4 %
Landlord/Landlady	3 %
In Business	2 %
Professors	2 %
Shepherds	2 %
Graduate of Law and Theology	1 %
Student of Medicine	1 %
Engineers	1 %
Writers	1 %
University Professor	1 %
Graduates	1 %
Postal workers (in 1922)	1 %
Carpenters	1 %
Stonemasons	1 %
Domestic employees	1 %
Children without professions	4 %
Unknown professions	17 %

Of this 17 %:

16 - lived in villages, perhaps farmers, landlords, businessmen, or working class
1 - worked in the Capital

8.8. - *Social Categories*

15 % - had superior learning
10 % - “famous” or “distinguished” people
4 % - nobles
4 % - clergy
8 % - intellectuals (including the reporters)
64 % - other classes (including campesinos, the small rural middle class, etc.)

9. *Processes of Observation*

- With the naked eye	99 %

- With the naked eye and binoculars	1 %

(We know indirect witnesses, referenced during this work, who made their observations with binoculars.)

10. *Description of the "Miracle"*

10.1. - *Rain Stoppage*

- stopping at the start of the phenomenon	34 %
- instantaneous stopping "as if by magic"	13 %
- merely reference the stoppage	21 %

10.2. - *Reference of the clouds at the start of the "Miracle"*

- Referred to the role of those clouds	31 %
- Existence of "dense clouds"	7 %
- Spoke of a special "cloud"	5 %
- "The Sun broke through the clouds"	10 %
- The cloud or clouds "parted"	18 %
- Opening of the clouds with light	3 %

10.3. - *What did they see appear?*

- The Sun	97 %
- Something other than the Sun	3 %

10.4. - *The situation of the "Sun"*

- at its zenith	3 %
- close to its zenith	1 %
- a luminous disk placed itself before the Sun	1 %
- the clouds descended	1 %
- the clouds were passing behind	1 %

10.5. - *Shape of the "object"*

- shape of the Sun without rays	78 %
- discoidal	13 %

- globe	3 %
- host	2 %
- round plate (chapa)	1 %
- round plate (placa)	1 %
- rounded veil	1 %
- not spherical as is the Moon (oblate spheroid)	1 %

10.6. - *Established comparisons (extra-Sun)*

- with the Moon	6 %
- disk of dull silver	6 %
- plate of dull silver	1 %
- globe of dull silver	1 %
- silvery disk	1 %
- ball of fire	1 %
- disk nacre like a shell	1 %
- metallic disk	1 %
- disk of misty crystal	1 %
- disk of dull glass	1 %
- plate of glossy silver	1 %
- globe of snow	1 %

10.6.1. - *Designations of those who do not refer to the Sun*

- luminous disk	1 %
- silver globe or sphere	1 %
- white snow form and silvery veil	
- of a round shape	1 %

10.7. - *Definition of the "solar metal"*

- silvery	15 %
- polished steel like that of a spoon	1 %
- lighter in color than aluminum	1 %
- dull glass	1 %
- misty crystal	1 %
- magnetic	1 %
- nacre like a shell	1 %
- mother-of-pearl	1 %
- white, opaque material	1 %

10.8. – *Obfuscating/shining characteristics*

- did not hurt the retina	40 %
- did not refer to this detail	60 %

10.9. - *Chromatic aspects*

- Reference to the chromatic aspects	66 %

10.9.1. - In the "Sun"	49 %
10.9.2. - In the atmosphere	36 %
10.9.3. - In the clouds	9 %

10.9.1. - *In the "Sun"*

- Iridescent only on the periphery	14 %
- Successive alternation of colors	4 %
- Chromatic succession provided by flashes of equal size and distance on the periphery	1 %

10.9.1.1. - *Colors observed in the "Sun"*

- yellow	11 %
- blue	9 %
- purple/violet	8 %
- green	7 %
- red	7 %
- rose	5 %
- rainbow colors	5 %
- orange	3 %
- white	3 %
- black	2 %
-"multi-colored"	18 %

10.9.2. - *Colors observed in the atmosphere*

- yellow	16 %
- red	8 %
- blue	7 %
- purple/violet	7 %

- rose	5 %
- orange	3 %
- amethyst	1 %
- green	1 %
- white	1 %
- rainbow colors	2 %
- "multi-colored"	6 %
- colors observed in blotches	6 %

10.9.3. - *Colors observed in the clouds*

- purple/violet	4 %
- red	3 %
- blue	2 %
- orange	2 %
- red	1 %
- yellow	1 %
- white	1 %
- rainbow colors	1 %
- "various colors"	2 %
- golden (in the "special cloud)	2 %

10.10. - *As to the luminousity*

- illuminated from behind	2 %
- the light appeared to be strained through glass	3 %
- compared to an eclipse	3 %
- was different from an eclipse	2 %
- the atmosphere darkened	8 %

10.11. - *Movement*

- referenced a "solar" movement	91 %
- gyrating movements	67 %
- trembling	11%
- dancing	8%
- brusque movements	5%
- moving from its place (excluding its descent)	3%

10.11.1 - *Gyrating movement*

- "it gyrated over itself" and "went away" separate?	24 %
- rotating in one and another direction	1 %
- rotation of only the periphery	2 %
- "like a wheel of fireworks"	27 %
- triple rotation with two intervals	8 %
- double rotation	2 %
- rotation "several times"	3 %

10.11.2.- *The downward movement*

- reference to this movement	61 %

10.11.2.1. - *Number of times it descended*

- one time	14 %
- two times	2 %
- three times	5 %
- "gave the impression that it was descended but it spun"	11 %

10.11.2.2. - *How it descended*

- as it spun	8 %
- descended as if "dancing"	1 %
- descended in a zigzag	1 %

10.11.2.3. - *How far it descended*

- to the trees	2 %
- to the height of a pine tree	1 %
- almost at our feet	2 %
- half the afternoon or more	1 %

10.11.2.4. - *How it ascended*

- as it descended (as it spun)	6 %
- as it descended (in a zigzag)	1 %

- in a spiral 1 %

10.11.2.5. - *To where it returned*

- to its regular place 5 %
- it hid itself behind the clouds 1 %
- it was hidden by the golden "cloud" 1 %

10.12. - *Increase in volume*

- reference an increase in its volume upon descent 2 %

10.13. - *Increase in temperature*

- reference heat when it descended 11 %

10.14. - *"Solar" Crew*

- reference the observation of beings 13 %

10.14.1. - *"Our Lady"* 6 %

- eyewitnesses 1 %
- references 5 %

10.14.2. - *"Saint Joseph"* 8 %

- eyewitnesses 2 %
- references 6 %

10.14.3 - *"Baby Jesus"* 6 %

- eyewitnesses 3 %
- references 3 %

10.14.4. - *Three characters together* 1 %

- eyewitness	1 %
10.14.5. - *A "Blessing" hand*	1 %
- references	1 %

11. ***Reactions of the witnesses and multitude***

- references to the reactions of the multitude	42 %
- references to the reactions of himself/herself	34 %

11.1. - *Reactions elicited*

- kneeling in the mud	21 %
- screams	18 %
- shouts of faith	18 %
- fear	17 %
- fear of the End of the World	11 %
- cries	11 %
- fear/awe	9 %
- euphoria	7 %
- conversions	5 %
- upheld hands	4 %
- confession of sins	4 %
- throwing of hats	3 %
- trembling	2 %
- fainting	2 %
- anguish	1 %
- distress	1 %
- goose pimples	1 %
- chest oppression	1 %

12. ***Duration of the "Solar" phenomenon***

- a few minutes	2 %
- some five minutes	2 %
- more than eight minutes	1 %
- eight to 10 minutes	1 %

- close to 10 minutes (including Alburitel)	7 %
- 10 to 15 minutes	1 %
- close to 15 minutes	1 %
- some 20 minutes	1 %

13. ***Secondary effects registered by the witnesses***

13.1 - Spontaneous healing at the time of the "Miracle"[1]

- references to cures	4 %
- witnesses cured	3 %
- mother of a witness	1 %

13.2. - Drying of clothing and the atmosphere

- reference the drying of one's own clothing	18 %
- witnesses that were not dried	5 %
- reference the drying of the atmosphere	2 %
- did not focus on this detail	75 %

13. THE OBSERVATORIES: "EVERYTHING NORMAL"

"Fátima was not an astronomical phenomenon, for *everything occurred in the atmosphere.* If the Sun had, in fact, moved, as it had seemed, that would have soon affected the other stars and planets, and what would have happened then?" Thus, did Dr. João Lopes Pires, technical experimenter at the Geophysics Institute of the University of Porto, speculate, with authority, to himself.[1]

In fact, in our opinion, everything occurred in the near atmosphere. Although, while Dr. Pires remits to meteorology the study of the "Miracle," thereby confessing the inadequacy of the astronomical perspective, we will say that meteorology as well can help little or not at all.

In the edition of *O Seculo* published on the evening of October 18, 1917, the scientific opinion of the day can be read. A reporter for that newspaper sought out engineer Francisco Oom, the director of the Lisbon Observatory. He wanted to get the opinion of that institution "on the cosmic phenomenon that thousands of people claimed to have witnessed at Fátima." The "illustrious astronomer" had the courtesy – and the prescience, given the axiomatic nature of his scepticism – to respond with the following:

> Had it been a cosmic phenomenon, astronomical and meteorological observatories would not have failed to register it. And that is precisely what is missing – *that inevitable recording* of all of the perturbations in the systems of the world, as minimal as they might have been.... A phenomenon, then... of a psychological nature? Why not? An effect, perhaps, no doubt curious in nature, produced by collective suggestion. In either case, it was something completely foreign to the branch of science that I practice....

Between Professor Oom and contemporary astronomers, no difference exists as to the impossibility of the phenomenon being analyzed by orthodox science. In general, mainstream science has failed to explore new pathways to explain the "Miracle" of October 13th. The reason such resistance exists within the scientific establishment, writes Father Maximiliano Cordero, a Dominican professor of Sacred Writings at the Pontifical University of Salamanca, is that to critically study the things of Fátima challenges the patriarchy of the Catholic Church and the Portuguese nation. He is not surprised that there might be sensitivity about a discourse that asks such questions, but adds that *"it is a duty to agitate" in regard to such matters* (Salamanca, July 1, 1974).[2]

By way of synthesis, we turn next to the meteorological hypotheses that might be formulated by orthodox science to frame a "natural" (as distinguished from a "supernatural") explanation for the events of October 1917.

One – *Aurora Borealis:* Beyond the fact that "the northern lights" is a phenomenon rarely observed as far south as Portugal, no observatory in the world recorded an *aurora borealis* during the relevant time. From the start, it was an unthinkable explanation.

Two – *Rainbow:* This is a static phenomenon. The atmosphere would not cause a rainbow to form as a spectral dispersal in circular movements, followed by sudden immobilizations and the full concatenation of maneuvers described by the witnesses whose statements are found herein.

Three – *Atmospheric refraction:* At the height at which the actual Sun was situated – 42° 44′– the refraction was only 1′ and 15" of an arc – almost imperceptible. The ultra-skeptical aimed to establish the variations of atmospheric density by citing variations in altitude, slope, temperature, etc.

In the case of a solar disk with a 30′arc, its diameter would represent a deviation comprised of the whole of an arc from its zenith to "the height of the pine trees!" Yes, this would have been a "meteorological miracle!"

Considering the angles by which mirages are possible, we are amazed by the weak value that the Sun should be given in calculating the atmospheric effects that were seen at Fátima. For an elevation of 10 degrees in relation to the horizon, the difference between the real position of the object and its reflected image would not have been greater than 5′of the arc.

In expressing his distrust of the refraction explanation, Michel Bougard wrote:

> The human eye is incapable of clearly distinguishing two details that might be distant with an angle of a little less than 4′. In order for the observed image to be due to refraction and not the location of the source, it is necessary to reach angles less than 14 degrees. So that there might be total reflection, it is necessary that the angle enters the luminous wave and the lowest temperature inversion layer is half a degree. It can therefore be calculated that the maximum angle that can exist between the real position of the source and its refracted image is on the order of one degree.[3]

In this way, one can see the narrow limits within which mirages are possible. They require small angles over or under the horizontal plane of vision, as well as a plane that is "real" – like the surface provided by a flat, rectilinear highway. Mirages also require that the distance between the source and the observer be a sufficient number of miles. Because we know that the position of the Sun was at its zenith during "The Miracle of the Sun" – the witnesses made reference to it – it is easy to conclude that *the astronomical refraction at the Sun's position in the sky over Fátima was null.*

Moreover, the Sun's maximum value of refraction (36′) is obtained when it is on the horizon. This produces "horizontal refraction." The color range of the EM spectrum, however, is opposite in order to the chromatic succession observed in the phenomenon of October 13th and the entire set of movements observed. Here, we must lend credence to the statement made by the Catholic apologist Sebastião Martins dos Reis, that "it cannot have been an astronomical or atmospheric phenomenon."[4]

Four – *Halo:* "For it to be a miracle it was necessary that there not be a natural explanation," mused Dr. Jesus Manuel da Costa, professor of Astronomy at the University of Compostelana.[5] Referring to a case he himself once testified about – three Suns rather than one seen in the sky above Tambre – he posed as a possible explanation "refraction of the solar rays in the different atmospheric layers." His hypothesis, however, does not harmonize with the descriptions of what was actually seen at Fátima, where the "solar" object was always described as a singularity.

In support of this failed hypothesis, Bougard once wrote:

> Three suns or moons are typical halos that are formed when the sky is veiled with cirrus stratus clouds, a whitish cloud made up of miniscule, hexagonal ice crystals in prism or plaques, which accumulate at an altitude of six to 10 kilometers. A luminous circle forms around the Sun. When it is not complete, two stains appear on either side of the source.

Note, however, that this was simply not observed on October 13th.

Beyond the solar halo (whose visual arc reaches 22 degrees while the Sun does not go beyond 15′) the alternative hypothesis half-heartedly pointed to was that of an *eclipse*. Two facts reveal the impossibility of that theory. First, prior to the incident, no observatory predicted an eclipse for October 13th. Second, four eclipses occurred in 1917, but none was observed in Portugal.[6]

The impression left Almeida Garrett, Jr. – that the clouds seemed to be running *behind* the Sun – now proves more real than imaginary. The light cirrus clouds of which he spoke could not have interfered with the perception of the object, situated only 1,000 meters above the ground, because those clouds were 6,000 to 14,000 meters in altitude.

For Doctor Diogo Pacheco de Amorim, the University of Coimbra professor who submitted for criticism the accounts of an appreciable number of witnesses to the "solar phenomenon," the explanation would wander closely to those previously cited.[7] Mindful of the "difficulty in interpreting colors amid the slackening of environmental light," Amorim admitted that it was ultra-difficult to justify the "solar" movements. Despite his disquiet, the patriarch of the UFO skeptics, astrophysicist Donald Menzel of Harvard, revived atmospheric refraction as a thesis.[8]

To be sure, "lenses of air" might serve in *cases of quite exceptional duration* to explain variations in the apparent diameter of the Sun and, possibly, variations in color. Some of the evidence supports such an idea. When considering how air might act as a lens, Amorim added to the debate the effect of increases in temperature. Menzel went even further. "The air is similar to glass," he stated. "And its irregularities could give rise to distortions."

The position taken by Amorim seems to us to have a weak foundation. Conditioned, as he was, by the information and theses of the era in which he approached the phenomenon, we cannot demand more from him – for example, substituting the mythical Sun of October 13th with an object more concrete and dear to the hearts of the 50,000 souls who saw it.

There is less historical leeway to explain away Professor Menzel's folly. To underscore the bankruptcy of Menzel's argument, and others like it, in regard to UFOs, we note that Project Blue Book, the US Air Force study into "flying saucers," found, even in cases later judged to be IFOs (Identified Flying Objects), that meteorological anomalies accounted for the smallest percentage of sightings. Upon examining thousands of cases, Blue Book found that in only 44 cases could an atmospheric cause – such as clouds, luminous phenomenon, or solar refractions – be established. This amounted to a tiny 0.3% of all UFO sightings.[9]

We believe that reliance upon the average meteorological data provided by the Coimbra Observatory – only 70 kilometers distant, in a straight line, from Fátima – is important to infer the chromatic variations associated with "our" UFO.

*

To summarize in a manner critical of the assertion that "atmospheric refraction" and related optical illusions caused "The Miracle of the Sun," we must remember the following:

First, the gyrating movements of the "Sun" began at the appearance of the "disk" between the clouds, and did not result from lengthy exposure to a luminous source, such as the Sun.

Second, its luminosity was quite attenuated, even without the obfuscating effect of what Dr. Lopes Pires described as "the remnants of thick fog or light atmospheric layer." One supports the purported hypothesis; another cannot be verified in accordance with the testimony.

Third, there are witnesses who said, *clearly and without question*, that it was not the Sun that was moving, but something that they defined as "different" (see the *designations given by those who did not see the Sun*). Their perspicacity, we believe, was superior to their religious prejudice.

Fourth, while it is easy to speak of "certain atmospheric conditions," these in no way help to resolve the problem posed by the meteorological hypothesis. If, "although motionless, the luminous source appeared animated by movements," how can justification be found for the stops, the immobilizations, the rotations in contrary directions, the descent to the height of the pines, the falls in a dropping leaf pattern, etc.?

Lastly, no optical illusion could have been responsible for the array of secondary effects detected in the atmosphere and felt by the witnesses. Eighteen percent reported rapid drying of their clothing. Eleven percent felt increases in temperature. It is not necessary, therefore, to examine other aspects – such as "spontaneous healings" or the observation of beings inside and perhaps outside the "pseudo-Sun" – to conclude that what was seen was not atmospheric in nature but rather an elaborate spectacle created by an alien super-technology.

14. THE HALLUCINATION HYPOTHESIS

The hypothesis that "The Miracle of the Sun" was the result of mass hypnosis was presented to the public as early as October 15, 1917. In the *Diário de Noticias*, we can read, "*suggestion* immediately seized the thousands of believers and curious" – by which it was meant, the power of suggestion. And further down in the article, we can read: "Thousands of *impressionable* people... dazzled by the very light of the Sun, that appeared for the first time that day, fell to the ground crying, and lifted their hands on high, which they instinctively joined." As sentimental prose, such descriptions will not cease to be pretty – but only that.

We begin with the exaggeration that the brilliance of the solar light distorted the perceptions of the crowd. Cova da Iria, in October, would not exactly have been a desert, producer of mirages and other optical illusions. It seems, then, that the theme of "suggestion" was animated by a measure of journalistic sensationalism.

We can say, right here, that hallucination is generically defined as being – "sensation not provoked by a real object (Larousse); manifestation of an idea that becomes, for the subject, a false illusion or still yet a false perception of an object."

a) Natural hallucination

René Sudre, in his work *Tratado de Parapsicologia* [*Parapsychological Treatise*], tells us, "The dominion of individual hallucination is already very restricted, but that of collective hallucination is even more so. One can even maintain that, outside of hypnosis, collective hallucination does not exist."[1]

Lester Grinspoon and Alan D. Persky note, "These (hallucinatory) images represent the exterior projection of such profound desires as self-affirmation, realization, blame, and self-punishment." They also underscore that "visual hallucinations occur with less frequency than those which are auditory, and are more typically observed in persons with infectious diseases or toxic reactions induced by drugs."[2]

Another example of hallucination is the nocturnal reverie experienced by certain drivers resulting from the monotony of the highway, which causes them to drive along in an *altered state of consciousness*. This is so-called figurative thought.[3]

If this psychopathological perspective were to have affected the witnesses of October 13th, it would be, nonetheless, difficult to reconcile the existence of some of the known conditions:

- a simultaneous hallucination of 50,000 people of the most diverse socio-professional backgrounds;

- the existence of such accentuated psychological traumas as self-affirmation, punishment, and so on in the anti-clerical individuals, such as the freemasons, who would never have gone to Fátima to participate in a collective form of "mystical insanity";

- the daytime setting of the event would have led to a state of permanent vigilance, engendered by the suspense of the moment, not to a demobilization of the senses.

b) "Supernatural" hallucination

If, as we are convinced, the "solar" phenomenon corresponded to something exterior to the witnesses themselves, "someone" would have had to be responsible for the movements perceived by the multitude. Some Catholic critics add, then, that there may have been a hallucination of a "supernatural" origin. This is tantamount to saying that a "miracle" happened.

Jesuit parapsychologist Dr. Óscar Quevedo supports this proposition, which, to us, is 180 degrees in opposition to the interpretive and acquisitive efforts made by the science of our time, taking refuge instead within the comfort of a marvelous fact only possible to God.

Dr. Quevedo's proposition, explicitly described by him to the *Diário de Lisboa*, was that, "Evidently, it was a matter of collective hallucination; evidently, the Sun did not spin around. Someone took advantage of the hallucinations of the 50,000 people."[4] That "someone" of whom he spoke, the reporter concluded, was Providence. In another text, Quevedo repeated his theme: "This was a collective hallucination provoked by God; it was supernatural."[5]

Dr. Quevedo agreed that a collective hallucination, of the kind purported to have occurred at Fátima, is refuted in psychology. Therefore, what remained for him was a "miracle." And it was a miracle that does not seem to have been a total success, because four or five people insisted that they saw nothing abnormal at all.[6] This puts us on the frontier, at once easy and difficult, where every unexplainable fact is abased and diluted on the basis of the time period in which it emerged.

If, however, four or five of the witnesses – the *known* witnesses, it is emphasized – saw nothing abnormal, that could depend upon their location at the site, the time that they arrived there, their attentiveness, their visual acuity, and so on. Were that not the case, we would have to conjecture that there was something amiss in the "supernatural" happening itself.

c) Limits and impossibilities of the hallucination

Leaving aside theoretical presumptions, let us broach again the conditions in place during the spatial-temporal framing of the phenomenon of October 13, 1917. We have determined that:

The descriptions of the "solar" phenomenon were due to an exterior stimulus, acting upon the witnesses, associated with the psychological mechanism of contagion and the projection of beliefs.

The limits and impossibilities of any alleged hallucination, be it natural or supernatural, having happened on that day, reside in the following:

i) The conditions of the observations previously described, whether environmental, or below the perceptual-physiological threshold of the witnesses, do not describe, to us, abnormalities;

ii) The content of the testimony itself. The witnesses were multiple in number, independent from one another as to their location, and in one conspicuous instance, an instrument aided perception (i.e., a couple used binoculars). All this leads us to conclude that the event was external to the witnesses;

iii) The psychosomatic reflexes experienced were intense and characteristic of terror. The fear and trepidation resulting from the approach of the "solar" object was captured in the testimony of Dr. Joaquim Lourenço, who was not even in Fátima but in Alburitel, some 13 miles distant.

It was also found in the testimony of Mother Maria do Carmo da Fonseca:

> Suddenly, the Sun tore the clouds and showed itself in a vertiginous, rotating movement. Suddenly, it descended, as if from an impetus, giving the impression that it was coming loose from the firmament to kill us all. Those people – some 20 people – began exclaiming in loud shouts, asking help from God and Our Lady, judging that they would die without delay. *And when the Sun gave a jump over them, the panic could not have been greater.* They threw themselves to the ground, and waited to be crushed – seconds that must have seemed like years! Thrown to the ground and seeing that death was delayed, [they] raised their heads a little bit and saw that the Sun had risen and was whirling around up above, emitting, without hurting one's sight, a multi-colored light, like never before seen. *That solar jump happened three times, and each time the crowd would throw itself to the ground, screaming, judging it to be the end of their lives.*[7]

The crux of the narrative permits us to dispense with more commentaries. Here the *criterion of fear* is patently shown, just as it is present in many close encounters with UFOs.

iv) The presence of non-believers, in great number, who could hardly be manipulated by the credulity of the faithful;

v) The sheer diversity of the descriptions – or the absence of them – becomes incompatible with the notion that a unique "program" was implanted into the minds of 50,000 witnesses;

vi) The drying of clothing was an incontrovertible fact, unaffected by the power of suggestion. It would have been a first in the annals of psychopathology for crazy minds to have managed to dry soaking wet clothing."

d) The belief system and the rumor about the phenomenon

That which people believe is normally organized into a system of beliefs. A novel, ambiguous, or anomalous event tends to be assimilated into this pre-existing belief system.[8] In Fátima, everyone knew that a "miracle" was going to take place, and that idea was rapidly integrated, in the presence of that widely known fact, into everybody's belief system. *The Sun could be the only daytime star visible at this juncture*. If the "miracle" had been realized at night, *it would not astonish us that the people "might have seen" the Moon or the stars spinning.*

As to this foreshadowing of the phenomenon, we will have to refer to the conclusion in the work by Amorim, in which he begins by alleging that Lúcia had anticipated, over three months beforehand, the *exact nature of the "Miracle,"* having announced that it would occur on October 13th.[9] That allegation was made during *The Official Interrogation of July 8, 1924*, when, in addition, it was said that Lúcia predicted "the Lady promised to make a final *sign* in the Sun." We note, in passing, that it is strange that *two days before* the "solar phenomenon," this same seer, in affirmations made to the Viscount of Montelo, would have merely stated that "the Lady was to have made a miracle," not explaining, concretely, *where* or *what* it would be.[10]

Logically speaking, we will have to concede more credit to the declarations of 1917, because we think the testimony found in *The Official Interrogation of 1924*, was a protracted, automatic response, "behaviorist" in its nature, emanating from the unconscious, where the solar myth permanently consolidated itself during the seven-year interim.

On the other hand, the force of collective rumor may have held sway. In the letter from Mother Maria do Carmo da Fonseca, published by Amorim, she stated, "it was known beforehand that the miracle promised by the Apparition would take place in the stars – in accordance with what people expressed." And when, further along, she wrote "there were those, who, on the morning of October 13th, occupied themselves in polishing fragments of mirrors, so as to be able to look at the Sun without hurting their vision," we think this shows that a general impression had spread, before the fact, that the Sun would spin at Cova da Iria. First, the letter cited by the University of Coimbra professor was written in 1958. Second, many of the witnesses had already observed (or had heard discussed) unusual phenomena in the "stars" in preceding months. From these clues, the spread of the rumor, and its *post hoc* objectification, are evident.

e) Psychosociology of perception in Ufology

Several of those present at Fátima noticed *another object, one that was not the Sun*, execute a series of maneuvers over the region. "Testimony to be ignored" – apologists will say. But such testimony exists, and it will have to be considered. These statements amount to a mere three percent in our sample. Yet, if we multiply that percentage by 50,000 people, we can suppose that, if, at the time, it had been possible to conduct a personal inquiry of *all* those present, 1,500 people would have claimed *that it was not the Sun* that spun over Cova da Iria. Undoubtedly, this is mere supposition, but it is within the bounds of reasonable speculation.

This means that there were people who escaped the control of the rumor, the contagion of accepted and consecrated belief. Does the notoriety it received, its privileged location, its isolation, its sensory and technical characteristics, justify its description? It is difficult to unveil its nature, because the solar myth comprises all social and professional categories that were present.

We have to consider these statements (and others potentially ignored), however, as important aspects of our alternative scenario: *the observation of a circular object, maybe actually a globe, concrete in form, and endowed with characteristics inherent to many UFOs*.

On this basis, substituting the Sun for "our" UFO, we can evaluate the possibility of a "model of spontaneous hallucination" for the UFO phenomenon.[11] In a necessarily brief comparison, let us see what was written about that hypothesis by Dr. Pierre Guérin, astrophysicist from the National Center for Scientific Research in France.[12]

This scientist called attention to the fact that the statistical studies of Dr. Claude Poher (see, *infra*) concluded, as to the origin of UFO observations, *there exists a phenomenon or physical object, real in nature, obeying the optical laws of absorption by the layers of the air that the visual characteristics of such an object would be subject to*. This interpretation excludes every kind of psychotic hallucination, with the exception of an hallucination of a new type, which, obeying the laws of optics, would nevertheless be encompassed within the statistics of Poher.

Pierre Guérin asked himself if that type of hallucination was plausible, and if the hypothesis was proven by its consequences. After analyzing some of the perceptual perturbations to which we have already referred, Guerin applied them to a sighting involving *strange and sometimes terrifying facts, rich in incomprehensible detail, observed in a state of complete vigilance, at times in the light of day, during long minutes....* We must remember what October 13th at Fátima was really like!

Definitively, the psychiatric literature has totally ignored Ufological symptomology. Psychiatrist Berthold Schwartz clinically examined 4,000 troubled people, and concluded that visions of UFOs are not provoked by psychological problems. Henry Davidson, director of the Essex County Medical Center, arrived at the same conclusion after examining 30,000 patients. Illo Brand also underscored that psychopathology induced by UFO themes cannot be confirmed.[13] In this respect, it would be convenient to emphasize that the frequently poor translators of Carl Jung are accustomed to insisting on the argument that UFO visions result from the unconscious of the witness – which explains nothing and leaves everything exactly the same. Jung himself, who did not furnish a hallucinatory vision of UFOs, but merely some dreams of the afflicted, contradicted that suggestion.[14]

We concur with Guérin that "if any themes exist associated with close encounters with UFOs or alien contact, they are apparently charged with unconscious human content; other themes, on the other hand, are almost systematically absent from UFO manifestations, near or far, like war, violence, and sexuality, that have profound roots in our psyches. In this way, one can see the *profound originality of the phenomenon* by that which is clearly demarcated, which the unconscious human mind would naturally segregate."[15]

That peculiar aspect of UFO information – the very originality of the phenomenon – has also been voiced by Douglas Price Williams, who has called attention to the difficult epistemological and methodological problems.[16] In 1917, as in 2005, the limits continue to rise up before us, notwithstanding previous obstacles. In the 18th century, humans also did not believe in meteors, because *these could not fall from the sky.* In 1917, they could not believe in flying objects that were technologically superior and magical, because magic was to be found in the "stars," from where the Lady had come where the Sun was situated.

15. MIMETIC ASPECTS OF THE "SOLAR" PHENOMENON

In light of the impossibility that the Sun itself descended to Cova da Iria, we must ask why this symbol was used in the frightening feat that, for the thousands below, became an aeronautical demonstration by those behind the Apparitions. The word "Sun" was accepted as it spread from witness to witness, and outward to posterity. But that identification, as we have already seen, was not total, since we possess nonconforming statements by those who managed to escape the "dictatorship" of the perspective of the great majority and the exalted religious environment. This, and other aspects, have led us to consider the importance of the *mimetic* factor in the occurrences of October 13, 1917.

Mimickery means *imitation*. Some animals imitate the natural environment in which they thrive, camouflaging themselves, physically or colorwise, within it, for offensive or defensive effect. But, as with every thing that imitates a reality not its own, mimickery is an incomplete function that is not totally achieved. In a similar way, the volume of typical descriptions gathered over the centuries has convinced some investigators that *functional mimickery* is part of the UFO phenomenon. It is not a matter, however, of a confirmed mechanism, rather of a set of relationships that are set up between the unidentified phenomenon and the witness.

Once established, this point produces others. Jean Jacques Jaillat has theorized that UFO mimickery would not be limited to the simple imitation of known natural and artificial realities external to the witness. It would extend to the translation, or taken in images, of more or less complex and symbolic psychological realities.[1] Gerard Marchais has theorized that the shapes of UFOs in different times would be the result of different means of comparison. The shapes of the UFOs in the same era would be a consequence of the social diversity of the different observers: for example, the farmer would see the occupant of a UFO collecting vegetables; the prospector, minerals; the jeweler would describe the phenomenon in the shape of a necklace.[2]

How, in Fátima, did the identification of the UFO with the Sun work? Could it have been the limitations of the period; the absence of any point of reference to other aerial objects beyond the first airplanes; or, adaptation of the phenomenon to the predictions made in the previous months that a "miracle" would take place in the "stars"? When these scientific questions are asked, it is difficult to establish definitive and rigorous canons for what was observed at Fátima. Yet, we are able to suppose that on October 13, 1917, an actual object, proximate in both time and space, produced *the exterior aspect of the phenomenon, circular in shape.*[3]

The premise that mimickery, not necessarily Ufological, was used, is applicable to our case. At Fátima, the real, known object was *the Sun, at that time and in that place*, at the moment of the phenomenon. Jaillat underscores that "at the level of natural, known realities are *astronomical* objects or phenomena, which retain their UFO preference."[4] But not only. Applying his premise to our case, we can say that *meteorological* phenomena served as environmental "camouflage" at Fátima. Witness the role that "special clouds" played in the Apparitions of 1917. Indeed, clouds with an apparent "camouflaging" function are found with great frequency in the annals of modern Ufology. In short, we can conclude that the nexus of the Sun and the UFO that is part of the Fátima incident is not exceptional, regardless of whether, as an imitative or pre-figurative element, that linkage was known to the observers of "The Miracle of the Sun."

a) Mimickery and camouflage – the "special clouds"

For Pierre Vieroudy, observations of mimetic forms "seen" floating in the sky have been constants throughout history. He includes in this category "the pseudo-sailboats of antiquity and the Middle Ages, the balloons and dirigibles of the 19th and 20th centuries, the ghost planes of 1946, the *false Moons and false Suns*, and so on."[5]

An element that, to us, is usually associated with these "lunar and solar masks" are the nebulous shapes, more or less dense, more or less colorful, that, as a general rule, do not respect the habitual comportment of their equals. They are the "special clouds" that at Fátima drew the attention of people in the multitude, a great number for whom such clouds served as barometers of what was happening. These "clouds" constitute new evidence of an activity that is not only mimetic in nature but also camouflaged in practice. It might be said that, to the extent they imitate authentic clouds, the "special ones" function as camouflage for something in their interior. The accumulation of cases of this type leads us to surmise that these "clouds" must be "harbingers" of themselves or something else. The same can be said for the "pseudo-Sun" seen above Fátima.

PARALLELS IN UFOLOGY

Not far from Coimbra, Portugal, January 7, 1977

This description evokes for us the case of the bizarre cloud that traveled over Portuguese territory on January 7, 1977, defying the force and direction of the wind, while the Portuguese Air Force tracked its trajectory on radar. This cloud, whose echo was identical to that which an airplane would produce on radar screens, remained stationary for nearly 15 minutes above the Mondego River, close to Coimbra, before calmly continuing its journey.[6] The Portuguese Air Force pilots who intervened refused to enter the "cloud." Could their decision have been based on a fortuitous premonition?

The Gallipoli Peninsula, during World War I

A similar case, far more dramatic and historic, is that of the well known "cloud" that appeared over the peninsula of Gallipoli in the middle of World War I, at the height of a pitched and gruesome battle between the Allied forces and the Ottoman Turks. The "cloud" stood out from a group of others, and descending over the field of battle, "enveloped" an English detachment, which was never seen again.[7]

b) UFO mimetics and the human psyche

Without caring to know, for now, if in Fátima the mimetic implications can be reduced, or not, to known, external realities (astronomical objects, in the case of the Sun; meteorological phenomena, in the case of the clouds), let us explore whether or not its alleged trans-historical character can be verified in the observations of our day. Several examples seem to prove it.

PARALLELS IN UFOLOGY

Near Vendôme, France, March 23, 1976

In 1976, Marc Boulaz, a 13-year-old student on Easter break, intended to watch the sky close to Vendôme, France, in the hopes of witnessing UFO phenomena. "I saw nothing, except for the Moon," he stated, after spending the night outdoors. What Marc was unaware of was that *the Moon could not have been seen during that period in its full phase*. It was Wednesday, March 23rd, and the Moon was waning. The new Moon would not appear until March 30th.[8]

Villareal de Ebro, Spain, November 2, 1968

Five soldiers traveling by car in Villareal de Ebro, near Zaragoza, Spain, on November 2, 1968, observed a large, yellowish disk. They presumed that they had been watching the sunrise. Soon, they became aware of the fact that this could not be so, because what they were observing was located to the West.[9]

At other times, in other places, it has been two Moons that have been observed, one on either side of the highway upon which a driver is making his way. Suddenly, one of the Moons turns itself off. In other situations, the mimetic extends to artificial objects, such as satellites, or the famous dirigibles in vogue in the United States in 1897, discussed in detail by Jacques Vallée in his famous UFO work *A Century of Landings*.[10] The ghost rockets, seen across Scandinavia at the end of World War II, or the "phantom train," observed near Morez, in Jara, parked upon a railway in front of two witnesses, belong to the same mimetic category.[11]

Jaillat thinks that there exists a duality between mimetics and the UFO phenomenon – an *exterior, or partial mimetic*, perceived in proximity to a real, known object, and an *internal mimetic,* one that seems to be an element of the UFO phenomenon as it is experienced internally by the percipient.[12]

Hence, the examples given would withdraw from consideration a trans-historic structure to the UFO phenomenon (observations of pseudo-Suns and other astronomical and meteorological objects representing that constant), substituting in its stead, according to the perspective of different eras, an attribute of malleability as to what is seen. For Jaillat, this mimickery by UFOs might be "a form of exterior manifestation of an unidentified organized system, attempting to adapt itself to external stimuli, by imitating some of the objects and images in our environment."[13]

We could ask, what would be the degree of mimetic perfection of that unidentified system? This is a pertinent question, because all of the evidence points to its imperfection. That imperfection is equally present in the cases discussed herein. It is also essential in order to understand the typical manifestations of UFO phenomena.

Next, we might ask, how would that unidentified system adapt itself to our environment? Obviously, by *false full Moons out of synchrony, by ghost planes that hover motionless in the air, by pseudo-Suns that jump their orbits and slowly descend only meters from the ground.*

Another pattern identified by Jaillat includes what he refers to as the "psychological realities," revealed, for example, in the language of the witnesses. We think a clue could reside there that might explain how the imitation is given meaning. Is it perceived from the observed object? Or does the witness "select" the image from comparative references found in his mind? At Fátima, the witnesses' professions seemed to influence how the object was seen, which would support the second hypothesis. The "solar object" was defined by an engineer, Mário Godinho, as a "magnetic disk," not unlike the "parachute-shaped" object seen by a military pilot on December 25, 1973 in Belgium.[14] In his turn, a farmer, José Joaquim da Assunção, used in his description an agrarian measure: "The Sun began to move erratically in the sky, as if within a half *alqueire*" [equivalent to 4.84 hectares]. In a similar manner, we can identify the existence of various definitions found in the environs of Cova da Iria. The "communion hosts" would be a representation of its ubiquitously Catholic environment, the same environs that existed, as a matter of fact, when the priests of Braga reported "flying hosts" in 1640.[15]

These questions, without making dogma of this aspect of the UFO phenomenon, turn on a possible reconciliation between the *objectivity* of the phenomenon – its real, exterior nature – and the interior *psychology* of the witnesses. If we accept the postulate that the mimetic function would be null in more conventional objects – discoid, fusiform, spherical – as Jaillat suggests, then the "solar" object of Fátima would not have imitated the Sun deliberately, but "accidentally," by the predisposition of the onlookers, among whom, moments before, had circulated the exclamation of the seers: "Look at the Sun!"

The statements provided tend to support the assertion of Marchais that if such a dichotomy were the case, "a UFO would not be definable except as a function of something known." Yet, we would add, it would still be *something that could be classified as something unknown*, in other words, unidentified. Fátima proves this.

The framework that we have elucidated enables us to briefly categorize the mimetic aspects of the phenomenon of October 13, 1917:

1) *Cultural identity* (social and professional) – the "magnetic disk" of the engineer; the "half *alquiere*" of the farmer;
2) *Symbolic identity* (religious) – the sacred "host" of the devout; the beings within (or next to) the Sun seen as "Catholic icons" by the people of a Catholic country;
3) *Astronomical and meteorological identity* (scientific) – the "Sun" and the "special clouds" mistaken for the actual Sun and unusual cloud formations.

In the interpretation of Jaillat, we would be able to see what the first two groups, influenced by *interior mimetics*, would say with respect to the "psychological realities," while the third group would represent objects closer to objective reality, where *exterior mimetics* were invoked.

16. THE PROCESS OF THE "MIRACLE" OR, THE ANTI-ABSURD EXPLANATION

The "Miracle" step-by-step reformulation
and confrontation of a hypothesis

Now that we are in possession of the major facts, gathered from a substantial number of witnesses, let us return to October 13, 1917, revisiting the very particular environment of Cova da Iria, armed with a reassuring sum of elements that, unlike us, our compatriots of that time did not possess. With the eyes and the words of our day, in which sightings of UFOs have become ubiquitous, let us see what could have happened in that singular alien demonstration of yesteryear.

1st phase – A "special cloud" appeared in the sky, approaching from the direction of Spain to the East. From that "cloud," which surrounded a portal bearing craft, a silver globe emerged, halfway over the course between the East and the South (where the Sun was situated). From this globe, a beam of focused light was emitted that served as a kind of transport sending the Being to the small oak tree.

2nd phase – While a dialogue ensued between the seers and the Being, the silver globe was seen again, appearing and disappearing in the vicinity of the "cloud" in intervals of three to four minutes.

3rd phase – The dialogue having concluded, the Being was "taken up" to the craft by the same means from which she came, reentering the silver globe, so that it appeared to the witnesses that "the doors had closed." Then the portal bearing "cloud" streaked across the sky to a position where it was superimposed in front of the Sun. One of the statements referred to a "ladder" near the Sun. This may have been a visual misidentification of a cigar-shaped UFO with windows running along its side.

4th phase – Starting from the mother ship, control of the whole phenomenon by the "unidentified beings" began to prompt the dissipation of the clouds surrounding the Sun, especially the low and medium lying ones. The rain stopped. The mass of "clouds" parted, intersected by rapid flashes of light in front of the Sun. This lateral separation or opening allowed a luminous disk to exit, possibly the same silver globe that had been observed before.

5th phase – The globe (or disk) then appeared as the putative "Sun" at mid-heaven, and began to execute its distinctive movements, which were independently observed from four different locations – namely, Cova da Iria, Minde, Alburitel, and Aljustrel.

6th phase – The disk descended to some 30 meters above the ground, oriented north-south, and released a wave of heat over the multitude, which dried people's clothing, and in places, the ground, while healing some of the afflicted situated in the zone affected by its trajectory.

7th phase – The UFO ascended once again and became clear (perhaps even transparent), which allowed some witnesses to detect beings within its interior, who seemed to greet the crowd.

8th phase – The "Sun" reentered the portal within the golden "cloud" as it moved away from its position vertically beneath the Sun.

Fig. 26 – The different phases of "The Miracle of the Sun," following the opening of the "black cloud."

The area of simultaneous observation and the spatial position of the UFO on October 13th

Let us now turn to the next stage of our critical analysis, and confirm that at the same time:

1st – The simultaneous observation of the essential movements of the "solar" object was possible from the four locations cited, and the descriptions reported at each contain little internal consistency, suggesting that what was reported was seen independently and did not enter the historical record by way of the cultural diffusion of a single account or accounts taken from a single location;

2nd – In the statements made in locations outside of Fátima, the psychological and symbolic associations of the Sun prevailed upon a diversity of values and perspectives which, naturally, we must consider. The data in the following chart attempts to reproduce merely the spatial location of a given moment: the instant at which the "Sun" broke through the barrier of the clouds. Evidently, as the object revolved towards a given locality, this suggested to respective witnesses a dimension superior to what they had initially seen [and corresponding to the position of the object during the 5th phase, *supra*].

3rd – From the location of the four towns, it is possible to see an object situated at a given height and a known vertical orientation. Thus, for a mathematical analysis of the topographical base, we do not include Leiria or Torres Novas in our calculations, for, though we do consider them areas of simultaneous observation, their distance would not have allowed for descriptions as clear and homogeneous as in the other four towns. These four are enough, however, for the objectives at hand.

Table 6: Spatial Location of the "Sun" Breaking Through the Clouds

Observation Site	Geographical Coordinates	Direction of Observation	Vertical Distance	Angle of Observation	Altitude of Location
Cova da Iria	39° 38′ N 8° 40′ 25" W	SSE	1 km	42°	352 m
Aljustrel	39° 37′ N 8° 39′ 50" W	NNW	1 km	42°	352 m
Minde	39° 32′ N 8° 40′ 30" W	NNE	10 km	5° 8′ 34"	350 m
Alburitel	39° 38′ 35" N 8° 31′ 15" W	NWSW	13.3 km	3° 52′ 17"	269 m

The data points considered were:

– The angle of observation of the Sun on that date – 42°
– The apparent diameter of the Sun on that date – close to 30 feet

Because these eyewitness observations indicate that they were made near Cova da Iria (toward the South) and in Aljustrel (in the direction of Cova da Iria), we can safely posit that the vertical of the point of observation was situated between those two locations. Similarly, since the figures in relation to the dimensions of the object are close in range, and in light of the proximity of the two localities – within two kilometers – we can, without a large margin for error, accept that point as halfway between Fátima and Aljustrel, which furnishes us, immediately, the probable directions of the observations.

The apparent diameter of the "Sun" being close to 30 feet, we can imagine that the diameter of an object destined to superimpose itself over the actual Sun and its brilliance, in our case, would be one degree. Under these conditions, we would have (right):

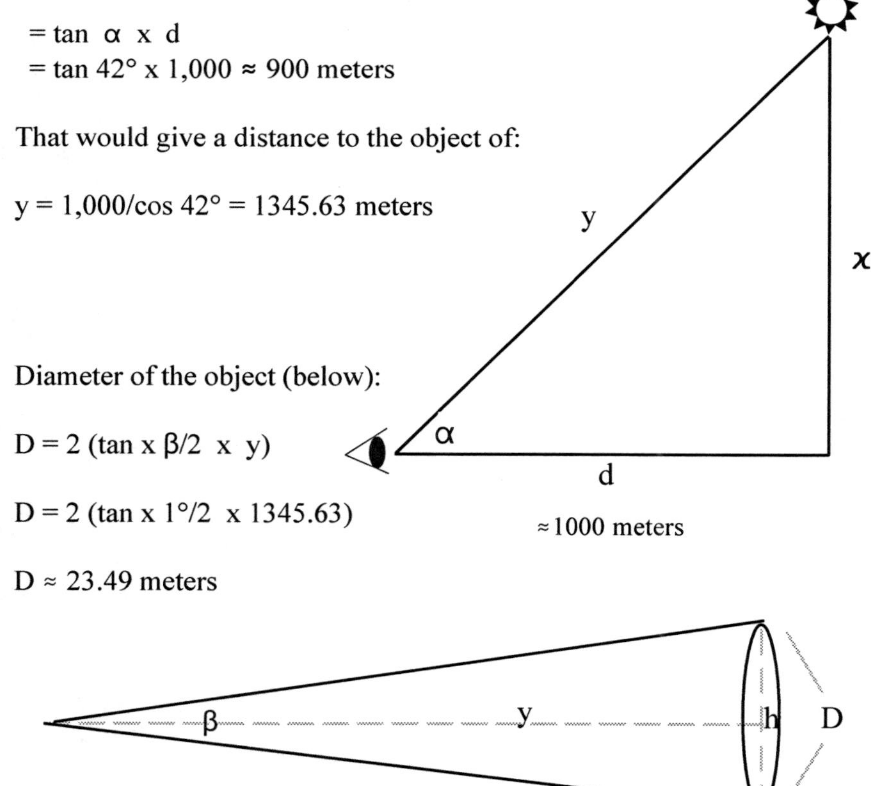

$= \tan\ \alpha \times d$
$= \tan 42° \times 1{,}000 \approx 900$ meters

That would give a distance to the object of:

$y = 1{,}000/\cos 42° = 1345.63$ meters

Diameter of the object (below):

$D = 2\ (\tan \times \beta/2\ \times\ y)$

$D = 2\ (\tan \times 1°/2\ \times 1345.63)$

$D \approx 23.49$ meters

Given that we considerably lengthened the angle of the apparent diameter of the object (close to 32 feet for one degree), we can, on the basis of what was previously established, conclude that:

1st – When the observations were made, the UFO was close to 1,500 meters from the witnesses, and at a distance to the plane of observation of close to 900 meters;

2nd – The actual diameter of the UFO was close to 25 meters;

3rd – The angle of observation, as well as the dimensions of the UFO, would be identical for Cova da Iria and Aljustrel.

In possession of these facts, we can now calculate the distances, angles of observation, and apparent diameters for the observations in Alburitel and Minde.

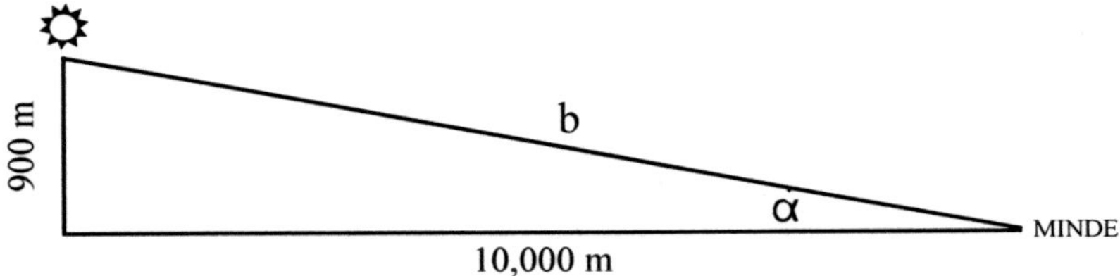

$\tan \alpha = 900/10{,}000 = .090 \Longrightarrow 5° \, 8' \, 34''$

$b = 10{,}000/\cos. \alpha = 10{,}000/.996 = 10{,}040.418$ meters

And for the apparent diameter, we will have:

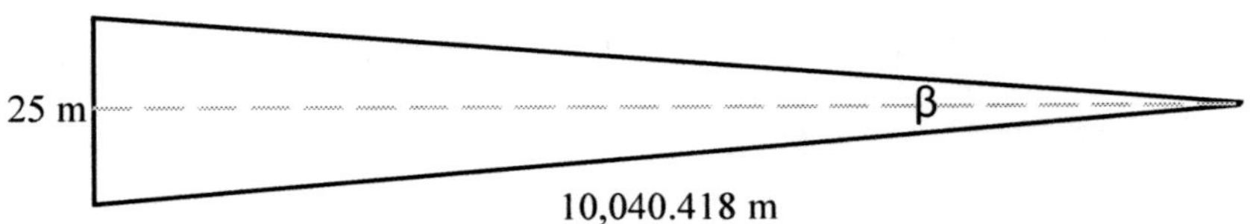

$\tan \beta = 25/10{,}040.418 = .0024899 \Longrightarrow \beta = 8' \, 34''$

In its turn, we will have for Alburitel:

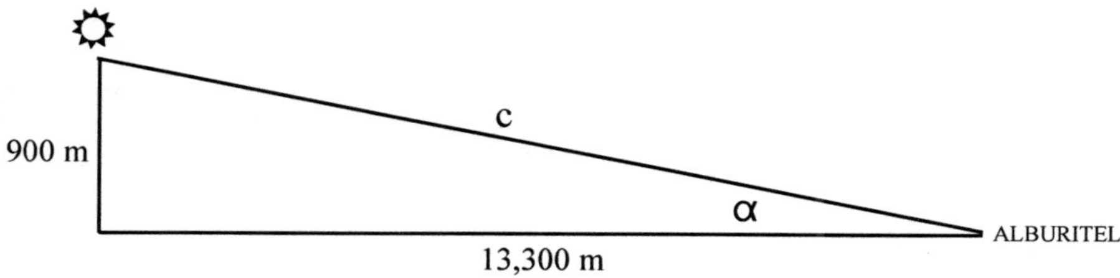

tan α = 900/13,300 = .0677 ⟹ 3° 52′ 17"

c = 13,300/cos. α = 13,300/.9977 = 13,330.418 meters

And we will have for the apparent diameter:

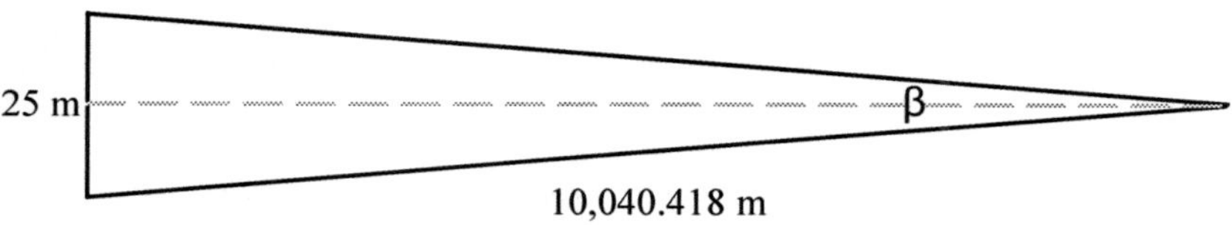

tan β = 25/13,330.418 = .0018754 ⟹ β = 6′ 27"

This data makes it possible for us to comprehend the different characteristics of the observations considered. Thus, as the UFO descended over Cova da Iria, merely a diminishment of the angle of observation would have been seen at the other locations. In this way, it is justified that among the crowd of 50,000 persons, an increase in the apparent diameter of the object would have been observed.

We emphasize that the results presented and attributed principally to the last two localities – Minde and Alburitel – are significant only when taken in relation to the airspace above Fátima, since it is probable – and the descriptions include eyewitness perceptions supporting the assertion – that the *UFO, in its movements, would have been quite close to these locations, especially Alburitel.*

By the same process, we confirmed that simultaneous observation of what was manifesting itself over the zone of Fátima would be possible, within a radius of almost 20 kilometers. Leiria, situated 18,400 meters from Cova da Iria, would not have seen (at least at the same time) the entire concatenation of events witnessed there. The testimonial statement of Guilhermina Silva supports this. In any case, in terms of what was possible visually and with reference to an object with the apparent diameter of the Sun, that observation is, theoretically, possible.

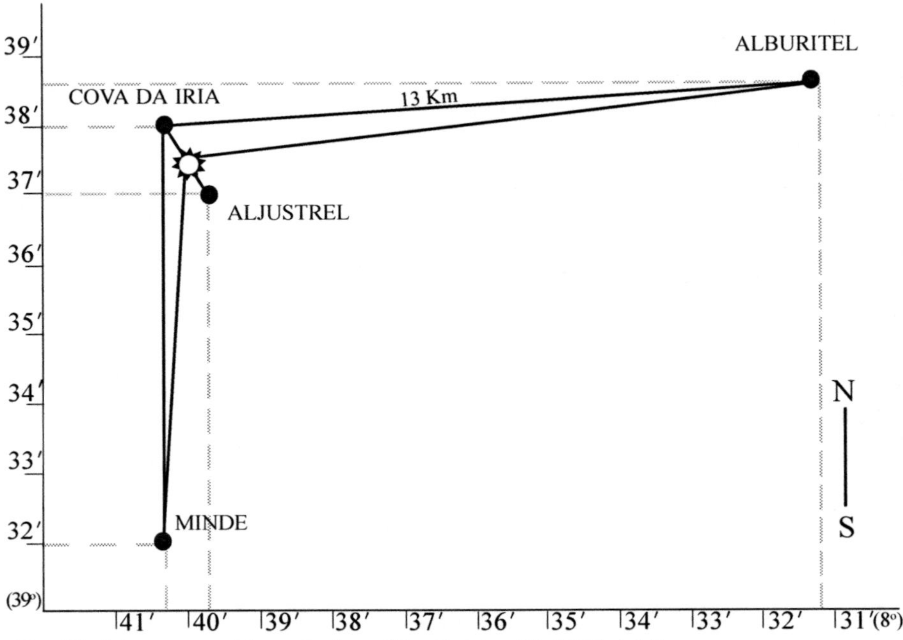

Fig. 27 – The topographic projection of the October 13, 1917 sighting.

Classical synthesis of the observation – verifying a "classic" of Ufology

The verification of the Ufological nature of the observations of October 13th in the region of Fátima begins by confronting the widely accepted results of the statistical studies of Dr. Claude Poher. These were recently confirmed by analyses performed by the Unidentified Aerospace Phenomena Study Group of Toulouse [GEPAN] under the aegis of France's respected Scientific Council.[1] Essentially, those results tell us the following.

The number of UFOs seen in the sky tends to grow with the visual angle of their altitude above the horizon, according to the law of Bouguer, which translates, in astronomical observation, the progressive growth of atmospheric transparency. According to this law, the rate at which atmospheric thickness diminishes is the measure at which it is seen each time higher in the sky. Thus, the number of UFOs observed annually is proportional to the pattern of visibility of the Sun in a particular region (that is, to the rate of atmospheric transparency). As we have concluded, these facts signify that UFO sightings originate from a real, physical phenomenon.

On the other hand, another graphic placed into evidence presents the statistical results of UFO sightings applied to a "theoretical law" that "squeezes" the possibilities of variations in the number of observations of objects in motion, expressed as a function of the distance of visibility.[2]

- Deduced theoretical law of the characteristics of human vision and of atmospheric transparency;
- Statistical study of UFO testimony.

Fig. 28 – This graphic shows the statistical results of the UFO sightings as interpreted according to a theoretical law that predicts the probability of variations in the number of moving sightings according to their distance and visibility (Courtesy of France-Empire).

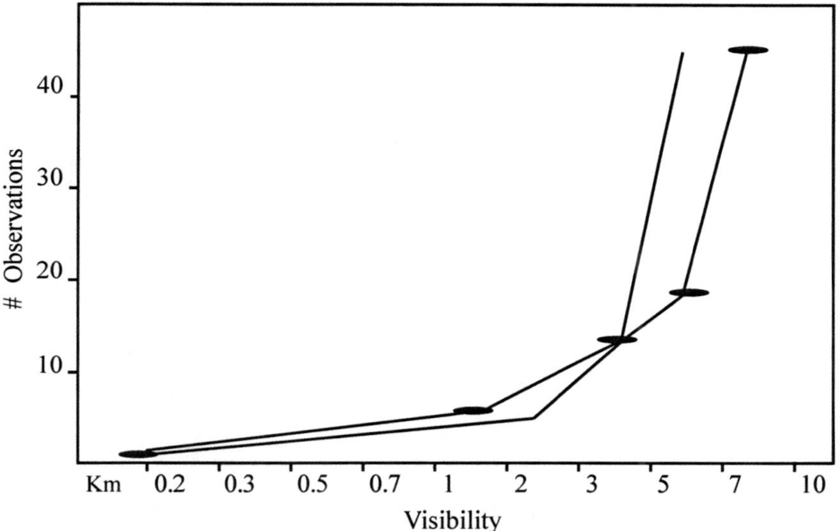

From this perspective, we are compelled to conclude:

1st – That the law established by Bouguer was fully and integrally confirmed in the case of October 13th. The angular height of the object was a very significant part of the data set, for it allows the principles of atmospheric transparency to prove the sequence of the phenomenon;

2nd – That the multiple observations of the same phenomenon, made at more than 12 kilometers, attests to the validity of the alluded graphic about the distance of visibility in the case of moving objects and in which can be correlated the characteristics of human vision and atmospheric transparency, and further still, statistical studies of UFO witnesses.

Poher himself, in a study in which he demonstrated the particular and novel characteristics of the UFO phenomenon, compared the respective average durations of reported sightings (from several seconds to several hours), thereby contributing valuable findings about the average duration of observations of UFO phenomena. For 140 observations, Poher found an average duration of 500 seconds, or nine minutes.[3] What is intriguing about his results is that this average duration corresponds to only an insignificant number of known atmospheric observations.

Fig. 29 – According to Bouguer's law, the number of UFOs sighted in the sky increases with the angular height of the visibility over the horizon (Courtesy of France-Empire).

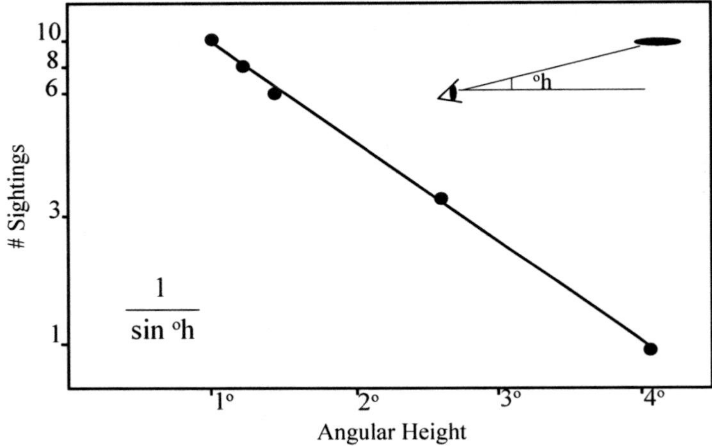

Relative number of accounts of observations

Where it is concluded that: *The average duration of the phenomenon considered on October 13th, at Cova da Iria, coincides absolutely with the statistical average considered by Poher.*

In defining what was actually observed on October 13th, we can apply with equal rigor the classification scheme first proposed by Vallée as to the location and spatial movement of the object: *observation Type III-A, related to a spherical, discoid object, which is stationary in the sky, associated with erratic descent of the object to the proximity of the ground* (the "falling leaf" pattern).[4] It is evident that, in its global strangeness, what happened at Fátima will have to be understood as a "close encounter of the third kind" as formulated by Hynek. Another aspect particular to the movement of the "Sun" is what it says with respect to the process of the appearance and disappearance of the UFO. Many cases, already cited, do nothing more than repeat a pattern seemingly intended as camouflage. Dr. Jacques Scornaux leans over backwards in his *Lumières dans la Nuit* [*Lights in the Night*] in an attempt to classify "the appearances and disappearances in the same locale."[5] The A-3 category signifies formation of a cloud allowing the UFO to appear and then dissipate immediately. The inverse process, categorized as D-3, includes cases in which a cloud is seen surrounding the UFO, but then dissipates without the object being seen again. From what is discussed herein, it seems logical to conclude that the phenomenon of October 13th constituted a variation on these very processes.

In summary, quantifying and qualifying the phenomenon with precision, we will have to consider:

- *Topographical basis:* a ray of close to 15 kilometers, considering the four little towns;
- *Demographic basis:* close to 50,000 people, including widely scattered witnesses;
- *Temporal visibility:* from eight to 10 minutes;
- *Spatial visibility:* daytime and good.

The proposition that the manifestations of October 13th were Ufological in origin is, therefore, unassailable, because of the high index of credibility of the event and the degree of strangeness that it presents, as a singular phenomenon, without any known alternate astronomical or artificial identity.[6]

Area covered by the secondary effects

We managed to identify within the space of the "Miracle" (corresponding to October 13th) the location of those witnesses who felt heat, who had their clothes dried, or who experienced sudden, unforeseen healings. For this, we furnished ourselves with a map, upon which was located people who testified to Haffert and whom he discussed in his work about Fátima. On the basis of that map, and adding to it other witnesses whose statements indicated their location, a persistent pattern emerged that startled us: *witnesses who later spoke of secondary effects related how they found themselves located in a band, more or less of a North-South orientation, with an approximate width of 70 meters. This band begins next to the southern road, passes by the oak tree of the Apparitions, and covers the great oak tree (which is still found in the area), under which the children awaited the "lightning" or the hour of the arrival of the Being.*

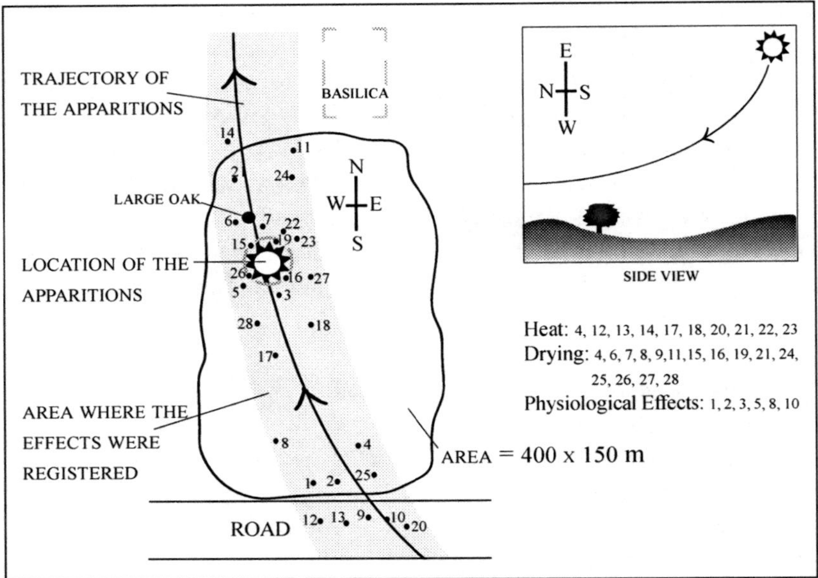

Fig. 30 – The scheme of the area where the secondary physical effects were reported on October 13, 1917 (Scale 1/3,000).

Identification of the Witnesses in the Area

(Numbers correspond to numbered sightings in Fig. 30.)

* Indicates probable location of those who could not remember exactly where they were standing.

1. Maria Emília Vilhena Barbosa *
2. Branca Vilhena Barbosa *
3. Joaquim Vieira *
4. Maria Teresa de Chainça
5. Maria do Carmo Maceiras *
6. Palmira Pinheiro da Costa
7. Carlos Silva
8. Higino Faria
9. Mário Godinho
10. Wife of Mario Godinho
11. Augusto Pereira dos Reis
12. Dr. Pinto Coelho *
13. Mariana Pinto Coelho *
14. Dr. Almeida Garrett *

15. João Carreira
16. Maria do Carmo Meneses
17. Bacharel Luís de Andrade e Silva *
18. Júlia Franco
19. Joaquim da Silva Jorge
20. Maria Augusta Saraiva
21. Dr. Pereira Gens *
22. António Ramos Mira
23. Ribeiro de Carvalho
24. Maria Cândida da Silva
25. Manuel António Rainho
26. Maria José Monteiro
27. Júlio Vicente
28. Inácio António Marques *

The final proof is found in a single account [7]

We sought, yet, additional confirmation. In 1979, we sent an eyewitness, still living, a simple set of questions about the phenomenon of October 13th. Through a cousin, Maria de Lourdes Simões, of Leiria (to whom we are grateful for her precious and kind collaboration), we obtained the essential answers. The trajectory of the descent of the "Sun" was clearly confirmed for us, adjusting itself perfectly to the paradigm that we had supposed, with its basis in the previously cited elements. Here is a redacted version of the interrogatory that resulted:

Q: Would you tell us your name, where you are from, and your age at the time of the miracle?

A: *Palmira Pinheiro da Costa, native of Leiria, and 21 in 1917.*

Q: Do you remember "The Miracle of the Sun?" What did you see on that day?

A: *I remember it perfectly. The Sun, a ball of bluish color, was revolving among the clouds, towards the Earth. At that moment, it rained torrentially, and after several moments passed, everything was dry, including our clothes.*

Q: On that day, where were you located? Try to locate yourself on the map by marking with an "x."

[She did so. See *Fig. 31*]

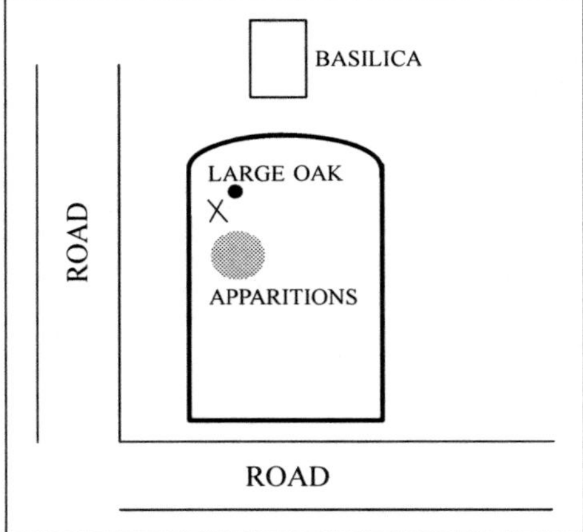

Fig. 31–The location of Maria de Lourdes Simões

Q: Was the Sun in its customary place? Or did it seem lower, toward the left or right side?

A: *It was farther to the left.*

Q: When the Sun appeared, did you see it come out from behind a cloud? Was it different or the same as the others?

A: *It was coming out from between dark and light clouds, as would befit a rainy day.*

Q: After the Sun appeared, what happened to the sky?

A: *The sky became clean.*

Q: Did you see the Sun descend? To what height?

A: *Yes. I have no idea of the exact distance.*

Q: Did it seem to you that it had increased in size?

A: *The same size, but a different color. And it did not make any impression when one stared at it.*

Q: Did you hear of people who were dried? Where were these people to be found? Were you one of these?

A: *I became dry, in the same way as those people who were around me.*

Q: There are those who say that the Sun came down upon the oak trees. But, at midday, the Sun was in the South. Might the Sun have made a curve like that which the design represents? If not, how was it?

A: *I remember its curve across the sky, but I was so frightened that I did not see everything well.*

Q: In what way did the Sun descend? Did it merely descend, or come in spins or zigzags?

A: *In spins.*

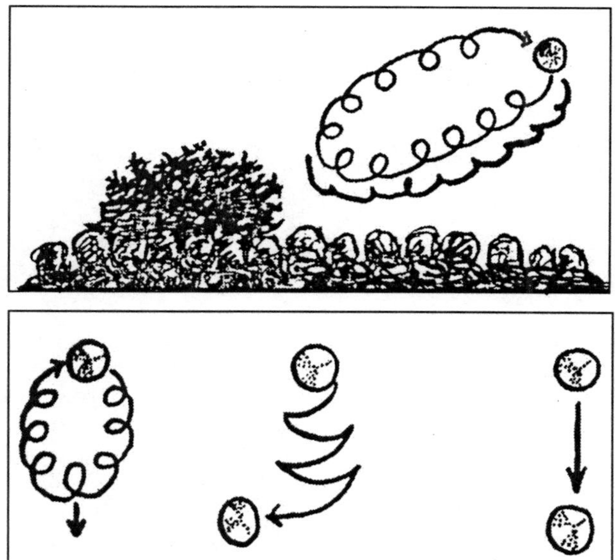

Figs. 32 and 33–Notations made by the eyewitness to indicate the direction and movements of the "disk."

Q: Did you see any colors in the atmosphere? If so, which ones?

A: *Everything looked silver, including the oak trees. Even my watch became silver.*

Q: Did the Sun spin in merely one direction?

A: *It only spun in one direction: clockwise.*

Q: At the time of the "Miracle," what was the weather like?

A: *It was raining, but it ceased immediately.*

Q: Did you hear any talk of people who were cured on the day of the 13th?

A: *I cannot recall. Afterwards, via the newspapers, is how I learned of the miracles.*

Q: Back to the drying. Did you only notice it as to your clothing? What about the ground and the trees?

A: *I only noticed it on my clothes.*

Q: How did the "Sun" seem to you? Define its colors and movements.

A: *Blue-silver. It was revolving among the clouds, disappearing and appearing.*

Q: When the Sun left its place and spun, in which direction did it go? Mark with an "x" the one that seems most correct to you.

[She did so. See *Fig. 34*.]

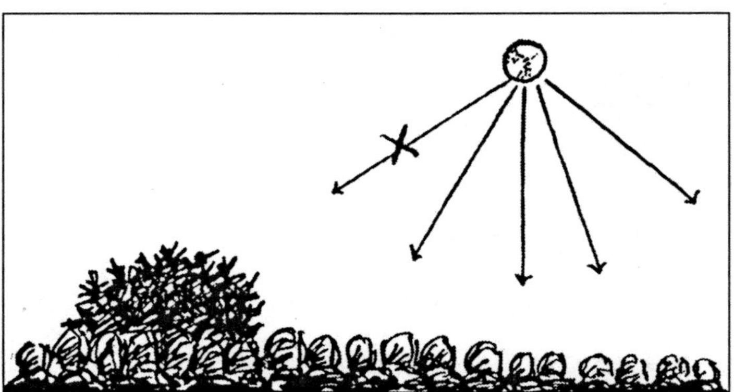

Fig.34–The direction of the Sun's descent, according to Maria de Lourdes Simões.

Q: When it returned to its place, how did it do so?

A: *While spinning.*

Q: Did you see it hide itself in any cloud?

A: *Yes.*

Q: Did you attend other Apparitions on the 13th day of a month? What did you see on those days?

A: *My mother always accompanied the seers and taught them how to address Our Lady. She asked them to solicit a miracle of the Virgin so that the people would believe. On another 13th, my sister accompanied by my mother and Lúcia made the request of Our Lady. On that day, several people, among them my sister, saw white roses scattered in the sky.*

*

We can verify the fact that this witness was located near the large oak tree, where other witnesses indicated that they experienced the drying of their clothing. In two drawings from the time are recorded the curve of the "Sun" on its descent to the Earth. From here the phenomenology of the case is explained, that, due to its very particularity, has served to discredit both the Apparitions and the actual events of October 13th. As to this fact, no one will any longer be able to accuse the witnesses of contradicting themselves or inventing evidence. In other UFO cases, the same sequence of events has been verified. Spontaneous healings, sensations of heat, and drying effects are manifestations perfectly limited to the zone closest to the vertical flight path of the phenomenon. What, in 1917, was a miracle, is today a perfectly intelligible fact understood within the framework of contemporary Ufology.

It is in this spirit that the synthesis of "Marian Apparitions" and the UFO phenomenon – a union of two faces of the same reality – may lead us, one day, to a final understanding of realities and universes that far surpass our own, but which, for today, as H.P. Lovecraft prophetically stated, are still located...

BEYOND THE REACH OF OUR FANTASY.

Notes

2. THE ANTECEDENTS OF THE "MIRACLE"

[1] Mrs. L. de S., *Raio de Luz*, November 1, 1917.

[2] This report by Avelino de Almeida was published in *O Século*, October 15, 1917.

[3] *O Mensageiro*, Leiria, October 18, 1917.

[4] MARCHI, João de, *Era Uma Senhora Mais Brilhante que o Sol*, 8th ed., Fátima, Missões Consolata, 1966, p. 195.

[5] *A Minha Peregrinação a Fátima* [*My Pilgrimage to Fátima*], Coimbra, October 1917. This was written on the 19th.

[6] TIZANÊ, E., *Les Apparitions de la Vierge*, Paris, Tchou, 1977, p. 71.

[7] HAFFERT, John Mathias, *Encontro de Testemunhas*, Fátima, Sede Internacional do Exército Azul, 1961, p. 96.

[8] Statement given to the authors on July 18, 1978.

[9] Rádio Fátima, transcribed in *A Voz*, May 16, 1957.

[10] BARTHAS, Canon C., *Fátima*, Lisbon, Aster, 1967, p. 386.

[11] Special Bulletin of the SBEDV, Rio de Janeiro, 1975, p. 61.

[12] Lúcia to the Dutch priest Jongen, in 1946. Published in *Stella*, February 1947, p. 18.

[13] Francisco to the Viscount of Montelo, October 19, 1917.

[14] Francisco to the Viscount of Montelo, October 13, 1917.

[15] Lúcia to the Viscount of Montelo, October 13, 1917. These interrogations can be consulted in REIS, Sebastião Martins dos, *A vidente de Fátima dialoga e responde pelas Aparições*, Braga, Franciscana, 1970, p. 89 *et seq.*

[16] *Stella*, October 1961, p. 4.

3. THE FUNCTION OF THE CLOUDS

[1] SPIELBERG, Steven, *Encontros Imediatos do 3rd Grau* [*Close Encounters of the Third Kind*], Internacional Portugália, 1977, excerpted from pp. 72, 145 and 150.

[2] HAFFERT, John Mathias, *Encontro de Testemunhas,* op. cit., pp. 80-81.

[3] MARTINDALE, C. C., *El mensage de Fátima,* p. 67, cit. in *Mundo Desconocido*, no. 3, August 1976, p. 18.

[4] ARMADA, Fina d', *Fátima - O que se Passou em 1917* [*What Happened in 1917*], Amadora, Bertrand, p. 283.

[5] Ibid., p. 298.

[6] *Jornal de Notícias,* Porto, October 1926.

[7] *Fátima, Altar do Mundo* [*Fátima, Altar of the World*], 2nd vol., Porto, Ocidental Editora, 1954, p. 98.

[8] HOBANNA, Ion, and WEVERBERGH, Julien, *Les Ovni en URSS et dans les pays de l'Est,* Paris, Robert Laffont, 1976, p. 260.

[9] HAFFERT, John Mathias, *Encontro de Testemunhas,* op. cit., p. 119.

[19] Ibid.

[11] ROUSSEL, Robert, *Ovni: la fin du secret, les dossiers confitdentiels de l'armée de l'air* [*UFOs: the end of the secret, the confidential dossiers of the air force*], Paris, Piente Belfond, 1978, p. 59.

[12] *Gazeta Flamenga de Harlém,* no. 14, in MASCARENHAS, José Freyre Monterroio, *Prodigiosas aparições e sucessos espantosos vistos no presente ano de 1716* [*Prodigious apparitions and frightening events seen in the present year of 1716*], Lisbon, 1716, p. 8.

[13] Cited by DURRANT, Henry, *O Livro Negro dos Discos Voadores,* Ulysses, 1970, p. 26.

4. A DESCRIPTION OF THE PHENOMENON

[1] *Arquivos Formigão.* Published in MONTELO, Viscount of, *Os Episódios*

Maravilhosos de Fátima, Guarda, 1921, pp. 22-23.
[2] *Beira Baixa,* October 20, 1917.
[3] *Stella,* January 1962, pp. 10-11.
[4] HAFFERT, John Mathias, *Encontro de testemunhas,* op. cit., p. 82.
[5] *Arquivos Formigão.* Letter written to the Viscount of Montelo.
[6] SANTOS, Gilberto F. dos, *Os Grandes Fenómenos da Cova da Iria e a História da Primeira Imagem de N. Sr.ª de Fátima,* 1956, p. 32.
[7] GENS, José Pereira, *Fátima - Como eu a Vi e como a Sinto* [*Memórias de um medico*], 1967, p. 25.
[8] MARCHI, João de, *Era Uma Senhora Mais Brilhante que o Sol,* 8th ed. Fátima, Missões Consolata, 1966, p. 207.
[9] Letter written to a colleague on the very day of October 13th, cited by MARCHI, João de, op. cit., p. 205
[10] HAFFERT, John, op. cit., p. 74.
[11] *Arquivos Formigão.*
[12] FERNANDES, Joaquim, *Ovnis em Portugal* [*UFOs in Portugal*], Porto, Nova Crítica, 1978, p. 99.
[13] *Insólito,* no. 27, Porto, September 1977, p. 12.
[14] FERNANDES, Joaquim, op. cit., pp. 28-29.
[15] DURRANT, Henry, *Os Estranhos Casos dos Ovni,* Amadora, Bertrand, 1977, p. 308.
[16] Idem., p. 114.
[17] Special bulletin of the SBEDV, Rio de Janeiro, 1975, p. 23.
[18] VALLÉE, Jacques, *Chroniques des apparitions extraterrestres,* Paris, Denoel, 1972, p. 297. It happened in Saint-Germain-de-Livet.
[19] *Jornal de Notícias,* Porto, October 19, 1957.
[20] BUENO, B. Sánchez, *Os Ovnis e a Vida no Universo* [*The UFOs and Life in the Universe*], Lisbon, António Ramos, 1978, p. 117.
[21] FERNANDES, Joaquim, op. cit., p. 147.
[22] DURRANT, Henry, *O Livro Negro dos Discos Voadores,* Lisbon, Ulysses, 1970, p. 27.
[23] Book XXXIII, chap. IV, cited by Father António Pereira de Figueiredo, in a note from the translator, in the *Livro de Ezequiel* [*Book of Ezekiel*], Lisbon, 1854, p. 520.
[24] *De divinatione, Book I,* chap. 43, in DURRANT, Henry, *O Livro Negro dos Discos Voadores,* op. cit., pp. 40-41.
[25] TOURS, Gregório de, *Historia Francorum* [*French History*], in DURRANT, Henry, op. cit., p. 45.
[26] PARIS, Mathieu de, *Historia Anglorum* [*English History*], in DURRANT, Henry, op. cit., p. 45.
[27] BOAISTUAU, Pierre, *Histoires prodigieuses* [*Historical prodigies*], Paris, 1575, in VALLÉE, Jacques, *Chroniques des apparitions extraterrestres,* French ed., 1969, p. 17.
[28] VALLÉE, Jacques, op. cit., p. 18.
[29] *Manuscris românesc* [*Roman manuscript*], Biblioteca Academicei, 2150, folio 1100, in HOBANNA, Ion, and WEVERBERGH, Julien, *Les Ovni en URSS et dans les pays de l'Est,* Paris, Robert Laffont, 1976, p. 288.
[30] *Correio da Beira,* November 10, 1917. The expression "speaking to the Earth" is

underlined in the original.

5. CHROMATIC EFFECTS

[1] *Arquivos Formigão. Also found in the work by* AMORIM, Diogo Pacheco, *O Fenómeno Solar de 13 de Outubro de 1917* [*The Solar Phenomenon of October 13, 1917*], Coimbra, 1961, p. 28.

[2] Idem., p. 26.

[3] *Arquivos Formigão.* Letter written on December 3, 1917.

[4] MARCHI, João de, *Era Uma Senhora Mais Brilhante que o Sol,* op. cit., p. 201.

[5] ARMADA, Fina d', *Fátima - O Que se Passou em 1917,* Amadora, Bertrand, 1980, p. 297.

[6] MARCHI, João de, op. cit., p. 201.

[7] *Fátima, Altar do Mundo,* 2nd vol. Porto, Ocidental Editora, 1954, p. 98.

[8] HAFFERT, John Mathias, *Encontro de Testemunhas,* Fátima, Sede Internacional do Exército Azul, 1961, p. 117.

[9] CRUZ, Marques da, *A Virgem de Fátima,* Brasil, Melhoramentos de S. Paulo, 1937, p. 28.

[10] DURRANT, Henry, *Os Estranhos Casos dos Ovni,* Amadora, Bertrand, 1977, p. 68.

[11] BUENO, B. Sánchez, *Os Ovni e a Vida no Universo,* Lisbon, António Ramos, 1978, p. 148.

[12] *Beira Baixa*, October 20, 1917.

[13] *Liberdade,* Porto, October 23, 1917.

[14] *Jornal de Notícias,* Porto, October 29, 1926.

[15] VALLÉE, Jacques, *Chroniques des apparitions extraterrestres,* Paris, Denoel, 1972, case 508, p. 352.

[16] Idem., case 622, p. 373.

[17] REIS, Sebastião Martins dos, *Na Órbita de Fátima*, Évora, 1958, p. 80.

[18] VALLÉE, Jacques, op. cit., p. 294.

[19] HAFFERT, John Mathias, op. cit., p. 128.

[20] Special bulletin of the SBEDV, Rio de Janeiro, 1975, p. 61.

[21] SANTOS, Gilberto F. dos, *Os Grandes Fenómenos da Cova da Iria...*, 1956, p. 37.

[22] BOURRET, Jean Claude, *La nouvelle vague des soucoupes volantes,* Paris, France-Empire, 1974, p. 71.

[23] McCAMPBELL, James, *Ufology,* Belmont, USA, Jaymac Company, 1973, p. 24.

[24] McCAMPBELL, James, *Ufology,* Belmont, USA, Jaymac Company, 1973, p. 24.

[25] MICHEL, Aimé, *The Truth about Flying Saucers,* Pyramid, 1967, p. 143, in McCAMPBELL, James, who also identify as a precursor the thesis advanced in KEYHOE, Donald E., *Flying Saucers from Outer Space,* Holt, 1953, p. 52.

[26] PETIT, Jean-Pierre, "Une propulsion magnetohydrodynamique pour les Ovni [A magneto-hydrodynamic form of propulsion for the UFOs]," *Inforespace,* no. November 30, 1976, p. 26 *et seq.*

[27] MEESSEN, Auguste, "Commentaire concernant les aspects physiques du phénomène Ovni," *Inforespace,* no. 40, July 1978, p. 2 *et seq.*

6. MOVEMENTS OF THE "SUN"

[1] HAFFERT, John Mathias, *Encontro de Testemunhas,* Fátima, Sede Internacional do Exército Azul, 1961, p. 91.
[2] Idem., p. 90.
[3] *Arquivos Formigão.*
[4] *Jornal de Notícias,* Porto, October 29, 1926.
[5] CAPUCHIN MISSIONARIES, *Camino da Luz* [*Path of Light*], 1955, p. 16.
[6] *Liberdade,* Porto, October 23, 1917.
[7] *Fátima, Altar do Mundo,* 2nd vol., Porto, Ocidental Editora, 1954, p. 98.
[8] CRUZ, Marques da, *A Virgem de Fátima,* Brasil, Melhoramentos de S. Paulo, 1937, p. 29.
[9] HAFFERT, John Mathias, op. cit., p. 77.
[10] Idem., p. 69.
[11] BROCHADO, Costa, *As Aparições de Fátima,* Lisbon, Portugália Editora, 1952, p. 122.
[12] HAFFERT, John Mathias, op. cit., p. 125.
[13] Idem., p. 78.
[14] MARCHI, João de, *Era Uma Senhora Mais Brilhante que o Sol,* 8th ed., Fátima, Missões Consolata, 1966, p. 201.
[15] HAFFERT, John Mathias, op. cit., p. 124.
[16] *Arquivos Formigão.* Letter written to a Brother, October 13, 1917.
[17] *Stella,* no. 161, May 1950, p. 17.
[18] GUIMARÂES, Vieira, *Tomar - Santa Iria,* pp. 200-201, in FARIA, P. O., *Perguntas sobre Fátima e "Fátima Desmascarada",* [*Questions about Fátima and "Fátima Unmasked"*], Porto, 1975, p. 208.
[19] BARTHAS, Canon C., *Fátima,* Lisbon, Aster, 1967, p. 387.
[20] REIS, Sebastião Martins dos, *Fátima - As suas Provas e os seus Problemas,* [*Fátima – Its proof and its problems*], Lisbon, 1955, p. 229.
[21] VIEIRA, Padre Alves, *Aos pés de N.ª S.ª de Fátima* [*At the feet of Our Lady of Fátima*] , Braga, 1952, pp. 80-81.
[22] *Arquivos Formigão.*
[23] MARCHI, João de, op. cit., p. 206. The witnesses name was Alfredo da Silva Santos.
[24] Ibid., p. 201.
[25] HAFFERT, John Mathias, op. cit., resp. pp. 128 and 87.
[26] Rádio Fátima, transcribed in *A Voz*, May 16, 1957.
[27] REIS, Sebastião Martins dos, op. cit., p. 231.
[28] VALLÉE, Jacques, *Chroniques de apparitions extraterrestres*, French ed., 1969, p. 16.
[29] BUENO, B. Sánchez, *Os OVNIs e a Vida no Universo*, Lisbon, António Ramos, 1978, p. 78.
[30] Idem., p. 147.
[31] OLMOS, Vicente-Juan Ballester, *Ovnis: el fenomeno aterrizaje,* Barcelona, Plaza & Janes, 1978, p. 345.
[32] FERNANDES, Joaquim, *Ovnis em Portugal, Porto,* Nova Crítica, 1978, p. 56.
[33] VALLÉE, Jacques, op. cit., p. 315.

[34] OLMOS, Vicente-Juan Ballester, op. cit., p. 305.

[35] ROUSSEL, Robert, *Ovni: la fin du secret, les dossiers confitdentiels de l'armée de l'air*, Paris, Pierre Belfond, 1978, p. 120.

[36] VALLÉE, Jacques, op. cit., p. 283.

[37] OLMOS, Vicente-Juan Ballester, op. cit., resp. pp. 307 and 301.

[38] OLMOS, Vicente-Juan Ballester, op. cit., resp. pp. 307 and 301.

[39] VALLÉE, Jacques, op. cit., Paris, Denoel, 1972, p. 344.

[40] BOUGARD, Michel, *Des Soucoupes Volantes aux Ovni,* Paris, SOBEPS, pp. 191-221.

[41] FRIEDMAN, S. T., "Flying Saucers are Real," in *Astronautics and Aeronautics,* February 1968, p. 16; *UFOs, myth and mystery,* communique at the Midwest UFO Conference, St. Louis, Missouri, 1971, cited by Auguste Meessen.

[42] PETIT, Jean-Pierre, "Une propulsion magnetohydrodynamique pour les Ovni [A magneto-hydrodynamic form of propulsion for the UFOs]," *Inforespace*, no. 30, November 1976, pp. 26 *et seq.*

[43] McCAMPBELL, James, *Ufology,* Belmont, USA, Jaymac Company, 1973, pp. 82 *et seq.*

7. THERMAL EFFECTS

[1] HAFFERT, John Mathias, *Encontro de Testemunhas,* Fátima, Sede Internacional do Exército Azul, 1961, p. 69.

[2] BOWEN, Charles, *En quête des humanoids* [*In Search of the Humanoids*], Paris, French ed., 1974, p. 71.

[3] BROCHADO, Costa, *As Aparições de Fátima* [*The Apparitions of Fatima*], Lisbon, Portugália, 1952, p. 122.

[4] KEYHOE, Donald, *Les étrangers de l'espace* [*Strangers from space*], France, Empire, p. 41.

[5] DURRANT, Henry, *Os Estranhos Casos dos Ovni,* Amadora, Bertrand, 1977, p. 79.

[6] VALLÉE, Jacques, *Chroniques des apparitions extraterrestres* [*Chronicles of the extraterrestrial apparitions*], Paris, Denoel, 1972, p. 404.

[7] BOWEN, Charles, op. cit., p. 60.

[8] REIS, Sebastião Martins dos, *Na Órbita de Fátima* [*In the Orbit of Fatima*], Évora, The D. Manuel Mendes da Conceição Santos Center for Studies, 1958, p. 80.

[9] *A Voz de Fátima,* December 13, 1922.

[10] *Fátima – Como eu a vi e como a sinto*, 1967, pp. 26-27.

[11] HAFFERT, John Mathias, op. cit., p. 91.

[12] Idem., resp. pp. 96 and 119.

[13] Letter written to the mother of Marta Maria do Carmo da Fonseca. *Arquivos Formigão.*

[14] ARMADA, Fina d', *Fátima - O Que se Passou em 1917*, Amadora, Bertrand, 1980, p. 316.

[15] BOUGARD, Michel, *Des Soucoupes Volantes aux Ovni,* SOBEPS, 1976, p. 192.

[16] VALLÉE, Jacques, op. cit., p. 310, cited by James McCampbell.

[17] McCAMPBELL, James, *Ufology,* Belmont, USA, Jaymac Company, 1973, p. 93.

[18] VALLÉE, Jacques, op. cit., p. 273, cited by James McCampbell.

8. MECHANICAL BREAKDOWNS AND SUCTION EFFECTS

[1] VALLÊE, Jacques, *Chroniques des apparitions extraterrestres,* Paris, Denoel, 1972, p. 312. The observation occurred in Criteuil-la-Madeleine, France, on October 21, 1954.

[2] VALLÉE, Jacques, op. cit., case 417, p. 335.

[3] *Phénomènes Spatiaux* magazine, no. 26, December 1970.

[4] MONTELO, Viscount of, *Os Acontecimentos de Fátima,* 1923, p. 20. Also found in *A Voz de Fátima,* March 13, 1933.

[5] NICAP, *The UFO Evidence,* 1964.

[6] McCAMPBELL, James, op. cit., p. 50 *et seq.*

[7] BRITISH UFO RESEARCH ASSOCIATION, *Vehicle Interference Project,* compiled by Geoffrey Falia, 1979.

[8] *Brotéria,* vol. XII, fasc. V, May 1931, p. 279.

[9] BOUGARD, Michel, *Des Soucoupes Volantes aux Ovni,* SOBEPS, 1976, pp. 211, 194, 211 *et seq.*

[10] BLUM, Ralph and BLUM, Judy, *Beyond Earth,* Corgi Books, 1978, p. 193 *et seq.*

[11] FIGUET, Michel and RUCHON, Jean Louis, *Ovni: le premier dossier complet des rencontres rapprochées en France,* Alain Lefeuvre, 1979, p. 57.

[12] Inquiry by CEAH (unpublished), 1980.

9. SIMULTANEOUS CURES

[1] VALLÉE, Jacques, *Le Collège Invisible,* Paris, Albin Michel, 1975, p. 37.

[2] *F. S. R.,* vol. XV, pp. 20-22, cited by DURRANT, Henry, *Primeiras investigações sobre os Humanóides Extraterrestres* [*First Investigations about Extraterrestrial Humanoids*], Lisbon, António Ramos, 1978, pp. 64-67.

[3] Ibid.

[4] Ibid.

[5] *Stella,* January 1962, p. 11.

[6] *Nossa Senhora de Fátima* [*Our Lady of Fátima*], 3rd ed., Porto, Livraria Apostolado da Imprensa, 1957, p. 87.

[7] *Encontro de Testemunhas,* Fátima, 1961, pp. 79-81.

[8] MONTELO, Viscount of, *Os Acontecimentos de Fátima* [*The Events of Fátima*], 1923, p. 12.

[9] *Stella,* no. 77, special issue of May 1943, p. 11.

10. THE CREW MEMBERS OF THE "SUN"

[1] HAFFERT, John Mathias, *Encontro de Testemunhas,* Fátima, International Seat of the Blue Army, 1961, p. 94.

[2] SANTOS, Gilberto F. dos, *Os Grandes Fenómenos da Cova da Iria,* 1956, p. 33.

[3] *Memórias e Cartas da Irmã Lúcia,* Porto, 1973, p. 351.

[4] SANTA TERESA, Frei Higino, *Fátima e Nossa Senhora do Carmo* [*Fátima and Our Lady of Carmel*], Coimbra, 1951, p. 35.

[5] REIS, Sebastião Martins dos, *A Vidente de Fátima Dialoga e Responde pelas Aparições,* Braga, Franciscana, 1970, pp. 62-63.

[6] Rádio Fátima, transcript published in *A Voz,* May 16, 1957.

[7] BENITEZ, J. Juan, *Documentos oficiales del Gobierno Español* [*Official Documents of the Spanish Government*], translation published in *Insólito*, special ed., no. 27, August-September 1977, p. 12 *et seq.*

[8] Special Bulletin of the SBEDV, Brasil, 1975, pp. 20-21.

[9] CRUTWELL, Rev. N. G. and CREIGHTON, Gordon, "UFOs in two worlds," *Flying Saucer Review,* no. 4, August 1971.

[10] OLMOS, Vicente-Juan Ballester, *Ovnis: el fenomeno aterrizaje,* Barcelona, Plaza & Janes, 1978, p. 295.

11. OBSERVATIONS ON THE SAME DAY

[1] AMORIM, Diogo Pacheco, *O Fenómeno Solar de 13 de Outubro de 1917,* taken from *O Instituto,* vol. 122, Coimbra, 1961, pp. 58-59.

[2] MARCHI, João de, *Era Uma Senhora Mais Brilhante que o Sol,* 8th ed., Fátima, Missões Consolata, 1966, pp. 207-208.

[3] HAFFERT, John Mathias, *Fátima,* 1961, resp. pp. 64 and 65.

[4] Ibid.

[5] AMORIM, Diogo Pacheco, op. cit., p. 57. *Arquivos Formigão.*

[6] Underlined in the original. *Arquivos Formigão.*

[7] CRUZ, Marques da, *A Virgem de Fátima,* Brasil, 1937, p. 32.

[8] *Arquivos Formigão.*

[9] AMORIM, Diogo Pacheco, op. cit., p. 53.

12. ANALYSIS OF THE STATISTICS OF THE WITNESSES

[1] We know that six witnesses felt cured. The other two alleged cases of healing were reports only and were not included in this statistical analysis.

13. THE OBSERVATORIES: "EVERYTHING NORMAL"

[1] Deposition taken on August 6, 1974 and published by FARIA, P. O., *Perguntas sobre Fátima e "Fátima Desmascarada,"* Porto, 1975, p. 276.

[2] Included also in op. cit., p. 274.

[3] BOUGARD, Michel, *La Chronique des Ovnis,* Paris, Jean-Pierre Delarge, 1977, pp. 19-22.

[4] REIS, Sebastião Martins dos, *Fátima - As suas Provas e os seus Problemas,* Lisboa, 1953, p. 257.

[5] Deposition of July 5, 1974. FARIA, P. O., op. cit., p. 275.

[6] Regarding the eclipses of the Sun in 1917: 1st - Partial eclipse of the Sun, January 22nd, visible in Paris and very visible in Spain; 2nd - Partial eclipse of the Sun, June 18th and 19th, not visible in Europe, but visible in Turkey, Southern Liberia, and Western Canada; 3rd - Partial eclipse of the Sun, July 18th, not visible in Europe, but visible in the glacial waters of Antarctica, Southern India, and lands adjacent to the South Pole; 4th - Partial eclipse of the Sun, not visible in Europe, but visible in Australia and Argentina.

[7] AMORIM, Diogo Pacheco, *O Fenómeno Solar de 13 de Outubro de 1917* [*The Solar Phenomenon of October 13, 1917*], Coimbra, 1961, p. 50 *et seq.*

[8] MENZEL, Donald H., *Flying Saucers,* Cambridge, Massachusetts, 1953.
[9] HYNEK, J. Allen, *The Hynek UFO Report,* London, Sphere Books, 1978, p. 259.

14. THE HALLUCINATION HYPOTHESIS

[1] Zehar Editores, 2nd ed., Rio de Janeiro, p. 352.
[2] GRINSPOON, Lester, and PERSKY, Alan D., "Psychiatry and UFO Reports," in *UFOs – a scientific debate,* ed. by Carl Sagan and Thornton Page, New York, The Norton Library, 1974, p. 213.
[3] PICARD, Michel, "À propos du modèle socio-psychologique de Michel Monnerie" ["À propos of the model of social psychology of Michel Monnerie"], *Inforespace,* no. 42, November 1978, p. 28.
[4] *Diário de Lisboa,* March 8, 1978.
[5] QUEVEDO, Óscar Gonzalez, *O que é a Parapsicologia?* [*What is Parapsychology?*], S. Paulo Loyola, 1971, pp. 108-109.
[6] *Diário de Lisboa,* March 8, 1978.
[7] AMORIM, Diogo Pacheco de, *O Fenómeno Solar de 13 de Outubro de 1917* [*The Solar Phenomenon of October 13, 1917*], Coimbra, 1971, pp. 58-59.
[8] HALL, Robert L., "Sociological Perspectives on UFO Reports," in *UFOs – a scientific debate,* op. cit., p. 213.
[9] AMORIM, Diogo Pacheco, op cit., pp. 6-7.
[10] Interrogations by the Viscount of Montelo on the day of October 11, 1917.
[11] MONNERIE, Michel, *Et si les Ovni n'existaient pas?* [*And if the UFOs do not exist?*], The Humanoid Associates, 1978.
[12] GUÉRIN, Pierre, "Trente ans après Kenneth Arnold: le point sur les Ovni" ["Thirty years after Kenneth Arnold: the point about the UFOs"], *Inforespace,* no. 43, January 1979, p. 2 *et seq.*
[13] PICARD, Michel, op. cit., p. 31.
[14] JUNG, Carl Gustave, *Un mythe moderne* [*A modern myth*], Gallimard, 1961.
[15] GUÉRIN, Pierre, op. cit., p. 8.
[16] PRICE-WILLIAMS, Douglas R., "Psychology and Epistemology of UFO Interpretations," in *UFOs – a scientific debate,* p. 224.

15. MIMETIC ASPECTS OF THE "SOLAR" PHENOMENON

[1] JAILLAT, Jean Jacques, "Premiers regards sur l'activité mimetique Ovni" ["First views about UFO mimetic activity"], in *LDLN,* no. 164, April 1977, p. 8.
[2] MARCHAIS, Gerard, "À propos d' Ovni et de psychisme humain" ["À propos of UFOs and the human psyche"], in *LDLN,* no. 185, May 1979, p. 4.
[3] JAILLAT, Jean Jacques, op. cit., p. 8.
[4] Ibid.
[5] VIEROUDY, Pierre, *Ces Ovni qui annoncent le surhomme* [*These UFOs which announce the superman*], Tchou, 1977, p. 73.
[6] *Insólito,* no. 34, August-September 1978, p. 13.
[7] BOUGARD, Michel, *La Chronique des Ovnis,* Paris, Jean-Pierre, 1977, p. 227.
[8] See Note 1.

[9] OLMOS, Vicente-Juan Ballester, *Ovnis: el fenomeno aterrizaje,* Barcelona, Plaza & Janes, 1978, case 90, p. 311.

[10] VALLÉE, Jacques, *Chroniques des apparitions extraterrestres*, Paris, Denoel, 1972, pp. 254-430.

[11] *Phénomênes Spatiaux*, no. 35, March 1973, pp. 21-31.

[12] JAILLAT, Jean Jacques, "Introduction à l'étude du mimetisme Ovni–1" ["Introduction to the study of UFO mimetics – 1"], in *LDLN,* no. 163, March 1977, p. 3.

[13] JAILLAT, Jean Jacques, "Mimetisme et psyquisme humain" ["Mimetics and the human psyche"], in *LDLN,* no. 170, December 1977, p. 11.

[14] WEVERBERGH, Julien, *Inforespace,* no. 31, January 1977, cited by JAILLAT, Jean Jacques, op. cit., see note in front.

[15] CALDAS, Silva, *Aparição de uma Hóstia no Ceo em Braga em 1640* [*Apparition of a Sacred Host in the Sky in Braga in 1640*], Braga, Imprensa Comercial, 1879.

16. THE PROCESS OF THE "MIRACLE" OR THE ANTI-ABSURD EXPLANATION

[1] GUÉRIN, Pierre, Trente ans après Kenneth Arnold: le point sur les Ovni [Thirty years after Kenneth Arnold: the point about the UFOs, *Inforespace,* no. 43, January 1979, p. 6.

[2] POHER, Claude, cited by BOURRET, Jean-Claude, *Le nouveau défi des Ovni* [*The new challenge of UFOs*], Paris, France-Empire, 1976, p. 242.

[3] POHER, Claude, op. cit., p. 252.

[4] VALLÉE, Jacques, *Challenge to Science: The UFO enigma,* London, Neville Spearman, 1967, p. 55.

[5] SCORNAUX, Jacques, "Essai de classification des apparitions et disparitions sur place" ["Essay of classifications of appearances and disappearances in place"], *LDLN,* no. 170 (cf. nos. 186 and 187 of the same publication).

[6] In order to acquire this technical data and resulting mathematical-cartographic evidence in this part, we collaborated with astronomer Dr. Nazaré Rego, mathematician Dr. Maria Clara Pereira, technical engineer Barrote Dias, and investigator Raul Berenguel, to whom we are grateful for their invaluable contributions.

[7] This testimony was not included in our statistical study.

Printed in the United Kingdom
by Lightning Source UK Ltd.
126777UK00001B/156/A

9 781933 665214